The Art of

TUNISIAN CROCHET

Developing technical and creative skills

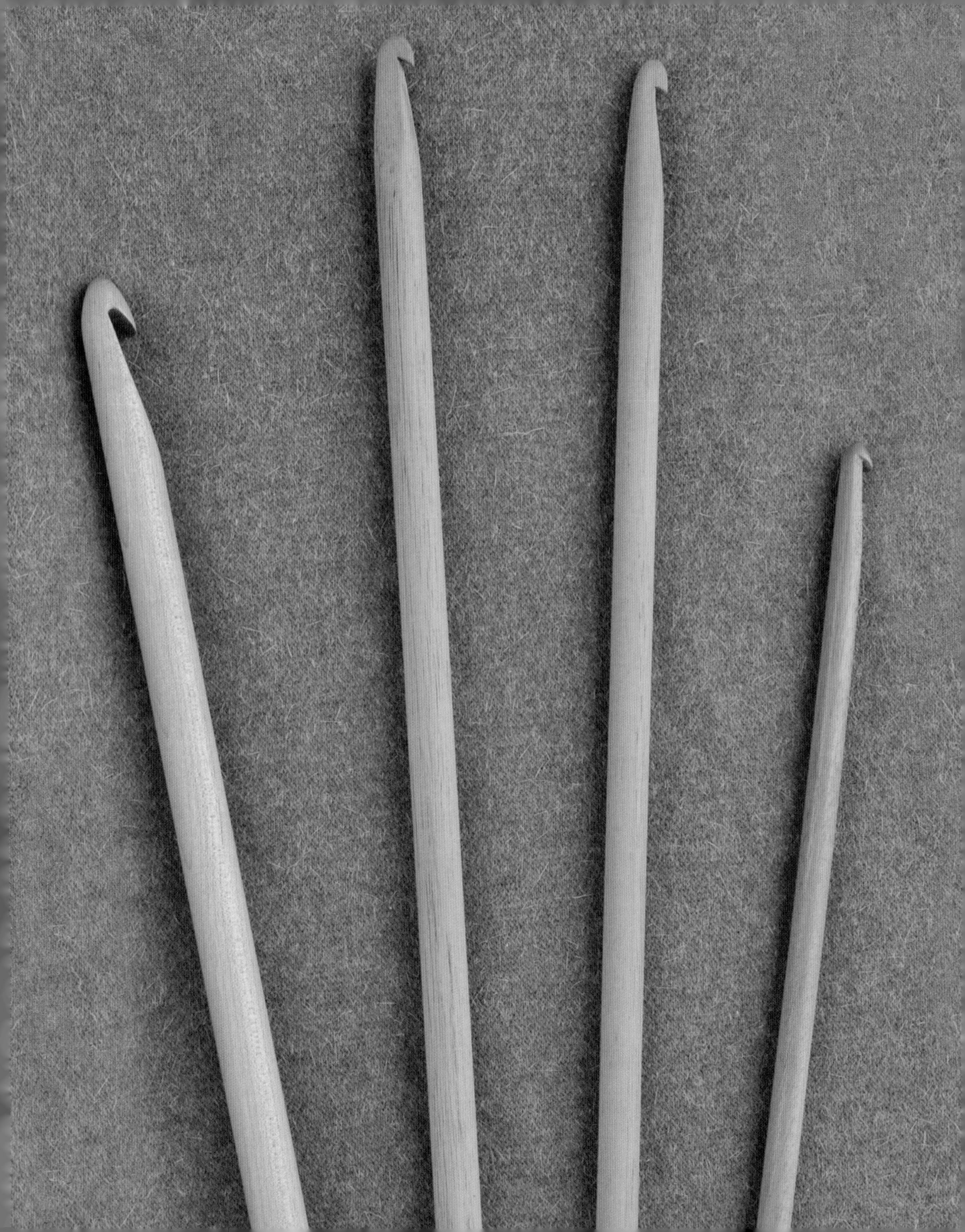

The Art of TUNISIAN CROCHET

Developing technical and creative skills

THE CROWOOD PRESS

Pauline Turner

First published in 2021 by
The Crowood Press Ltd
Ramsbury, Marlborough
Wiltshire SN8 2HR

enquiries@crowood.com

www.crowood.com

British Library Cataloguing-in-Publication Data
A catalogue record for this book is available from the British Library.

ISBN 978 1 78500 924 2

Cover design by Kelly-Anne Levey
Typeset by Kelly-Anne Levey
Printed and bound in India by Parksons Graphics Pvt. Ltd., Mumbai.

CONTENTS

CONVERSION CHART

For Frequently Used Hook Sizes and Yarns

Wool hooks			Cotton hooks			Tunisian	Yarn thicknesses	
metric	Old UK	USA	metric	Old UK	USA	metric	UK terms	USA terms
2.00mm	14		0.60mm	6	14		Cobweb/ 1-2 ply	Lace/Fine/ Light fingering
2.25mm	13	1/B	0.75mm		13			
2.50mm	12		0.70mm	5	12		2 ply	Fingering
2.75mm	11	C	0.80mm		11		3 ply	Sock
3.00mm	11		1.00mm	4	10	3.00mm		
3.25mm	10	D	1.15mm		9			
3.50mm	9	4/E	1.25mm	3	8	3.50mm	4 ply	Sport/baby
3.75mm		F	1.50mm	2.5	7			
4.00mm	8	6	1.60mm		6	4.00mm		
4.25mm		6	1.70mm		5			
4.50mm	7	7	1.75mm	2	4	4.50mm		
5.00mm	6	8/H	1.85mm		3	5.00mm	DK/8 ply	Dk/light worsted
5.50mm	5	9/I	1.95mm		2	5.50mm		
6.00mm	4	10/J	2.00mm	1	1	6.00mm	Aran/10 ply	Worsted/ Medium
6.50mm	3	10½/K	2.25mm		0	6.50mm		
7.00mm	2		2.50mm	0	00	7.00mm	Chunky/Bulky	Bulky
8.00mm	0		2.75mm			8.00mm		
9.00mm	00	15/N	3.00mm	00		9.00mm		
10.00mm	000	P				10.00mm	Super Chunky	Super bulky
15¾mm or 16mm		Q				15mm or 20mm		

ABBREVIATIONS

Abbreviations in Patterns

Note: UK crochet terminology is used throughout this book.

Instructions to work the traditional crochet stitches listed below can be found in *Crochet for the Absolute Beginner* (*see* Bibliography and Further Reading for further details).

3trcl three-treble cluster

C contrast colour

C1, C2, and so on
contrast colour 1, contrast colour 2, and so on

ch chain

dc double crochet

dc2tog double crochet the next 2sts together

dc3tog double crochet the next 3sts together

dtr double treble

htr half treble

M main colour

RS right side

RtrB raised treble back

RtrF raised treble front

slst slip stitch

st(s) stitch

Tdtr Tunisian crochet double treble

Tgs Tunisian crochet garter stitch

tog together

Tpuff Tunisian crochet puff stitch

tr treble

TRtr Tunisian crochet raised treble

TRtrB Tunisian crochet raised treble back

TRtrF Tunisian crochet raised treble front

Tslst Tunisian crochet slip stitch

Tss Tunisian crochet simple stitch

Ttr Tunisian crochet treble

Ttrtr Tunisian crochet triple treble

Tx Tunisian crochet cross stitch

Txtr Tunisian crochet extended treble

WS wrong side

yoh yarn over hook

A sample of Tunisian simple stitch showing the side with the square look facing, which is generally acknowledged as the right side of the fabric.

A sample of the other side of Tunisian simple stitch, which resembles the look of the back side of a piece of knitted stocking stitch.

CHAPTER 1

INTRODUCTION

Where Did Tunisian Crochet Begin?

Crochet is the youngest of the needlecrafts. One has only to look in the catalogue of the Great Exhibition, 1851, to realize that entries under crochet, or Tunisian crochet, did not exist. This catalogue lists every craft and trade imaginable at that time. If you search hard enough, you can find a small list of crochet taking up less than one column in this massive three-column catalogue. It is to be found under 'embroidery' in a section allocated to tambour; as so little crochet was available around 1851, it can be assumed the organizers recognized that crochet is worked with a hook and placed the tiny list of items together with this technique of embroidery, which also uses a hook. Tunisian crochet, even under the word 'tricot', could not be found. The oldest printed reference using the name 'Tunisian crochet' is to be found in the *Encyclopedia of Needlework* by Th. de Dillmont, published in 1884. In this beautiful gem of a book of needlework, there are six pages given to Tunisian crochet (pp. 336–41).

Speculation as to where and when Tunisian crochet emerged as a needlecraft continues, but, despite extensive research, there is no definitive answer. Until someone can bring forward proof of its existence prior to the early nineteenth century, we can confirm its existence only from the latter half of the eighteen hundreds. As to where – the colourful unsubstantiated possibilities are rife with conjecture.

The history of Tunisian crochet as known in the twenty-first century is vague, and, after extensive research to find validating material in order to discover the source of Tunisian crochet, it is still unclear. Just looking at the various names given to Tunisian crochet underlines the difficulty in answering the question 'where did Tunisian crochet begin?'

What is Tunisian Crochet?

Is that crochet or knitting?

This is one question frequently asked when someone watches Tunisian crochet being worked. It is an understandable question when observing a fabric being made with yarn and a long hook: the viewer at first sees all of the loops on the hook, as for knitting, and then, a little later, they disappear, as for crochet. Observers unfamiliar with a Tunisian crochet hook assume that the hook is a knitting needle and the resulting material is being made with just one knitting needle! Although many are curious, only a few outgoing people will ask what this craft actually is.

There are numerous names given to this style of crochet. These names are part of its history. In order to bring it into the current decade starting in 2020, it is possibly best to clear away the confusion surrounding what to call this type of needlework. If it can be shown at the outset that there is a valid reason for this needlecraft to be called Tunisian crochet and not one of the many other names that it has accumulated over the years, some of the confusion could be alleviated.

> A true, widely accepted definition of crochet is as follows:
> 'Crochet stitches begin with one loop on the hook and end with one loop on the hook.'

This definition is true whether the hook is a classic crochet hook for working with yarn, a fine lace hook for working thread-based lace or a Tunisian crochet hook. A facsimile of a crocheted fabric produced with only the fingers, instead of a hook, is not crochet according to this definition.

Although Tunisian crochet can appear to look like knitting, after the first stage of the process when all of the loops are on the hook, the second stage removes all of the loops until only one loop remains, therefore 'Tunisian crochet' is technically a correct name.

It is interesting to note that, in the mountainous regions of South America, knitting is made in the round on five needles that have one sharp end and one hooked end. It is the hooked end that is inserted into the loops. Long tubes of knitting of varying diameters are produced in this way. As the tubes vary in diameter, they can be cut to make a bodice, and sleeve for a garment, or for some other article.

The hook required for working Tunisian crochet is longer than the standard crochet hook. The hook needs to be able to accommodate all of the loops produced for the first stage of working a row.

Without having any knowledge of Tunisian crochet, however, it is understandable that an observer would assume that what they are seeing is a strange form of knitting. Because of this perspective, it is plausible that what we are referring to as 'Tunisian crochet' could be called 'Tunisian knitting', but it is necessary to remember that having all of the loops on the hook is only half of the process. Unlike knitting, which retains these loops on the needle (or needles) throughout, Tunisian crochet removes the loops during a second stage of the process, leaving only one loop on the hook, before repeating these two steps to produce a fabric.

Alternative names given to Tunisian crochet

Researching the origin of the names for Tunisian crochet was intriguing. Given the background of each different name and how it came to be used to describe Tunisian crochet, all have valid reasons for being given to Tunisian crochet as a name. Listed here are most of the alternative names that you may encounter relating to Tunisian crochet, in their order of review in the following sections.

- Tunisian knitting
- tricot
- Afghan crochet
- Princess Frederick William stitch
- shepherd's knitting
- railway knitting
- blanket knitting

Fortunately, the confusion is lessening, as 'Tunisian crochet' is now becoming the accepted name globally.

Tunisian knitting

It is doubtful that this needs any explanation. When working in public on a long, straight Tunisian crochet hook, in a fairly short time, comments such as 'I have never seen anyone knit with one needle', 'What kind of knitting is that?', 'That is quite a thick needle you are knitting with', and so on, are sure to be heard. These frequently heard comments quickly confirm why Tunisian crochet is sometimes called Tunisian knitting!

At the stage when all of the loops are placed on to the Tunisian crochet hook, Tunisian crochet can appear to be some kind of knitting to an uninformed observer. The loops are on the hook for 50 per cent of the time, and, during the picking-up stage, the actions can seem to be a process of casting on for knitting; however, this is relevant to only the time before the loops are worked off the hook to go back to there being one loop only. When all of the loops are on the hook, it is necessary to acknowledge that most people will primarily be looking at the back of the work, for the front of the Tunisian crochet to be facing the crocheter whilst they are working the first stage of the process. Thus, the viewer sees only the back, or rough side, of the Tunisian crochet, which looks exactly like the back of a piece of knitting worked in stocking stitch. Inevitably, 'knitting' is the word that will pop into their mind. Personally, I am reluctant to call the rough side of Tunisian crochet the 'wrong side', as both sides of Tunisian crochet play their part when producing a design.

Tricot

Tricot was the first name given to Tunisian crochet in Britain. It can be loosely translated as 'French knitting'. My research led me to discover that 'crochet' came from the French name 'croc', or hook. Therefore, it makes sense that other words from the French language would intrude. Much early information on tricot was written by members of the French aristocracy residing in Britain.

An image of Queen Victoria crocheting was released to the press at the end of the nineteenth century as a call to the British public to support the efforts of the military forces during the Second Boer War. The earliest record in the royal archives of any member of the royal family taking an active interest in crochet is this one of Queen Victoria, dated 1889. Interestingly, in the image, Queen Victoria is using a tricot hook, which in those days was similar in thickness to that of knitting needles. In that period, the thickness of yarn produced was quite fine, and a double-knitting (DK) yarn would have seemed coarse and clumsy, even if the yarn itself was soft and pleasant to work with!

Queen Mary was later known to be a skilled needlewoman whose repertoire included crochet.

Afghan crochet

In the USA, Tunisian crochet was called Afghan crochet for many years, and reference is still made to Tunisian crochet under that name. 'Afghan' crochet hooks were initially thicker than crochet hooks, making it a faster method with which to make a throw or Afghan blanket. In the USA, creating Afghans, blankets and knee rugs with the Tunisian crochet simple stitch (*see* Chapter 2) increased in popularity during the 1970s, and this interest has been maintained since then. To avoid confusion between the Afghan blanket and the Afghan style of crochet, the European name of Tunisian crochet has gradually infiltrated the written word in the USA.

Princess Frederick William stitch

It would be remiss of me to exclude the reference to the name Princess Frederick William stitch. It is found mainly in older patterns produced in the USA. Princess Frederick William stitch was often used in place of the term 'Afghan' as a stitch, in the hope of elevating its status, as it has an elite sound, linking it to the British royalty. The date that this term emerged seems to have been after Queen Victoria's rally call to the women of the British Empire to provide comforters for the brave men fighting for peace.

Queen Victoria, crocheting with a tricot hook.

Shepherd's knitting

Scotland was, and still is, a country known for the quality of its needlecrafts. The climate and temperature of Scotland is renowned for being damp, windy and, in most regions, colder than the rest of Great Britain. It makes sense, therefore, that spinning, weaving, felting and knitting were predominant activities, in an effort to keep one's family members warm and dry.

The Black Isle in Scotland seems to be the first place where the title of 'shepherd's knitting' appears. When I once admitted to being puzzled as to why they used the name 'shepherd's knitting', a mature lady from that area of Scotland who was working Tunisian crochet in one of my workshops informed me that all those working Tunisian crochet in that area associated the long hook with the shepherd's crook. They believed that the crook was a more accurate name for the long Tunisian crochet hook, particularly as the small, thin hooks that they were using for other crochet projects were used in a different way. No one seems to know when Tunisian crochet began being worked in that region, only that 'Granny did it!'

Railway knitting

This name seems to have been handed down through two generations, and it is claimed to date back to the 1880s in Canada. The date is feasible, as Canada was under British rule from 1763–1867, so it is possible that the technique could have been taken across the Atlantic by British travellers.

There is speculation as to how the technique gained this name. The author of *The Railway Knitting Workbook* has given the supposition that it could have been the vertical lines of Tunisian crochet simple stitch resembling the symmetry of railway lines, or because Tunisian crochet was used on the long train journeys from the east coast of Canada to the west coast, and vice versa – an eighty-four-hour journey.

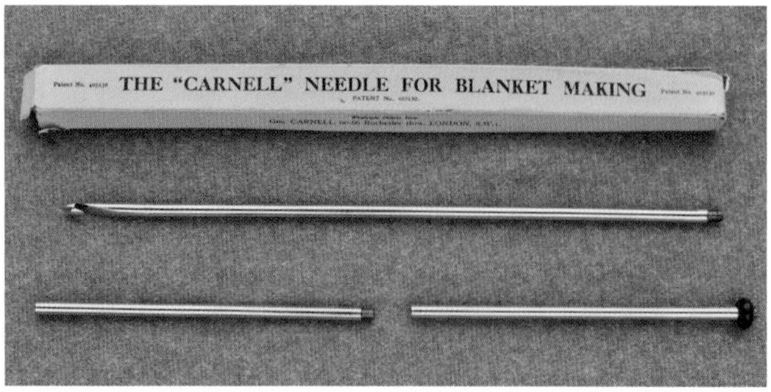

The Carnell needle for blanket making has three sections.

Blanket knitting

Because Tunisian crochet was mainly used for the making of blankets in the early years of it being counted as a craft, the source of its name is self-explanatory. Its use for blankets prompted one manufacturer to make a hook that was thick enough and long enough to make warm blankets. The hook is in three sections to allow the crocheter to make the hook longer when necessary, to accommodate more loops for a wider blanket.

Why Did It Take So Long for Tunisian Crochet to Become Popular?

It was only upon entering the twenty-first century that Tunisian crochet became popular, although it had been in existence for approximately 150 years before that. Until the introduction of digital communication with smartphones, tablets, Facebook and YouTube, and so on, it was difficult to find any patterns for this style of crochet. Recently, Tunisian crochet has become more well known, partly due to the advent of short home-made videos being posted electronically, demonstrating the craft and what can be achieved with it.

Unfortunately, many of the earlier patterns used the same size of Tunisian crochet hook as would be selected for knitting needles if using the same yarn to produce an equivalent knitted item. As a result, much of the twentieth-century Tunisian crochet was made on hooks that were much too small, resulting in very dense fabrics that were stiff and unable to drape, as well as requiring a lot of yarn. An observation was made that, for children in the Victorian era, who were meant to be seen but not heard, the density of the resulting crocheted garments would be tantamount to these children wearing straightjackets!

Even when a Tunisian crochet pattern was available, a further complication arose, because of the confusion over what comprises a 'row'. Some designers referred to picking up the loops on to the hook as one row and taking off the loops from the hook as another row. Yet other designers classed the picking up of the loops and their removal as one row. Patterns produced by myself and my company Crochet Design list both stages as one row, simply because the Tunisian crochet craft fits the definition of crochet, therefore the row should end with one loop on the hook, just as it started with one loop on the hook. Whichever stitch pattern is used, the process of working Tunisian crochet does end up with only one loop on the hook at the end of a row. In some way, it requires both the picking up of loops and their removal, and so it still fulfils the definition of crochet.

The Scope of Tunisian Crochet

A whole world of colour and texture opens up to anyone enjoying the combination of logic and artistic inspiration that Tunisian crochet can provide. The two stages of Tunisian crochet allow numbering, counting and planning to be used, because of the need to have all of the loops on the hook at one time prior to removing them, so satisfying someone with a logical mind. At the same time, the limitless number of stitch and yarn combinations is most gratifying to someone with an artistic temperament.

Suggestions for some of the ways that Tunisian crochet can be used are provided here:

- Quickly made, simple projects for presents or for sale at charity events can be produced.
- Accessories to liven up a favourite outfit can often be achieved in one or two evenings.
- The oddment stash of leftover yarns can be utilized for knee rugs, chair covers, blankets and throws.
- Fashion designs for men or women, babies, children and teens are able to be produced with Tunisian crochet.

- Unique emblems, symbols, logos, and so on, can be incorporated readily into a design featuring Tunisian crochet simple stitch with its even square pattern.
- All manner of household items, from lacy curtains, cushions, bathroom accessories and even upholstery fabrics, for use in such items as chairs with a drop-in seat, can be made.
- Art forms either on a garment or as a picture are both rewarding and fun to produce.

A little bit of Tunisian crochet magic

During my teaching career, I have been privileged to teach many people with both temporary and permanent disabilities. In addition to those with physical disabilities, there are those who attend a class or workshop as a respite from the stress of their everyday life. It is heart-warming to see so many mindfulness groups emerging, where all forms of crochet are being included to reduce stress. We see community groups working on projects either to raise funds for charity or to send donations to disadvantaged areas, both at home and abroad. There is a special place in my heart when it comes to the long, straight Tunisian crochet hook.

Although nowadays short Tunisian crochet hooks with a wire of the desired length attached can be purchased, the classic long, straight hook has some advantages over the shorter version. For instance, I have included a picture of the first ever Tunisian crochet sampler made by a lady who had become paralyzed in one arm. She could not have achieved this with the shorter-length crochet hook to which a wire is attached. The story behind this achievement is worth relating, as it can open the door to many frustrated needlecrafters for whom one of their hands or arms can no longer be used, either temporarily or permanently.

I was demonstrating Tunisian crochet at the National Exhibition Centre in Birmingham, England, many years ago, using the long hook and attracting a crowd. A lady rushed up to me shouting, 'Can I do that with one hand?' I answered 'Yes', only to be challenged by her irritated husband. Apparently many other crafts had stated only one hand was needed, and he was angry about the false hope given to his wife. Inevitably, the crowd grew larger at this exchange. I asked him, 'If I do this type of crochet using only one hand, will you let your wife try for herself?' He agreed. I placed the long hook in my belt and used only the hand holding the yarn to make the stitches. His wife then tried and succeeded sufficiently to learn enough

It is the mixture of various types of yarn and working partial rows of Tunisian simple stitch that has created this Tunisian crochet picture.

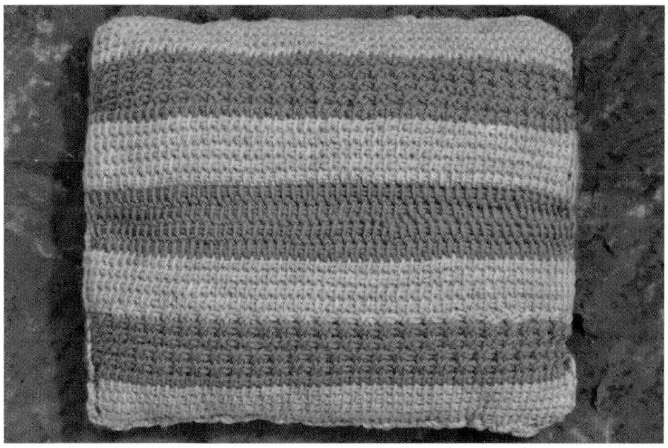

An example of first attempts of working Tunisian crochet with one hand only.

to be able to continue at home, with the instructions and long Tunisian crochet hook.

A few months later, a parcel arrived in my office, containing the cushion shown in the photograph. She informed me this was her first attempt and to keep the cushion because now she could produce a better standard of Tunisian crochet, although her arm was still paralyzed. I treasure this cushion, which is a symbol of hope to a lot of people.

Working with just one hand, the Tunisian crochet hook can replace the classic crochet hook to produce all styles of traditional crochet. Placing the Tunisian crochet hook in a belt and using the hook head only results in conventional crochet. Select the same size Tunisian crochet hook as that recommended in the pattern. The yarn does the work, and the hook is not moved, so any basic crochet pattern can be reproduced in this manner.

CHAPTER 2

THE FUNDAMENTALS OF TUNISIAN CROCHET

Tunisian Crochet Hooks

Even today, obtaining hooks for working Tunisian crochet can be a challenge, because not all yarn shops have them in stock. As more interest is being taken in needlecrafts generally, producers of tools and equipment have realized the need to satisfy both the professional and the hobbyist needlecrafter. This has resulted in an increase in the number and type of Tunisian crochet hooks being produced, although they are still not readily available everywhere; as a last resort, they can usually be purchased by mail order.

Tunisian crochet hooks can be grouped into three types:

- classic Tunisian crochet hooks
- double-ended Tunisian crochet hooks
- Tunisian crochet hooks with wire extensions

Classic Tunisian crochet hooks

The classic Tunisian crochet hook is similar in length to a long, straight knitting needle. It has a hook at one end and a stopper at the other.

The first Tunisian crochet hooks manufactured were of metal. Production then progressed specifically to aluminium, being the most common material for the manufacturing of non-steel knitting needles. In the twenty-first century it is possible to purchase mass-produced Tunisian crochet hooks made of plastic, aluminium, bamboo and wood. The larger-sized Tunisian crochet hooks are frequently available as hand-tooled wood. The hook does not have to be glossy or finished with lacquer for it to be useful for working Tunisian crochet. A beeswax finish will suffice, as long as the wax has been polished to remove any sticky residue. Of course, the quality of lathe-turned and hand-produced wooden hooks depends upon the skill of the machinist or woodworker.

OPPOSITE PAGE:
This Tasseled Boa is quick and simple to make.

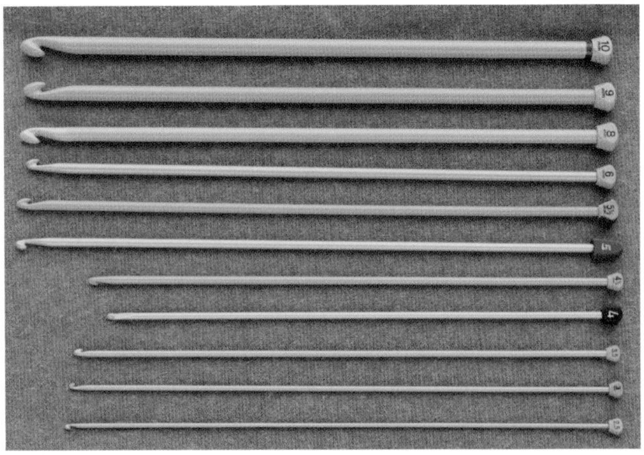

A selection of classic Tunisian crochet hooks.

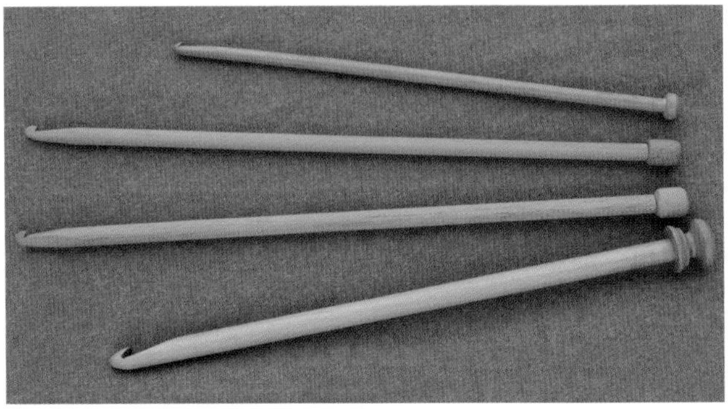

Wooden hand-turned classic Tunisian crochet hooks.

A selection of double-ended Tunisian crochet hooks.

When purchasing any hand-produced Tunisian crochet hook, look out for the following points:

1. The hook is smooth and sanded to a gloss finish, with no snags or splinters in the wood.
2. The hook head has been formed with a rounded top, to allow the vertical strands and stitches to be easily picked up.
3. The claw end of the hook head is not without shape – if it is thin and flat, it can cut the yarn as it is being worked.
4. The inside of the hook head is an area that may get missed when the wood is being sanded to a smooth finish, but it is to the inside of the hook head that the yarn has to go! Check whether there has been attention to detail and appropriate finishing of this vital area of a wooden Tunisian crochet hook.

Tunisian crochet hook sets can be purchased, with the hooks typically ranging in size from 2.00mm to 8.00mm; however, your local yarn shop may carry only a few sizes, unless they have a strongly crochet-based clientele. A wider range of hooks is more likely to be found at needlecraft or yarn-craft exhibitions and fairs. In such places, the range of Tunisian crochet hook sizes can be as large as 1.50mm to 25.00mm. Prior to visiting such events, check who will be exhibiting, particularly if the reason for your visit is solely to buy a Tunisian crochet hook or set.

The classic Tunisian crochet hook has the additional advantage of being able to be used as though it were a small crochet hook by anyone unable to utilize both hands.

Double-ended Tunisian crochet hooks

Double-ended Tunisian crochet hooks are produced in the same sizes and materials as are the classic Tunisian crochet hooks. Originally, the double-ended Tunisian crochet hook was available only in the same length as the classic Tunisian crochet hook. Now, however, shorter-length double-ended Tunisian crochet hooks have become available, which are ideal for making changes in the stitch direction when designing more adventurous Tunisian crochet fabrics.

The double-ended Tunisian crochet hook is more versatile to use than is the single-ended hook, making it possible for reversible Tunisian crochet fabrics to be produced, and the turning of the work when using such a hook reduces the resulting fabric's natural curl. It opens up many other techniques that would be difficult to work with a single-ended Tunisian crochet hook. With the aid of a little plasticine or play dough that does not harm the yarn, a stopper can be moulded for temporary use, turning the double-ended Tunisian crochet hook into a classic Tunisian crochet hook, when desired.

The beauty of using a double-ended Tunisian crochet hook is its ability to produce reversible fabrics. For instance, garments produced with two different colour combinations and using two different types of yarn can be designed to be reversible, allowing the wearer a choice of two alternative-colour outfits.

Tunisian crochet hooks with wire extensions

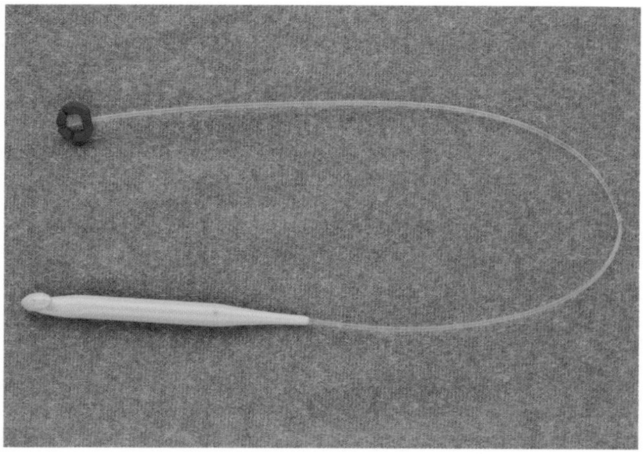

A Tunisian crochet hook with a wire extension and stopper.

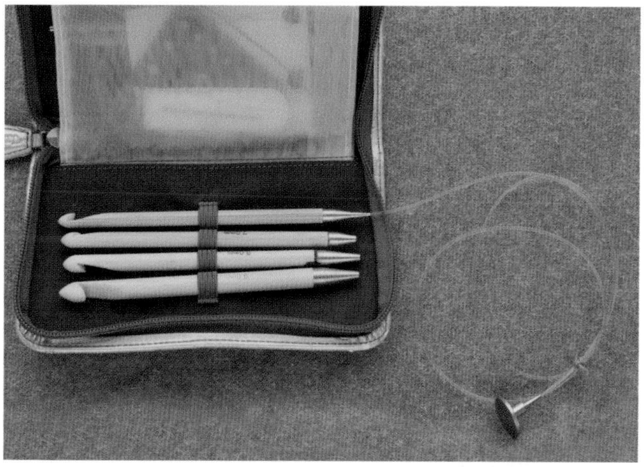

A selection of Tunisian crochet hooks with wire extensions.

The shorter Tunisian crochet hook with a wire extension is also available in a wide range of hook sizes. Not everyone wants to work with a long hook, but there are certain things to remember when producing an item worked in Tunisian crochet with a shorter hook and its wire extension. Most importantly, when purchasing such a hook, even from a reputable firm, it is necessary to check the screw or attachment part of the hook. I personally recommend the Japanese Tulip range, as from experience I can say that the screw is long and very finely turned, preventing it from coming undone even after a lot of use.

Some Tunisian crochet hooks with wires work well initially, but, if the screw end of the wire is short, it will eventually work loose from the hook. There are many other manufacturers producing hooks with wire extensions that work well, but do check the length of the screw and how closely the ridges of the screw sit next to each other.

Another part of a hook with a wire extension that needs to be checked is the wire itself. It must not be so springy that it is impossible to keep your work lying flat. Without the work lying flat, there may be tension problems.

The end of the wire will have either a secure or a moveable stopper. Both operate well, depending on what you need the stopper to do as the Tunisian crochet project is being made. The wires themselves can vary in length, and it is often useful to have a range of these wires handy. A set of Tunisian hooks with wires contains a removable stopper, allowing another hook to replace it and turning it into a double-ended hook.

One additional advantage of working with a wire extension is its usefulness when working borders, because of its flexibility.

Yarns

The fibre content of a yarn is only significant if it affects the project at hand, for example, in terms of drape, thickness, caring for the item and the intended recipient or user of the crocheted item. There is no limit to the different fibres contained in a yarn, which can be based on either a single fibre or a mixture; both types of yarn produce excellent results. In other words, you can use string, wire, thread and knitting yarn (smooth or textured) for working a Tunisian crochet article. Fine cottons are suitable for heirloom items when worked with an appropriately small Tunisian crochet hook. Heavily textured fashion yarns can be incorporated into a suitable design to be worked with Tunisian crochet once the correct size of hook has been selected. The size of hook should be large enough to allow the texture of the yarn to show its beauty and not be of a size that flattens and removes the texture incorporated in the yarn.

Yarns gain their different appearances by the way that they are produced. For instance, mercerized cotton has an additional final process to ensure its longevity of life and its ability to retain its colour through the years. On the other end of the smoothness spectrum, textured yarns (ones that include crimps, coils, loops, long hairs and other distortions) gain their texture during a heating or plying stage. The myriad colours available primarily depend upon the processes used during dyeing.

A selection of smooth 4-ply, DK- and aran-weight yarns.

A selection of yarns of different textures, some of which are heavily textured.

A selection of thinner bedspread-weight mercerized cotton threads.

There are a few things to be aware of when working with more than one colour:

- The inclusion of dye in the yarn will change its physical weight. Different dyes have different weights that can impact how far a ball of yarn will go in terms of how many stitches or how much fabric it can produce. Even when the same thickness of yarn is purchased from the same spinner and in the same range, there will be a difference in how much length is included for the same gram weight of the ball depending on its colour. How the yarn is dyed is relevant when designing a project.
- Space-dyed yarns that change colour after only a few stitches can be used for an overall pattern, but, when selecting a complementary colour to accompany such a yarn, choose one that blends with the finished look and not one of the colours used to make the multicoloured yarn because, paradoxically, that colour will clash with the completed fabric overall.
- The use of longer lengths of colour present in a spaced-dyed skein or cake needs to be carefully planned if the design to be worked includes any seams. These yarns provide wide stripes of colour when the yarn is used to work back and forth or around and around over the same number of stitches on each row or round, which can be beautiful. However, when an article has been designed to include clean bands of colour, as for the Accent-on-Autumn design (*see* Chapter 5), it would be unwise to have one of the selected yarns as a space-dyed one. The very nature of the yarn produces higgledy-piggledy breaks in such stripes, which can be off-putting to the wearer or viewer.

Other materials, tools and accessories

The following is a list of materials that may be needed when working Tunisian crochet. Many are similar to those used for other needlecrafts, and you may already have many of these items amongst your craft supplies.

Basics

Scissors

These are a necessity! Ideally have two pairs of scissors at hand: a small pair of very sharp, pointed embroidery scissors, for cutting close to the crocheted fabric without causing harm, and a pair with longer blades, for cutting material and paper into shapes to act as a template.

Not everyone likes to use the same pair of scissors for material and paper, in which case purchase an additional pair to keep solely for paper.

Large-eyed sewing needle

These are needed for securing the ends of the yarn. The ones available for knitting are also suitable for crochet. However, the better-known brands of tapestry needles have a wider range of thicknesses and a large eye to accommodate the yarn.

A selection of different thicknesses of sewing needles is good to have at hand, not only for ease when threading the yarn through the eye of the needle but also to have a sewing/tapestry needle slender enough to avoid distorting the crochet.

Stitch markers

This tool has many different names, but a small, regularly used type of stitch marker that is readily available is a stitch locker.

Typical stitch markers and stitch lockers may be too small for use with some of the thicker yarns, and it may be necessary to revert to using small nappy pins that are smooth at the loop end or safety pins, or to use a length of yarn (being careful to ensure that it will not pull out whilst you are working on your project).

Tape measure

This is necessary to ensure the size appropriateness of a finished project. Even more importantly, a tape measure is essential for measuring tension. A ruler can be an advantage, particularly if a template of paper is being made first. Ideally, choose a tape measure that shows both centimetres and inches.

A variety of materials to substitute as yarn. Starting at the top and looking back and forth: strung wooden beads; a selection of colourful leather thong on reels; elastic bands, which can be linked to form a thread; tape; metal wire, which could include jewellery wire and fuse wire; linen thread; pipe cleaners; elaborate sequin ribbon, and of course other ribbons could be used; and strung shells.

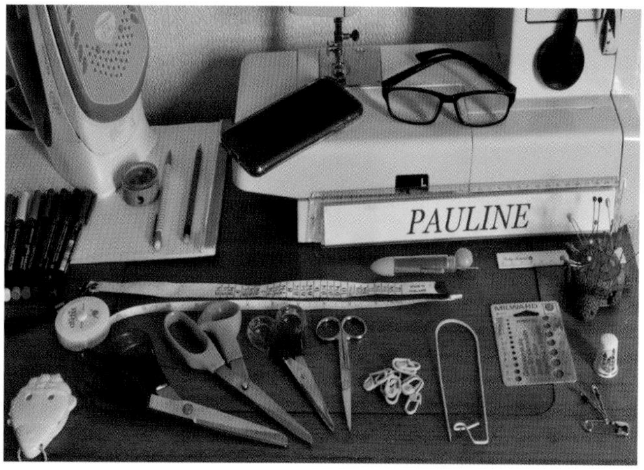

Extra items that can be acquired as necessary for your practice of Tunisian crochet. From left to right: iron; note-taking equipment; row counter; tape measures; scissors; sewing machine; camera or mobile phone; magnifier of some sort, whether glasses or another lens; rulers; sewing needles; stitch markers and holders; straight pins; needle and hook-gauge; thimble; safety pins.

A sample of Tunisian simple stitch with the square look facing, which is generally acknowledged as the right side of the fabric.

A sample of the other side of Tunisian simple stitch, which resembles the look of the back of a piece of knitted stocking stitch.

Notebook and pens or pencils

These materials are a must. Even those of you with excellent memories can forget some of the finer details of a design or pattern, particularly when using an unfamiliar technique. Jotting down legible notes can save time, energy and money, as well as reducing frustration!

Possible extras

Coloured pencils

These are a useful addition when designing with more than one colour but also for highlighting important aspects of a pattern and other information.

Eraser

This is an obvious necessity when using pencil (my preferred tool for note-taking)!

Stitch holder

This is handy to have because, for Tunisian crochet, there are times when the loops already on the hook need to be removed whilst another process is ongoing. A knitter's stitch holder is something to keep handy and could really be included in the first group of basic materials, tools and accessories.

Bent large-eyed sewing needle

This is used for those occasions when two pieces of Tunisian crochet go round a corner and need to be joined together. A bent large-eyed sewing needle can make tackling this challenge easier.

Camera

With today's digital technology, it is easier to keep a visual record of your work. You can use a camera designed for the purpose, or take pictures with your smartphone or electronic notepad.

Steam iron

This should be at hand purely for emergencies and needs to be used with care. Acrylic yarns can be distorted by steam, and other fibres may change shape upon exposure to heat.

All crochet, including Tunisian crochet, ideally ought not to be pressed. Mercerized cotton and some other materials can prove to be an exception. However, adding fabric as a lining or as a backing normally requires the fabric to be ironed or pressed first.

Tunisian Crochet Simple Stitch

Tunisian crochet simple stitch, more commonly referred to Tunisian simple stitch (Tss), is the basic stitch of Tunisian crochet, producing a fabric that looks different on both sides. The flatter side has an appearance of canvas, with squares predominating, whilst the opposite side is textured and appears similar in look to that of the reverse side (the purl side) of knitted stocking stitch. In the majority of instances, it is the flatter side that is considered to be the right side. However, for crochet, there is no right and wrong side until the fabric is made to have a right and a wrong side.

Making a slip knot; it is important to ensure that the short end tightens the loop on the hook.

Principles of working Tunisian crochet

As with all styles of crochet, Tunisian crochet starts with a single loop placed on to the hook and finishes with one final loop on the hook that needs to be secured. This is true no matter how complicated the in-between processes become. The initial loop is provided in the form of a slip knot, which is then followed by a length of chain stitches. It is vital that the slip knot is made in such a way that the short end, rather than the end from the ball of yarn, is the one that will tighten. If the slip knot tightens from the ball end, the result will be an ugly little knot protruding at the end of the first row.

The slip knot here is not flush with the edge of the work.

Begin by making a length of chain stitches with a crochet hook that is smaller in size than the Tunisian crochet hook selected to work the Tunisian simple stitch. Place the last loop on to the Tunisian crochet hook, and keep the smooth side of the chain facing (this is, the front side that looks like a row of embroidered chain stitches, lying horizontally, rather than the back side that looks like a row of raised dashes or bumps, lying end to end). The hook is inserted under the top strand of each chain stitch (that is, picking up only one strand of yarn).

The number of chains worked should be exactly the same number as that required for working the Tunisian simple stitches needed. The strand of yarn is caught and pulled through the top of the chain to make a loop that is left on the hook. For one row of Tunisian crochet, all of the chain stitches need to contain one loop (that is, to have one loop extending perpendicularly out of it). At this point, the work resembles knitting rather than crochet. To complete the row, it is necessary to sequentially remove the loops on the hook until just one loop is left on the hook.

The slip knot needs to be eased to the edge of the work by manipulating the short end of the yarn.

The construction of a knitting stitch.

The construction of a crochet stitch, with the addition of another strand of yarn.

The construction of a Tunisian crochet stitch, requiring two interlocking loops.

During the removal of the loops, one hooped loop is being pull through another hooped loop on the hook; this effectively doubles the amount of yarn held within each stitch compared to that of a knitted stitch. This is the reason why it is necessary to double the size of Tunisian crochet hook being used from that of the size of knitting needle recommended on the ball band of the particular yarn being worked.

It must be stressed that the size of knitting needle to use that is advised on the yarn ball band or in a knitting pattern is a guide, not a firm instruction, to selecting the size of either a standard crochet hook or a Tunisian crochet hook that would be suitable for working this particular yarn. Note that only a few yarn manufacturers recommend an accurate size for crochet.

Tunisian crochet began to be popular only relatively recently, and, in order to remove any confusion concerning the necessity for using a size of Tunisian crochet hook approximately double the size of the needle recommended for knitting with, let me explain the reason.

Let us refer to the front and back of a loop on the Tunisian crochet hook as involving two strands: this is the equivalent of a knitting stitch, but Tunisian crochet does not stop there. When producing a piece of typical crochet, the top of each crochet stitch has three strands, and the crochet hook is inserted under two of these strands. Tunisian crochet, however, involves pulling another loop, similar to one of knitting, through the loop already on the Tunisian crochet hook, resulting in each Tunisian crochet stitch containing four strands of yarn. Therefore, a much larger hook is necessary for the resulting fabric to be as flexible as one produced by knitting, in order to accommodate all of these loops within a suitable amount of space to allow drape.

A quick trial run – producing the basic Tunisian simple stitch

If you have never worked Tunisian crochet before, try this process with only eight stitches that are worked with ordinary crochet hooks (a smaller one for making the foundation chain and a larger one for working the Tunisian simple stitch, standing in for a Tunisian crochet hook).

This little experiment will give you a feel for the technique and show why it is necessary to work on what appears to be a hook that is too large! The size of the hook used for working the chain should be one size larger than the recommended knitting needle for the yarn being used.

The size of the hook for making the Tunisian crochet stitches should be double that of the size recommended for the knitting needle with which to knit the yarn.

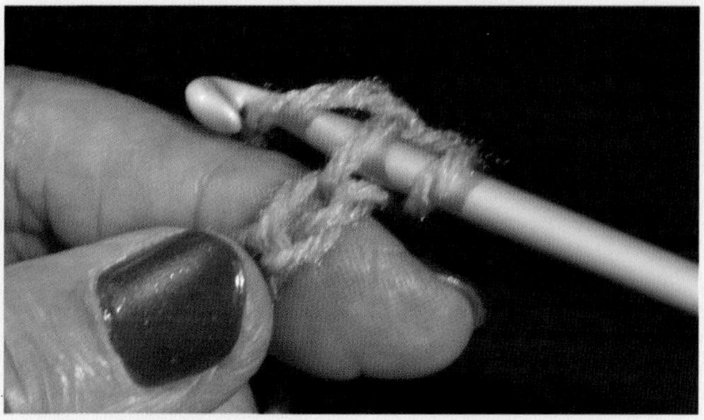

Insert the Tunisian crochet hook under the top loop of the chain to collect the yarn to be pulled through the chain to make a loop that is left on the Tunisian crochet hook.

Set-Up

Step 1: With the selected yarn, make a slip knot that will slide into the finished fabric (*see* the section 'Principles of working Tunisian crochet'). Place this slip knot on to the smaller crochet hook.

Step 2: With the smaller crochet hook, make 10 chains (10ch); place the last chain made on to the larger crochet hook that will be acting as a Tunisian crochet hook.

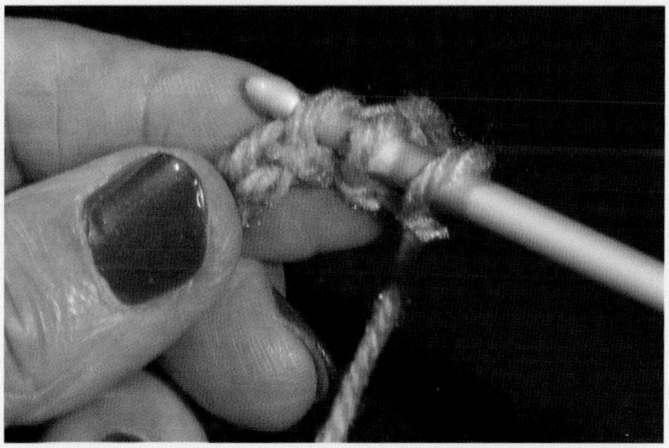

Continue picking up one loop from under the top strand of each chain in turn, until all of the chains have been worked.

Row 1, Stage 1

Step 1: Insert the larger crochet hook into the 2nd chain stitch from the hook head, by passing the hook head under only the *top* strand of this chain stitch (not the two strands normally recommended for working traditional crochet).

Step 2: Put the yarn over the hook head (that is, 'yarn over hook' or yoh), and pull the caught yarn under and through the single strand (that is, the top strand of the chain stitch). [2 loops on hook]

Step 3: *Keeping the loop just made on the hook, pick up the top strand of the next chain, yoh, and pull the yarn through as for Step 2.

Step 4: Continue repeating this procedure from * in Step 3 until all of the chains have been worked. [10 loops on hook]

This completes the first-stage picking-up part of the first row, which is similar to casting on for knitting.

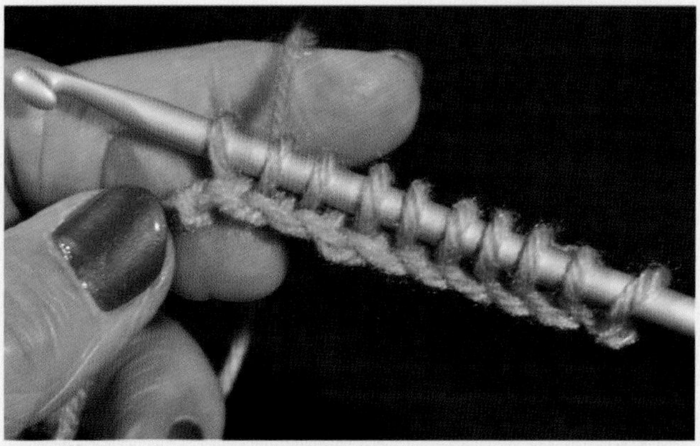

All of the loops corresponding to individual chains of the foundation chain are on the hook – this is the knitting aspect of Tunisian crochet.

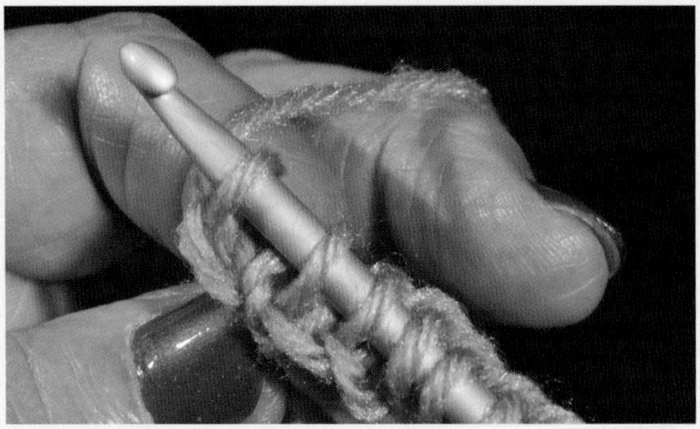

One chain is made to lift the hook at the start of the row for this step.

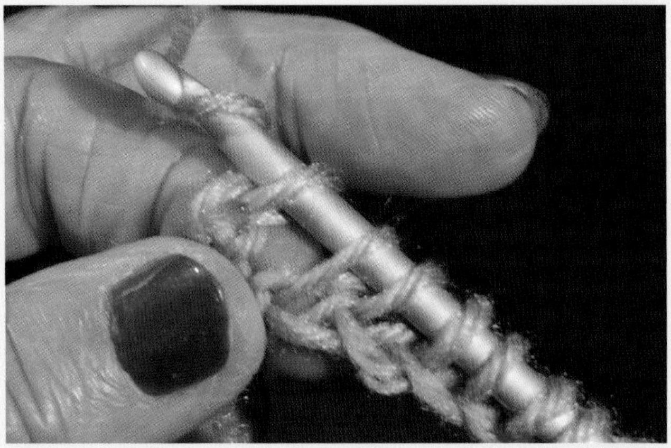

Work yoh and pull the yarn through the first two loops on the hook; this is the one closest to the head of the hook and the next loop along the shaft of the hook.

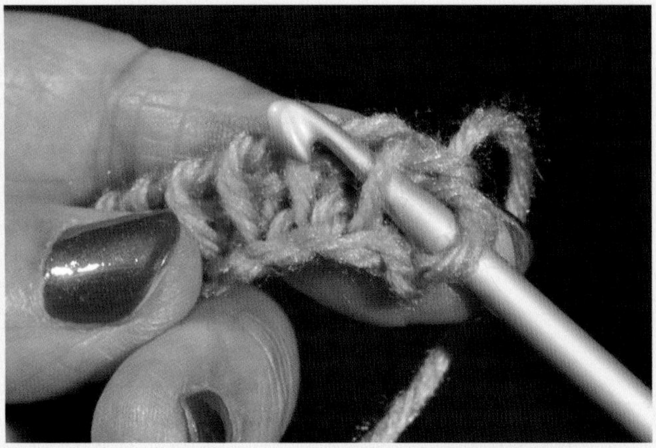

Insert the hook under next vertical strand, to form the next loop on the hook.

Row 1, Stage 2

There was no turning chain (often abbreviated as 'tch' in published patterns) present at the start of the row as the loops were all picked up, and the hook was kept in position through the centre of the loops and not above them. Now, however, the hook needs to sit on top of the stitches and therefore requires one chain to be made to lift the hook prior to the loops being removed during this Stage 2 step.

Step 1: yoh, pull the caught yarn through the first loop on the hook to create 1 turning chain, to lift the hook to the correct position for working the rest of this row.
Step 2: *yoh, pull the caught yarn through the next 2 loops on the hook. The yarn held in the hook head is pulled through the working loop just made and the next loop on the hook.
Step 3: Repeat from * to end of the row.
There is 1 loop left on the hook.

The first row or foundation row has been completed. Remember that there is no turning chain at the beginning of a Tunisian simple stitch row. At this point, this loop on the hook *must* be counted as the first stitch.

Row 2, Stage 1

Step 1: *Insert the hook under the next vertical strand of the previous row, yoh, and pull the yarn through this vertical strand, to result in another loop on the hook.
Step 2: Repeat from * until all of the vertical strands of the previous row have been worked, including the one at the end of the row, which can easily be missed.
Note: This last-stitch pick up can be recommended to be worked differently; however, it is necessary to do what I recommend here, because the result is as needed for working the stitch-pattern trial pieces and patterns presented later in the book.
Step 3: Check whether all of the stitches have been worked! It is easy to count the stitches whilst the picked-up loops are still all on the hook.

Row 2, Stage 2

All of the loops currently on the hook need to be removed to complete the second stage of Row 2.

Step 1: Make 1ch to lift the hook (that is, to serve as the turning chain and bring the hook up to the correct level for working the row) – in other words, yoh and pull the yarn through the first stitch on the hook. This ensures that the left-hand side of the piece is kept straight.
Step 2: *yoh, and pull the yarn through the next 2 loops on the hook.
Step 3: Repeat from * to the end of the row.
There is 1 loop left on the hook.
Repeat Row 2, Stages 1–2, until the required length of the fabric is reached.

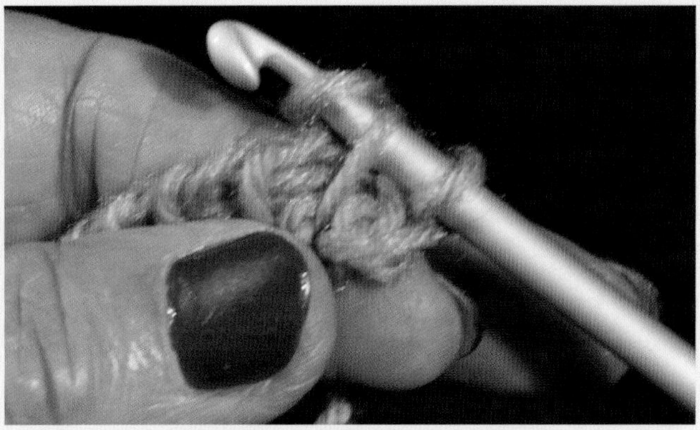

Work yoh and pull the yarn through and under the vertical strand.

Last row

Having now got the hang of the basic stitch, all that is left is for the previous row to be neatened, by hiding the holes that are currently present between the vertical strands of this row.

On the last row to be worked, make sure that the hook is again inserted under the vertical strands (not into the visible holes between the vertical strands), otherwise the last row will have an open look, which would be out of keeping with the rest of the fabric.

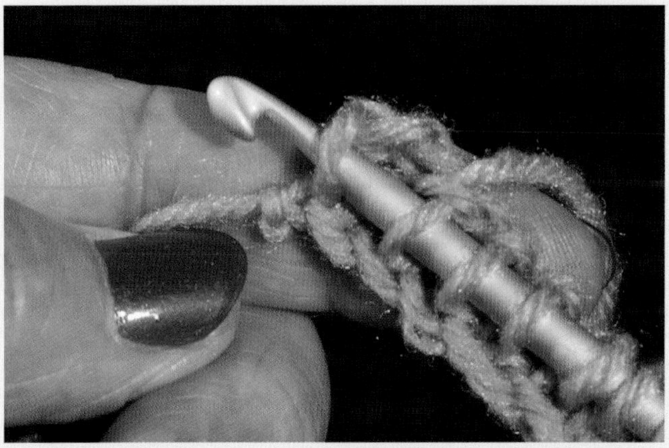

Be careful not to miss this last vertical strand of the row.

Step 1: Change to using the smaller hook (the same one used for working the foundation chain), and make 1ch, to keep the side straight.
Step 2: *Work 1 double crochet (dc) under the next vertical strand by inserting the hook under the vertical strand yoh, pull the yarn through the strand, yoh and pull the yarn through the next 2 loops on the hook (= 1dc made); repeat from * until one vertical strand remains to be worked at the end of the row.
Note: Now, just one vertical strand remains and needs to be worked with 1dc in a suitable way to avoid a hole appearing. Do this as follows:
Step 3: Pick up one loop on to the hook by inserting the hook under the top horizontal strand before the last vertical strand of the row and under the last vertical strand of the row, and then yoh, pull the yarn through both strands at once, yoh and pull the yarn through the next 2 loops on the hook (= last 1dc of row made)

Fasten off.

The top row of a piece of Tunisian simple stitch appears to have holes; when a length of Tunisian simple stitch fabric has been completed, a double crochet is worked under each vertical strand across the row to rectify this.

Points to look out for

To save time and undue effort, keep an eye open for the following points when working Tunisian crochet. It often helps to imagine the loops after they have been picked up as replicating an enormously long treble.

The process of collecting the yarn in the hook head and removing two loops at a time until only one loop remains on the hook is the same process as working a very tall treble for traditional crochet.

The work leaning: that is, the vertical strands of the fabric slant to the right.

Action: Check whether the hook is being inserted into the second vertical strand and not through the work. If in doubt, look at the illustrations for the steps of the trial piece.

Insufficient stitches: for instance, if stitches are being lost on each row.

Action: Check whether the last strand is being picked up as described for Step 3 of the earlier 'Last row' section. Alternatively, check whether it is the vertical strand and not a horizontal strand that is being picked up when working Row 2, Stage 1.

Lack of height: although the tension is correct widthways, there may be insufficient rows to reach the height required.

Action: Ensure that the hook sits on top of the work when the loops are being picked up. Frequently, if the hook is allowed to sit in front of the stitches, this shortens the loops on the hook. This then makes the Tunisian crochet fabric shorter than the tension needed, as well as making the fabric denser, resulting in more yarn being used than is necessary. This usually occurs when crocheting in a hurry with a familiar Tunisian crochet stitch pattern.

The following Tasselled Boa pattern is worked in exactly the same way as the sample of basic Tunisian simple stitch, and it requires no finishing of edges. The sides of a narrow length of Tunisian simple stitch automatically curve inwards, with the fabric shaping itself into a roll. One large tassel added at each end helps it to hang well during wear.

Rectangles and squares

The easiest shape to produce is a rectangle. A rectangle is just a piece of unshaped crochet with its opposite, parallel sides being of the same length. The Tasselled Boa is an example of a very long and narrow rectangle. It is made by following the instructions for Tunisian simple stitch for a specified number of rows. Make a boa in a different colour to suit each of your outfits!

A square is made in the same way, stopping when the length of the sides equals the width of the fabric. With thick yarns, an allowance sometimes has to be made for the height of the last row of double crochet. This is achieved by stopping working the Tunisian crochet stitches one row early, to allow for the height of the finishing row of double crochet. It is not necessary to take that into consideration when working with thinner yarn.

The Square Cushion Cover and the Colourful Cushion Cover are examples of working a square.

TASSELLED BOA

Materials

Approximately 100g 4-ply soft acrylic yarn (if using a yarn of a different material, the required yarn weight may vary)
5.00mm crochet hook
6.50mm Tunisian crochet hook
Large-eyed sewing needle
15cm piece of stiff card/piece of wood/ something similar, to make the tassels. As a last resort, a smartphone can be used, having remembered to switch off the phone first!

Tension

Not important for this item, as it depends on the chosen yarn

Size

Not important for the boa as it is based on personal preference

The quickly made but stylish Tasselled Boa.

Pattern instructions

Boa body

Step 1: Leave a length of yarn long enough to attach a tassel before making a slip knot and placing it on to the 5.00mm crochet hook.
Step 2: With the 5.00mm crochet hook, work 21ch.
Step 3: Change to using the 6.50mm Tunisian crochet hook. Work Rows 1–2 as for Tss (that is, Row 1, Stages 1–2 and Row 2, Stages 1–2) on these 21sts.

Securing the loops of a tassel.

The tassel securely attached to one end of the boa.

Step 4: Repeat working Row 2 (that is, Row 2, Stages 1–2) until 164 rows in total have been completed.
Step 5: Work as for the last row of Tss (that is, by working double crochet stitches across the row).
Step 6: Break off the yarn, leaving a length of yarn long enough to seam together the edge of one short end of the boa and attach a tassel.

Tassels – two made alike

Step 7: Wrap the yarn around the card/wood/other object 100 times, for a large tassel. (For a smaller tassel, work fewer wraps.)
Step 8: Thread a needle to one end of the yarn, and carefully slide the loops off of the card whilst maintaining their alignment.
Step 9: Approximately 2cm down from the top fold of the loops, tightly wrap the threaded end of yarn several times around the loops.
Step 10: Secure the end of yarn by sewing it through the wrapped part of the tassel.
Step 11: Fasten off. The long loops of the featured tassels are left uncut, but, if preferred, cut the loops of your tassels.

Finishing

Step 12: At one end of the long strip of Tss, fold in the sides of the fabric so that the corners of the short edge meet in the middle, leaving the side of the fabric with the square look on the outside.
Step 13: Use the length of yarn still connected to the boa body to secure the edges of the folded fabric in place and attach one tassel, by spreading the upper parts of the loops to span the short end of the boa and secure them in place. Ideally sew the tassel firmly using many stitches.
Step 14: Repeat for the other end of the boa, to seam it and attach the second tassel.
Step 15: Sew in all yarn ends.

SQUARE CUSHION COVER

Two pieces of Tunisian simple stitch are seamed together to form this basic simple Square Cushion Cover.

Materials

3 × 100g ball West Yorkshire Spinners DK-weight yarn (approximately 225m/100g)
6.00mm crochet hook
7.00mm Tunisian crochet hook
1 × cushion pad, 42cm/16½in × 42cm/16½in
Note: The third ball of yarn may not be required, depending on the size of the cushion cover being made.

Tension

Measured over Tss: 13 stitches and 13 rows to 10cm

Size

38cm/15in × 38cm/15in, including the completed edging

The pattern is for producing a 38cm × 38cm cushion with a Tunisian crochet cover. Different sizes can be obtained by reducing the number of chain stitches and rows worked, for example, to make covers for small scatter cushions, or by increasing the number of chain stitches and rows worked, for larger cushions. The secret is to make certain that both the back and the front are of the same size and form a tidy square when arranged back to back. The crochet pieces need to be slightly smaller than the cushion pad, to avoid the cover wrinkling when in use.

Pattern instructions

Covers – two made alike

Step 1: Make a slip knot and place it on to the 6.00mm crochet hook. With the same hook, make 45ch.
Step 2: Place the last chain on to the 7.00mm Tunisian crochet hook. Work Rows 1–2 as for Tss.
Step 3: Repeat working Row 2 until the work measures the same in height as for its width (ideally, 34cm/13½in).
Step 4: Check whether the work is a square.
Step 5: Change to the 6.00mm crochet hook. Make 1ch to lift the hook. Work1dc per st by inserting the hook under each vertical strand in turn to the end of the row, producing a straight edge of dc, making the pad insertion easier. Fasten off.

Finishing

Step 6: With the fronts of the covers together, secure the two pieces by matching each stitch and each row of the covers so that they are opposite to and aligned with each other. Sew the two pieces together along three sides – the right side, top and left side – with a whip stitch.
Step 7: Turn the cushion cover the right way out, with the front sides of the fabric outermost. Insert the cushion pad and securely close the bottom opening using a whip stitch.

Alternatively, place two markers indicating the length of the zip at the bottom side of the cushion. With the front sides facing you, double crochet around the sides and top of the cushion cover by working through both pieces until a marker is reached. dc between the markers to form the opening for the zip. Continue working as given for the Colourful Cushion Cover (*see* the section 'Edging').

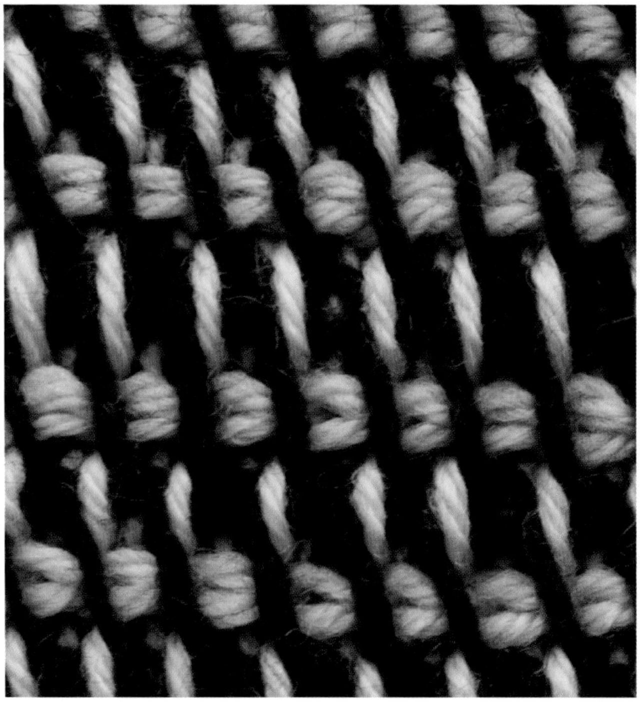

A second colour converts the Tunisian simple stitch into the Tunisian tweed stitch.

COLOURFUL CUSHION COVER

Spaced-dyed yarn can be used to create interesting design features such as the Colourful Cushion Cover.

Materials

1 × 100g ball space-dyed DK-weight yarn with a long colour run
2 × 100g balls DK-weight yarn of a complementary single shade
6.00mm crochet hook
7.00mm Tunisian crochet hook
1 × cushion pad, 42cm/16½in × 42cm/16½in
2 × stitch markers
30cm zip of a colour matching the spaced-dyed yarn
Note: The second ball of the single-shade yarn may not be required, depending on the size of the cushion cover being made.

Tension

Measured over Tss: 13 stitches and 13 rows to 10cm

Size

38cm/15in × 38cm/15in, including the completed edging

Using a space-dyed yarn is what makes this cushion cover appear to have a planned basic coloured design. A striped-print West Yorkshire Spinners self-striping yarn of the Colour-Lab DK series is the yarn selected for this project.

It has enough length before the colour changes to introduce interesting patterning for a piece of fabric of the desired width for this cushion cover. The back is worked in a plain shade of the same yarn, chosen to complement the space-dyed front.

Pattern instructions

Front

Step 1: With the single-shade yarn, make a slip knot and place it on to the 6.00mm crochet hook. With the same hook, make 45ch.
Step 2: Place the last chain on to the 7.00mm Tunisian crochet hook. With the space-dyed yarn, work as described previously for Tss on these 45sts to make the cover for the Square Cushion Cover (*see* Steps 2–3 of that pattern). (Note: The work should measure 34cm in width.)
Step 3: Continue until the work measures 34cm in length.
Step 4: Check whether the work is a square.
Step 5: Change to using the 6.00mm crochet hook and single-shade yarn. Make 1ch to lift the hook, and work 1dc under each vertical strand in turn to the end of the row.
Fasten off.

Back

Step 6: Make a slip knot and place it on to the 6.00mm crochet hook. With the same hook and single-colour yarn, make 45ch.
Step 7: Place the last chain on to the 7.00mm Tunisian crochet hook. Do not change yarns. With Tss, make a square of the same size as for the front (*see* Steps 2–5 of the front), but *do not* break off the yarn: keep the yarn attached after the finishing double-crochet row has been worked.

Edging

Step 8: With the backs of the covers together, secure the two pieces by matching each stitch and each row of the covers so that they are opposite to and aligned with each other.
Step 9: Mark the position of the start and end of the opening for the zip on the bottom side of the cushion cover.
Step 10: With the front side of the cushion cover facing you (and therefore with the back of each cover together), begin joining both pieces together: work double crochet along the left side of the cushion cover, making certain that the hook goes through both pieces of fabric and checking that the rows of Tss are properly aligned and no holes are being made.
Step 11: Continue working double crochet along the top side of the cushion cover. Avoid any holes appearing at the join by picking up the vertical strand of the nearest row of fabric for both pieces of the cover. (Note: The cushion pad will hide any additional bulk that this way of joining may produce.)
Step 12: Join the right side as for the left side (*see* Step 10).
Step 13: Join part of the remaining, bottom, side as for the top side (*see* Step 11), from the corner to the nearest marker for the zip.
Step 14: Continue working double-crochet stitches *into the fabric of the front piece only* up to the second marker for the zip.

Step 15: Complete joining the bottom side as for the top side (again, *see* Step 11), from the second marker to the corner.

Step 16: Work 1 full round of crab stitch on these double-crochet stitches, whilst retaining the opening for the zip. Fasten off.

Step 17: With the back side of the cushion facing you, work 1 row of double crochet and 1 row of crab stitch on the unworked stitches of the zip opening (that is, for the back piece only).

Finishing

Insert and attach the zip to the underside of the cushion-cover fabric at the zip opening using your preferred method, sewing thread and choice of stitch. Sew in all yarn and thread ends. Insert the cushion pad, close the zip, and check whether all of the yarn and thread ends are secure.

Alternatively, insert the cushion pad and close the bottom of the cushion by sewing the edges of the opening together with a whip stitch.

A close-up of one corner of the Colourful Cushion Cover that is worked with a double-crochet and crab-stitch edging.

CHAPTER 3

EXPLORING TUNISIAN SIMPLE STITCH

There are numerous possible ways to be creative with Tunisian crochet. However, to produce a professional finish to any project, there are some techniques that need to be understood and put into practice. This does not take away the fun, it just reduces the time lost in having to pull back and start again. It also saves on money. Making something beautiful and usable is normally the endgame. Taking the analogy of building a brick or stone house is appropriate when making a Tunisian crochet article.

Start with the best materials and implements that are necessary and affordable at the outset. Except for the yarn, everything can be used again. Ensure that you know how to use all of your materials, tools and accessories. This is the foundation and beginning of any Tunisian project, in the same way that a strong enough foundation is laid that will withstand the weight of the proposed building. Although the actual foundation of the building is covered up later, it is the base that determines the building's durability. Similarly, having the correct implements, materials and techniques at hand ensures that the resulting Tunisian crochet fabric is suitable, durable and, when necessary, can support embellishment.

Understanding the idiosyncrasies of Tunisian crochet is important. Be aware of its restrictions as well as its limitless possibilities! Become familiar with those techniques that are similar to crochet and the ones that lean more towards knitting. This knowledge increases confidence and reduces uncertainty when developing a new design.

OPPOSITE PAGE: The first side of the reversible, unisex All-Square Sleeveless Jacket, inspired by a pattern of Maris Groter.

It is well worth the time and effort to try any unfamiliar technique as soon as you come across it. By experimenting and understanding a new idea immediately, the time it takes to execute the more complicated processes is reduced. In particular, it expands the number of imaginative stitches that might be included in a design.

How to work the basic Tunisian simple stitch (again, abbreviated Tss) is covered in Chapter 2. Other than how to finish the last row with double crochet, to avoid a lacy or loose finish, nothing else has yet been explained.

However, Tunisian simple stitch is incredibly versatile, and all of the peculiarities found in Tunisian crochet can be explored through this basic stitch.

For instance, here are some of the things possible to explore with Tunisian simple stitch:

- Working an edging or border
- Adding colour
- Tunisian crochet garter stitch
- Increasing
- Decreasing

Each of these elements is looked at in more detail throughout this chapter.

A double crochet is worked by first inserting the hook under the next vertical strand of the previous row.

The completed double crochet forms part of the neat finish for the top edge of the fabric.

Double crochet stitches are worked until the last stitch and corner of the top edge are reached.

At the corner, the hook must be inserted under two strands as shown, to avoid a hole appearing.

Working an Edging or Border

Double crochet across the last row

Unlike the usual form of crochet, which has no right or wrong side unless it is made to have a right or wrong side, producing Tunisian crochet with a single-ended Tunisian crochet hook results in a fabric that is different on each of its two sides.

The surface with the square look is normally considered to be the right side (RS), being flatter and smoother. The reverse, often referred to as the wrong side (WS), has a look of knitting (actually, like the purl side of a piece of stocking-stitch fabric) and is used as the right side only when specifically intended as such as part of a design. For instance, a project incorporating panels or small inserted shapes may have the 'wrong side' facing in order to create texture to enhance a design and to set off the embedded panels or shapes.

Because it is usual when working Tunisian crochet to have the same side facing at all times, there is a tendency for the fabric to curl. Fortunately, most patterns have additional borders and edgings that counteract this effect. Alleviating the curl of a Tunisian crochet fabric is more difficult when the size of the hook chosen to work the fabric is too small. The tighter the stitches are, the greater the tendency for the fabric to curl.

Tunisian simple stitch by itself produces a solid fabric. Therefore, to prevent taking away from this appearance, it is essential to be able to complete the Tunisian crochet fabric without unnecessary holes appearing at the top, bottom and side edges.

A standard crochet hook of two sizes smaller than the size of the Tunisian crochet hook being used to work the main part of the fabric is required. At the start of a row, with one loop on the hook, pick up a loop from under the next vertical strand as if continuing to work Tss. Instead of keeping the picked-up loop on the hook as when working Row 1 of basic Tss, once this loop has been picked up from the vertical strand, yoh and pull the yarn through the next two loops on the hook, to complete a double crochet. Continue working in double crochet until you reach the end of the row (that is, work as given for the 'Last row' of the section in 'A quick trial run – producing the basic Tunisian simple stitch'– *see* Chapter 2). Had the double crochet been made by inserting the hook through the work in the spaces between the vertical strands across the top row instead of by picking up loops for working the double-crochet stitches from under the vertical strands, the finished result would be one of holes.

Double crochet down the left-hand side

Adding a double-crochet border into the sides of a piece of fabric of Tunisian simple stitch can be a challenge. The end of each row of the left-hand side of the fabric has only one strand of yarn present to work with, which, if used on its own, will create an unacceptable hole.

To add a border of double crochet without holes, a second strand of yarn needs to be found and picked up at the same time as the loose single strand on the very edge. The following method produces a firm finish that wears well.

Step 1: First, rotate the fabric by 90 degrees clockwise, so that what was the vertical left-hand side of the fabric is now the horizontal top edge. Now, look for the two (formerly horizontal, now vertical) parallel strands (that look like an equals sign) forming the first stitch of the take-off stage (Row 2, Stage 2) of the last row of Tss worked.
Step 2: Insert the hook through the right-hand strand (was top strand) of this stitch and the single strand at the top edge (was left-hand side) of the fabric, yoh and pull the yarn through.
Step 3: Proceed to make 1dc (that is, yoh and pull the caught yarn through the two loops on the hook).
Step 4: Continue in this way until reaching the left-hand corner that connects to the left-hand vertical edge (was bottom edge) (that is, the first row of Tss, worked into the foundation chain).
Note: It may be necessary to work an additional 1dc into each corner of the fabric (so 2dc in total) to achieve a sharper point.

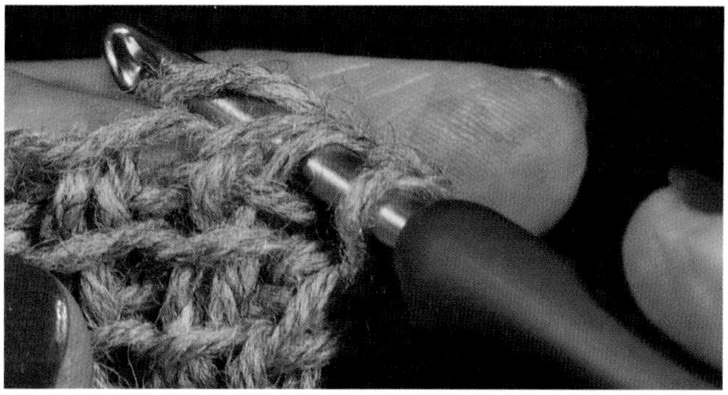

To work double crochet down the first side edge of the fabric, having rotated the fabric as shown, pick up the (now) top strand of the row below and the last vertical strand of the row.

Work two double-crochet stitches in the last stitch of the first side edge of the fabric, to help to turn the corner.

Double crochet across the bottom edge

There are two ways to add double crochet along the bottom of the work, where the foundation chain lies.

Work one double crochet for each stitch in turn along the bottom of the fabric by inserting the hook under the vertical strand adjacent to the bottom edge.

Method 1

At each stitch in turn across the row, simply insert the hook between the two horizontal strands (the equals sign) resulting from Row 1 and *at the same time* pick up the single strand remaining from the foundation chain, and use them together to work 1dc.

Method 2

Pick up 1 loop from under the vertical strand closest to the edge of the fabric at each stitch position in turn across the row to the end of the row, and use it to work 1dc (that is, after picking up a loop, yoh and pull the yarn through the next 2 loops of the hook).

Work one double crochet for each embroidered-look chain in turn along the second side edge by inserting the hook under the chain strands as shown.

If holes appear, as can be seen here, change to using Method 2.

For Method 2, to work each double crochet, pick up a loop from under the bottom strand of the parallel lines and the front loop of the embroidered-look chain as shown.

Double crochet up the right-hand side

To complete the border or edge of the piece of Tss fabric, a final side of double crochet needs to be added to give a neat overall result. Before adding an edging of double crochet, the look of this edge will appear similar to that of traditional crochet stitches with a chain-top finish.

Method 1

Work 1dc by picking up 1 loop from under the two horizontal strands of the chain that can be seen at the top of the work that has the look of an embroidered chain stitch. Should holes appear, use Method 2.

Method 2

To avoid holes or gaps, have the work turned by 90 degrees so this side has a horizontal orientation. Pick up the bottom strand of the last stitch of the take-off process from Row 2, Stage 2, which looks similar to that of an equals sign; and also the *front* loop of the chain at the top of the work (the chain that is at the side of the fabric when held in its original vertical orientation) for each row end in turn.

Crab stitch

Crab stitch is essentially a backwards double crochet. To work crab stitch, do not turn the crochet at the end of the previous row of double crochet; the crab stitch is simply worked in the opposite direction, that is from left to right, along the previous row.

Step 1: At the end of the previous row of double crochet (or other crochet stitch), make 1ch to lift the hook.
Step 2: Insert the hook under the top two strands of the next stitch to the right of the hook.
Step 3: To be able to work the yarn held at the back of the work, drop the hook head on to the yarn, rather than placing the yarn over the hook head as usual.
Step 4: Tilt the hook upright, with the hook head pointing down, to allow the hook head to pull the yarn through to the front of the work. At this point, check there are two loops on the hook as it is easy to make a backward slip stitch, in which case no texture would appear as a result of working the stitch.

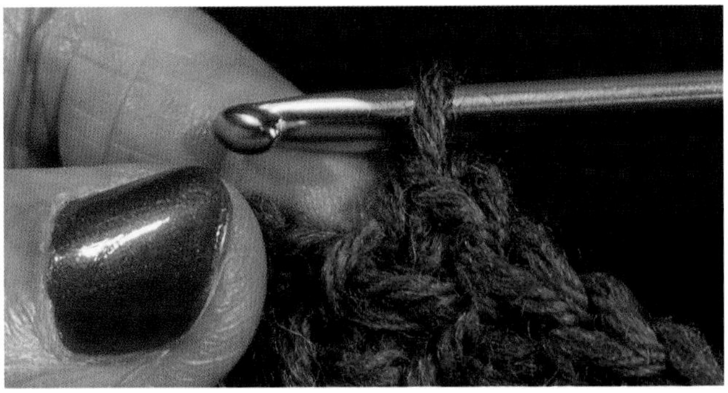

The hook is at the end of the previous row of double crochet and is ready for making one chain to lift the hook.

Having made one chain, insert the hook under the top of the double-crochet stitch to the right of the hook (the last stitch of the previous row), picking up both strands of the top of the stitch as usual.

Drop the hook head on to the yarn being held at the back of the work.

Step 5: Twist the hook into its normal working position. There should now be 2 loops on the hook, as usual for working a double crochet.

Tilt the hook, to pull through the yarn, and ensure that two loops are now on the hook.

Move the hook back to its normal working position.

The previous crab stitches have been completed, and the hook is ready for the making of the next one.

Step 6: yoh and pull the yarn through the 2 loops on the hook, to leave 1 loop on the hook (= 1 crab stitch).
Repeat Steps 2–6 to continue to work crab stitch to the end of the row or round.

Change colour when only two loops are left to remove from the hook.

With the new colour, continue working across the row as for Tunisian simple stitch.

Here you can see the resulting clean lines of colour at the edge of work.

Modular designs

Large projects can be produced by working long strips, small squares, and other unshaped pieces that can create a range of items, including the following:

- A sofa throw or knee rug worked with a lightweight soft or brushed yarn
- A bedspread worked with a DK-weight yarn, or with a 4-ply yarn, to alleviate some of the physical weight of this item
- A floor mat worked with a smaller Tunisian crochet hook and with a hard-wearing yarn
- A bathroom mat worked with a cotton yarn, to absorb moisture

To execute these larger designs:

Step 1: Plan the patchwork design of panels, long strips and/or square/rectangular/other-shape motifs.
Step 2: Make the required pieces, finishing each piece with a double-crochet edging around all sides.
Step 3: Join the pieces together by sewing or with double crochet and (optional) crab stitch.
Step 4: Add a final border around the outside edge of the assembled piece. This can be another round of double crochet followed by a round of crab stitch or something more decorative.

Adding Colour

Clean, straight stripes

Changing colours to produce clean, straight stripes is not difficult. For the Accent-On-Autumn Coat (*see* Chapter 5), colours are changed at the edges by employing a method that ensures that the stripes end crisply, with no colour dragging into the next band of colour.

Remember that the main characteristic of the Tunisian craft is crochet (rather than knitting); therefore, to avoid the first colour bleeding into the next colour band, proceed as follows:

Stage 1

Step 1: Work across the row with the current colour by picking up 1 loop from under each vertical strand in turn to the end of the row.

Stage 2

Step 1: Make 1ch.

Step 2: *yoh, pull the yarn through 2 loops; repeat from * to the end of the row, stopping when there are still 2 loops left on the hook.

Step 3: yoh with the new colour and pull it through the remaining 2 loops on the hook. The loop made with the new colour is now the start of the next row.

Colour changes within a row

Because all of the loops are present on the hook having worked in one direction for Stage 1, some knitting techniques can be utilized with Tunisian crochet. One of these is to be able to work with two colours (or more) within the same row. It is a method used by knitters when working a Fair Isle pattern.

For the use of two (or more) colours in a row to be achieved neatly, it is necessary to twist the two yarns together at the back of the fabric every time after working two to four stitches. This ensures there are no long strands of yarn floating around for fingers, buttons, zips, and so on, to catch. In addition, if the yarn producing the fabric being worked is an easily-snapped soft wool, it reduces the possibility of the yarn being broken if it is caught by something. Even worse, if this technique was used for a child's design without the twisting together of the yarns or with a yarn that does not easily snap, the damage to little fingers could be horrific.

Tunisian crochet tweed stitch

By using two yarns of different colours, Tss can be worked to obtain a tweed effect. For the first time when you work tweed stitch, choose two yarn colours of the same thickness that contrast strongly. You need colour to achieve this effect! The yarn of the second colour is attached when all of the loops worked with the yarn of the first colour have been picked up and placed on to the Tunisian crochet hook. Smooth rather than textured yarns are easier to work with initially.

An example of Fair Isle-style Tunisian crochet.

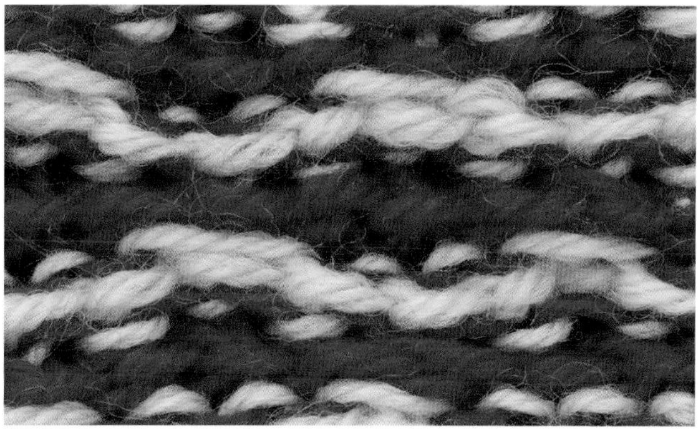

The back of a sample of Tunisian crochet colourwork, showing no long, floating strands.

It is changing the yarn colour being used at the end of every row, once all of the loops are on the hook, that causes the colours to intermingle, resulting in a tweed effect.

Set-Up

With the yarn of the first colour, make a slip knot that will slide into the finished fabric (*see* the section 'Principles of working Tunisian crochet' in Chapter 2). Place this slip knot on to a crochet hook of an appropriate size for the two chosen yarns. Work a length of chain stitches, and place the last chain on to a Tunisian crochet hook of an appropriate size for the two chosen yarns.

Row 1, Stage 1

With the first yarn colour and the Tunisian crochet hook, pick up and place 1 loop on to the hook for each chain in turn, starting with the 2nd chain from the hook.

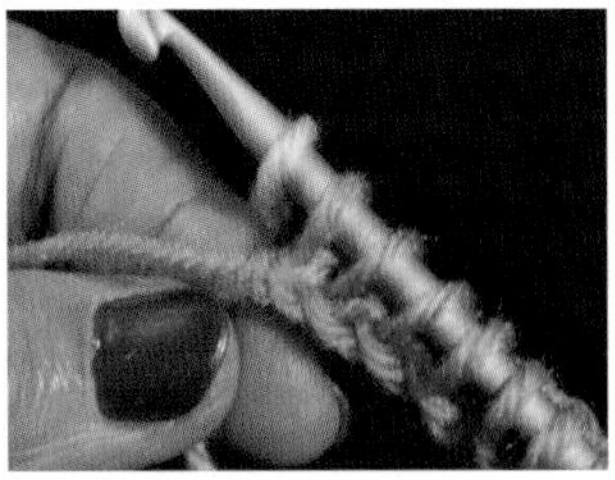

Introduce the new colour once all of the loops are on the hook.

The new colour is used to remove all of the loops on the hook.

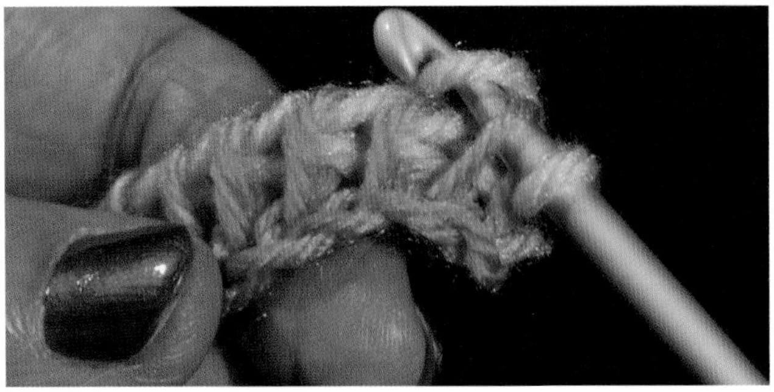

Still with the new colour, pick up all of the loops and place on to the hook as for Tunisian simple stitch.

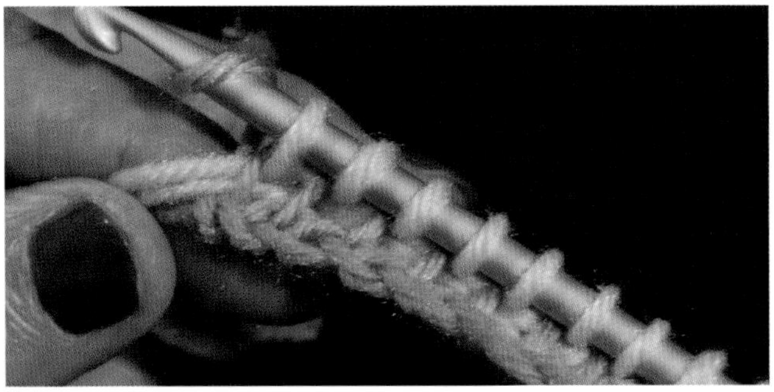

Once all of the loops are again on the hook, change to using the original colour.

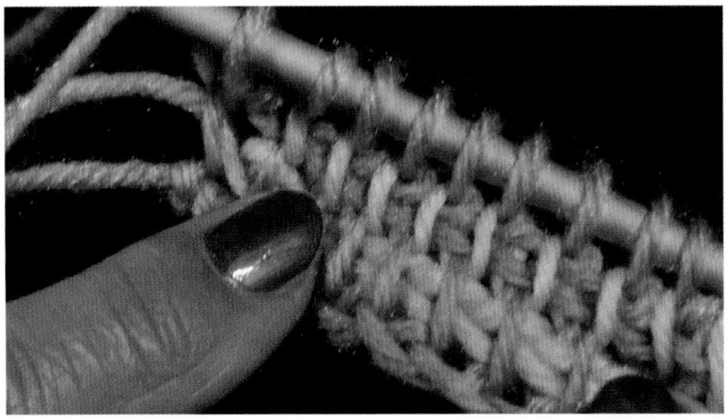

Continue changing the colour being used each time that all of the loops are on the hook.

Row 1, Stage 2

Step 1: Leaving the first yarn colour attached to be used later, yoh with the second yarn colour, pull the yarn through the first loop of the hook (that is, the last loop worked during Row 1, Stage 1), and make 1ch.

Step 2: Remove all of the remaining loops of the first yarn colour as for Tss Row 1, Stage 2 by working with the second yarn colour.

Note: At this point, the two yarn colours are attached but with the yarns at opposite ends of the work.

Row 2, Stage 1

Step 1: With the second yarn colour just used to work the previous stage, pick up 1 loop for each vertical strand across the row as for Tss Row 2, Stage 1.

Step 2: Once all of the loops are on the hook, both yarns are again at the same end of the work.

Row 2, Stage 2

Step 1: Change to using the first yarn colour instead of the second yarn colour. Have the second yarn colour behind the first as you make 1ch with the first yarn colour.

Step 2: Remove all of the loops of the second yarn colour as for Tss Row 2, Stage 2 by working with the first yarn colour.

Repeat this process from Step 2 of Row 1, Stage 1 to Step 2 of Row 2, Stage 2, until the desired length of the fabric is reached.

Many hours of fun can be had working tweed stitch by doing nothing more adventurous than changing either the colour of the yarn or the type of yarn being used. There is no end to the combination of yarns that can be experimented with! To begin with, try some of the following combinations:

- Two balls of the same yarn with one a little darker in shade but of the same colour.
- Two balls of yarn with one ball being smooth and the other textured but of roughly the same colour.
- One ball of yarn of a single colour and the second ball being of a short space-dyed yarn.
- A ball of basic DK-weight yarn with a ball of shiny ribbon yarn.
- A ball of an irregularly textured yarn that has both thick and thin parts to it with a ball of basic DK-weight yarn of a complementary colour.

SMARTPHONE AND TABLET COVERS

An example of the Smartphone Cover worked with Tunisian crochet tweed stitch.

Materials

1 × 100g ball West Yorkshire Spinners ColourLab DK (225m/100g) in main colour (M)
1 × 100g ball of DK-weight yarn in contrast colour (C)
6.00mm crochet hook
7.00mm Tunisian crochet hook

Tension

Measured over tweed stitch: 7 stitches and 7 rows to 5cm

Size

Smartphone cover: 10cm/4in × 15cm/6in, including the completed edging
Tablet cover: 20cm/8in × 28cm/11in, including the completed edging

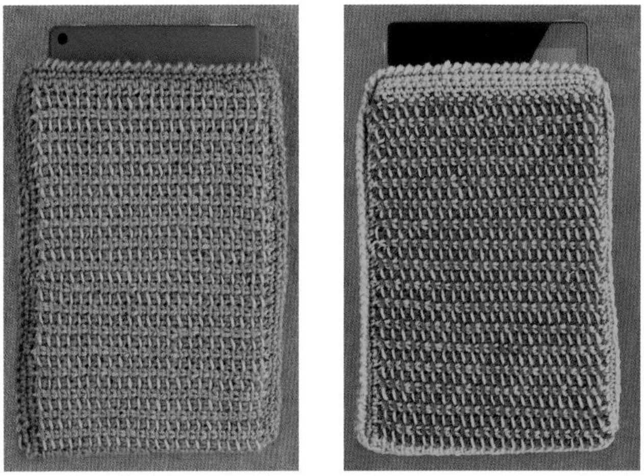

An example of the Tablet Cover worked with Tunisian crochet tweed stitch, front and back.

This pattern is a good way to practise working tweed stitch and adding a border. Remember that one row equals both the picking up of the loops and the removal of them (Stages 1–2). For the materials listed here, there is sufficient yarn to make two sets of covers. The following instructions give the smartphone-cover figures first and the tablet-cover figures second, in brackets.

Pattern instructions

Cover

Step 1: With M, make a slip knot, place it on to the 6.00mm crochet hook and make 14(28)ch.

Step 2: Work as follows:

Row 1, Stage 1: Change to using the 7.00mm Tunisian crochet hook. Pick up 1 loop on and place on the hook for each chain. [14(28)sts]

Row 1, Stage 2: With all of the loops on the hook, change to using C. With C, remove all of the loops as for Tss. [14(28)sts]

Row 2, Stage 1: With C, pick up 1 loop from under each vertical strand.

Row 2, Stage 2: With all of the loops on the hook, change to using M. With M, remove all of the loops as for Tss.

Row 3, Stage 1: With M, pick up 1 loop from under each vertical strand.

Row 3, Stage 2: With all of the loops on the hook, change to using C. With C, remove all of the loops as for Tss.

Step 3: Continue by working Rows 2–3 another 7(15) times.

Step 4: Work Row 2 once.

Step 5: Without changing colour, work 2 rows as for Tss, for the bottom of the cover.

Step 6: Continue by working Row 3 and then Row 2 another 9(17) times. Fasten off C.

Note: M is now in a position to work an edging around all four sides of the case prior to forming a pocket for the smartphone[tablet]. [14(28)sts]

Edging

Step 7: Make 1dc in each stitch across the top of the cover fabric in turn, remembering to pick up 1 loop from under each vertical strand in order to work each dc.

Step 8: Work double crochet along the first long side of the cover, working into the edge of the main tweed-stitch part of the fabric, following the instructions given earlier (*see* Step 10 of the section 'Edging' for the Colourful Cushion Cover).

Step 9: Work double crochet along the bottom of the cover fabric, again picking up 1 loop from under each vertical strand in order to work each dc.

Step 10: Work double crochet along the second long side of the cover, again working into the edge of the main tweed-stitch part of the fabric.

Finishing

Step 11: Fold the work in half along the single-colour rows of Tss at the bottom of the cover (*see* Step 5), and match the top edge to the bottom edge. Check whether the stitches of the side edges match and align properly, and temporarily secure the folded cover fabric with stitch holders or short lengths of yarn.

Step 12: Work double crochet down the new first (half-length) long side of the cover by working through both sides of the folded fabric, stitch for stitch.

Step 13: Return to the top of the cover by working one row of crab stitch into the double-crochet row just worked.

Step 14: Work double crochet along the top edge of only one side of the top opening.

Step 15: Work double crochet down the other new second (half-length) long side of the cover by working through both sides of the folded fabric, stitch for stitch, to complete making the pocket of the cover.

Step 16: Return to the top of the cover by working one row of crab stitch into the double-crochet row just worked.

Step 17: Work double crochet along the top edge of the other side of the top opening not worked in Step 14. Join the last dc worked with a slip stitch to the first dc worked at the start of the first row of double crochet (worked in Step 12).

Step 18: Work around the opening of the cover by working crab stitch into each dc of both sides of the opening. Fasten off. Sew in all yarn ends.

SQUARE-WITHIN-A-SQUARE CUSHION COVER

The front piece of the Square-Within-A-Square Cushion Cover is worked in three pieces that are connected together before the working of the edging.

Materials

2 × 100g balls West Yorkshire Spinners ColourLab DK (225m/100g) in M
1 × 100g ball DK-weight yarn in C, either a single shade or a space-dyed yarn
6.00mm crochet hook
7.00mm Tunisian crochet hook
1 × cushion pad, 42cm/16½in × 42cm/16½in
(Optional: 30cm zip of a colour matching M)

Tension

Measured over Tss: 13 stitches and 13 rows to 10cm

Size

38cm/15in × 38cm/15in, including the completed edging

The Tunisian crochet tweed-stitch central square is joined to the sides of the plain Tunisian simple stitch frame with a whip stitch.

The basic Tunisian simple stitch can be combined with tweed stitch to create designs of plain and busy colour sections. The idea works well for articles worked in stripes and where the back is unlikely to be visible, for example, rugs, bedspreads and throws. With this in mind, a suitable project to start with could be the front and back of a cushion cover. The DK-weight yarns selected for working this Square-Within-A-Square Cushion Cover with a tweed-stitch insert are a plain shade of deep teal and a matching space-dyed yarn for just the central square of tweed stitch on the front of the cover. (Note that the back does not include a central panel.)

Pattern instructions

Front

Set-Up: With M, make a slip knot and place it on to the 6.00mm crochet hook. With the same hook, make 45ch. Place the last chain on to the 7.00mm Tunisian crochet hook.

Step 1: Work as follows:

Row 1, Stage 1: With the 7.00mm Tunisian crochet hook, pick up 1 loop and place on to the hook for each chain across the row, starting with the 2nd chain from the hook. [45 loops on hook]

Row 1, Stage 2: Remove all of the loops as for Tss Row 1, Stage 2. [45sts]

Work in Tss for 11 rows (that is, with each row comprising Tss Row 2, Stages 1–2) with all 45sts.

Step 2: With M and with the first 11sts only, work 23 rows in Tss (11 loops on hook at the end of Stage 1, including the first loop already on the hook at the start of each row). Break the yarn, leaving a long enough end to sew in later.

Step 3: For the next unworked stitch (that is, the 12th stitch of the original 45sts), join in M by picking up 1 loop from under the vertical strand of this stitch (counts as the first loop for Stage 1 of the front-piece centre section):

Row 1, Stage 1: With M, pick up 1 loop and place on to the hook from under the vertical strand of each of the next 22sts [23 loops on hook]

Row 1, Stage 2: Change to using C. Remove all of the loops as for Tss.

Row 2, Stage 1: With M, pick up 22 loops and place on to the hook from under each of the next 22 vertical strands. [23 loops on hook]

Row 2, Stage 2: With C, remove all loops as for Tss.

Step 4: Work 21 rows more as for tweed stitch, finishing by removing all of the loops with M. Break both yarns, leaving long enough ends to sew in later.

Step 5: For the next unworked stitch (that is, the 35th stitch of the original 45sts), with M, work 23 rows in Tss. Break the yarn, leaving a long enough end to sew in later.

Step 6: With M, pick up 1 loop from under each vertical strand of the first 11-stitch strip worked in Tss. [11 loops on hook]

Step 7: Continuing with M, pick up 1 loop and place on to the hook from under each vertical strand of the tweed-stitch panel. [34 loops on hook]

Step 8: Still continuing with M, pick up 1 loop and place on to the hook from under each vertical strand of the second 11-stitch strip worked in Tss. [45 loops on hook]

Step 9: With M, remove all of the loops as for Tss. [45sts; 1 loop on hook]
Step 10: Work a further 10 rows in Tss (that is, with each row comprising Tss Row 2, Stages 1–2).
Step 11: Change to using the 6.00mm crochet hook. Work 1dc under each vertical strand in turn to the end of the row. Fasten off.

These steps form a single-colour Tss frame around the front cover containing the Tweed stitch square. Working with the reverse side (what will be the inside of the front of the cover) facing, attach the two sides of the tweed-stitch central panel to the main frame.

With the main yarn, whip stitch the two adjacent edges together, make sure that the same amount of sewing is worked for each join. This ensures that the central panel sits squarely in the frame and will not look untidy once the cushion pad has been inserted.

Back

Step 12: With M, make a slip knot and place it on to the 6.00mm crochet hook. With the same hook, make 45ch. Place the last chain on to the 7.00mm Tunisian crochet hook.
Step 13: With the 7.00mm Tunisian crochet hook, work 45 rows in Tss on these 45sts.
Step 14: Change to using the 6.00mm crochet hook. Work 1dc under each vertical strand in turn to the end of the row. Fasten off.

Edging

Follow the edging instructions given for the Colourful Cushion Cover, making sure that, when the two pieces have been secured together, the zip opening is of the correct size for the length of zip to be inserted.

Finishing

Insert and attach the zip to the underside of the cushion-cover fabric at the zip opening using your preferred method, sewing thread and choice of stitch. Sew in all loose yarn and thread ends. Insert the cushion pad, close the zip, and check whether all of the yarn and thread ends are secure.

Alternatively, insert the cushion pad and close the bottom of the cushion by sewing the edges of the opening together with a whip stitch.

A sample of garter stitch in DK-weight yarn used together with a brushed acrylic, side 1.

A sample of garter stitch in DK-weight yarn used together with a brushed acrylic, side 2.

A sample of garter stitch using two DK-weight yarns together, one of a plain colour and one space-dyed, side 1.

A sample of garter stitch using two DK-weight yarns together, one of a plain colour and one space-dyed, side 2.

Trial piece of Tunisian garter stitch

The loops from the foundation chain are now on the hook. All of the loops from the foundation chain are now on the double-ended hook.

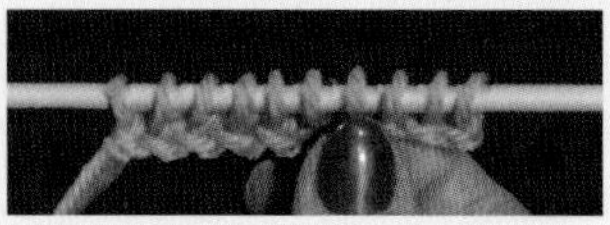

The loops are sent to the other end of the hook and the work is turned at the same time.

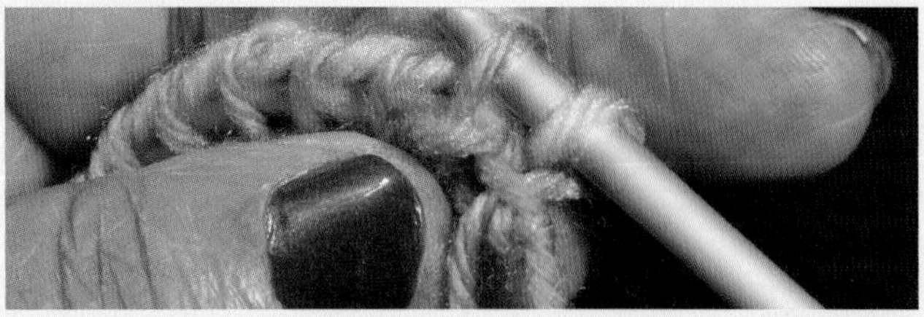

Without turning the work, with C, pick up a loop and place on to the hook from under each vertical strand in turn.

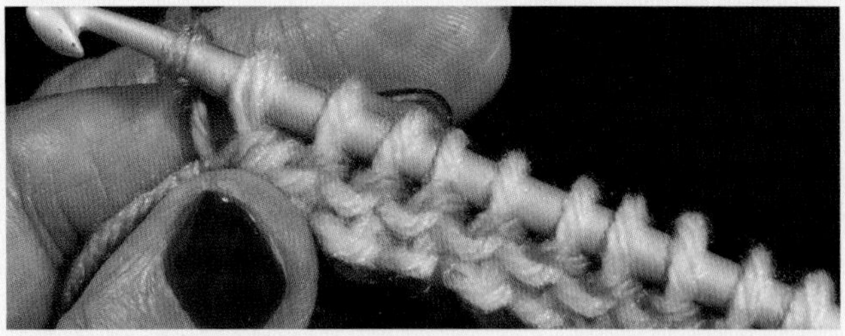

By sliding the loops to the other end of the hook and turning the work, the first colour, M, is again available for use.

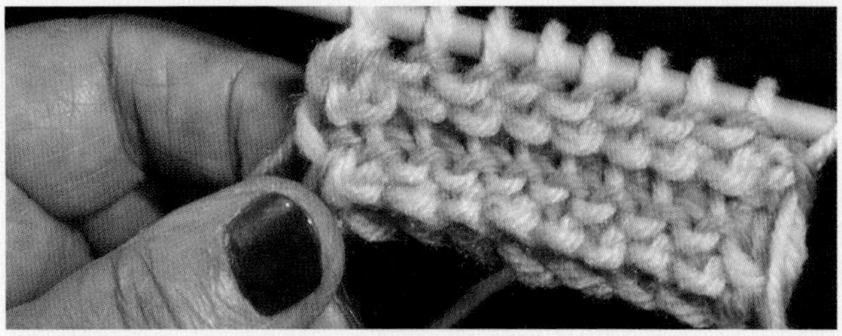

After working some more Tunisian garter stitch fabric and with all of the loops again on the hook, the two yarns are again at opposite ends of the work.

Set-Up

With M, make a slip knot that will slide into the fabric (*see* the section 'Principles of working Tunisian crochet' in Chapter 2), place it on to a crochet hook of an appropriate size for the yarn, and make a length of chain stitches. Place the last chain on to a double-ended Tunisian crochet hook of an appropriate size for the yarn.

Row 1, Stage 1

Step 1: When working into the foundation chain, with M, pick up 1 loop and place on to the hook from under the top strand of each chain, starting from the 2nd chain from the hook. However, later, when working into the previous row of the Tunisian crochet fabric, pick up 1 loop and place on to the hook from under the vertical strand of each stitch in turn across the row.

Step 2: When all of the loops are on the hook, slide them to the other end of the hook. *Turn the work!*

Row 1, Stage 2

Step 1: Change to using C instead of M. With C, make 1ch by pulling the yarn through the first loop on the hook (that is, the loop closest to the head of the left-hand end of the hook).

Note: At this point, the two colours, M and C, are attached to the work, but the yarns are at opposite ends of the hook.

Step 2: With C, remove all of the loops as for Tss. *Do not turn the work when there is only one loop left on the hook!*

Row 2, Stage 1

Step 1: With C, pick up 1 loop and place on to the hook for each vertical strand in turn as for Tss.

Step 2: When all of the loops are on the hook, slide them to the other end of the hook. *Turn the work!*

Row 2, Stage 2

Step 1: Change to using M instead of C. With M, make 1ch by pulling the yarn through the first loop on the hook (that is, the loop closest to the head of the left-hand end of the hook).

Step 2: With M, remove all of the loops as for Tss.

Do not turn the work when there is only one loop left on the hook!

Continue in Tunisian garter stitch by picking up one loop of yarn for each vertical strand and placing each loop on to the hook with the same yarn colour that has just removed the loops. Once all of these loops are on the hook, slide the stitches to the other end of the hook and turn the work, to allow a yarn colour change to be made. Repeat this process, working Row 1, Stages 1–2, and Row 2, Stages 1–2, until the required length of the fabric is reached, finishing with the yarn colour that made the foundation chain of stitches.

Tunisian Crochet Garter Stitch

Tunisian crochet garter stitch, more commonly referred to as simply Tunisian garter stitch (Tgs), is a reversible form of Tunisian simple stitch. Tunisian simple stitch has the look of stocking stitch of knitting, with one side smooth and the other side textured. To work Tunisian garter stitch, the classic Tunisian crochet hook that has a hook at one end and a knob or stopper at the other needs to be replaced with a double-ended Tunisian crochet hook that has a hook at both ends. Having a hook at each end enables the production of a Tunisian crochet fabric that is similar to knitted garter stitch.

The first noticeable characteristic of Tunisian garter stitch is that the fabric no longer curls. This result is achieved because, unlike classic Tunisian simple stitch, the hook is turned each time the loops have been picked up and are sitting on the hook. Turning the work means that the same side of the fabric is no longer facing at all times, so this removes the reason that causes Tunisian simple stitch to naturally curl.

The second obvious characteristic of Tunisian garter stitch is that Tunisian crochet worked with a double-ended crochet hook looks the same on both sides when the same colour is being used for both procedures of working the basic Tgs row (that is, Stages 1 and 2). Usually two colours are used to make a reversible material. However, if a monochromatic look is desired, the single-colour yarn needs to be divided into two balls to allow the yarn to be available to continue crocheting with it without interruption after turning the hook.

By working Tunisian garter stitch with two contrasting colours or two different types of yarn, one side of the fabric will show one colour or characteristic predominantly, whilst the other side will have the second colour or characteristic conspicuously displayed. The versatility of a garment or accessory designed in this manner increases the number of different ensembles that it can be associated with.

Working Tunisian garter stitch with a double-ended Tunisian crochet hook is not dissimilar to working Tunisian crochet tweed stitch. The only difference is that the hook carrying the work is turned before making the colour change.

Having produced a little Tunisian garter stitch in two colours, it is easily noticed that, as mentioned earlier, one side of the work has one colour prevalent whilst, on the other side, it is the other colour that dominates. Not only is there texture on both sides but also the fabric no longer curls.Many designs become possible by utilizing this reversible fabric technique. Some examples of the variety that a different combination of yarns and colours make are

A sample of a DK-weight acrylic/silk-mix yarn used together with a DK-weight ribbon yarn, side 1.

A sample of a DK-weight acrylic/silk-mix yarn used together with a DK-weight ribbon yarn, side 2.

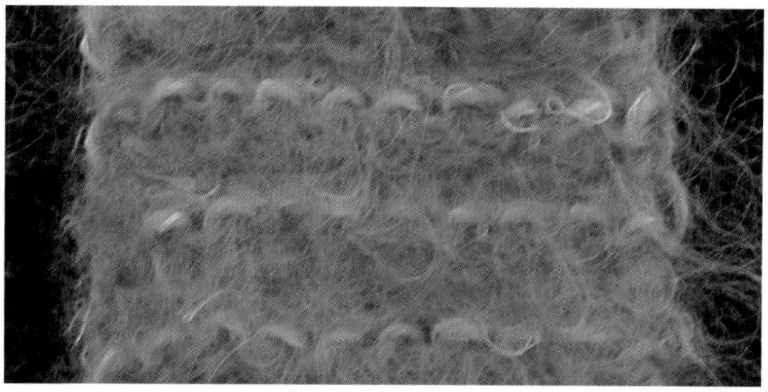

A sample of a DK-weight angora yarn used together with a light 4-ply eyelash yarn, side 1.

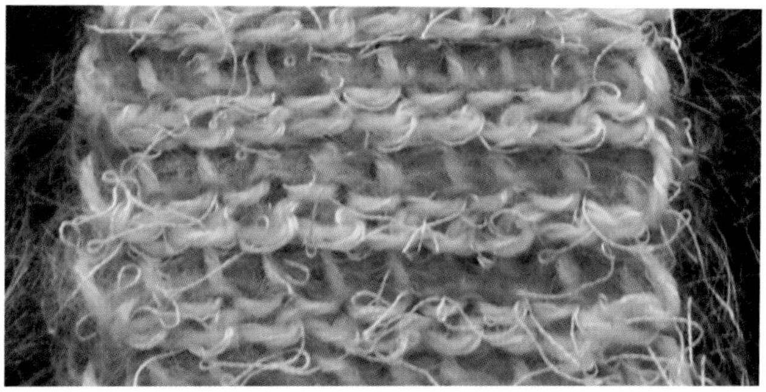

A sample of a DK-weight angora yarn used together with a light 4-ply eyelash yarn, side 2.

A sample of an eyelash yarn used together with a 3-ply cotton yarn, side 1.

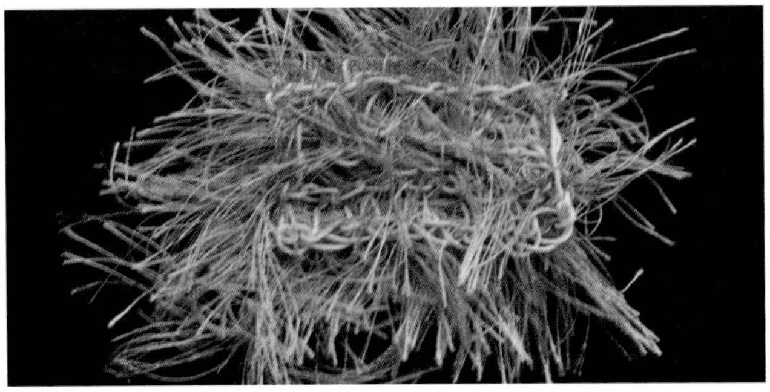

A sample of an eyelash yarn used together with a 3-ply cotton yarn, side 2.

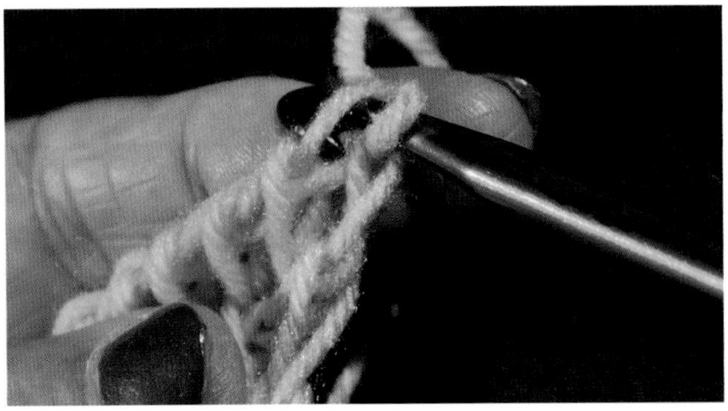

Picking up the top horizontal strand of the previous row.

Now insert the hook under the as-yet-unused next vertical strand.

illustrated here to tempt you to experiment for yourself: the front and back of these combinations are shown. It is very rewarding to discover by doing, rather than just being told or shown.

The possible combinations are endless, so enjoy yourself and have fun experimenting and combining different yarns and different colours to provide continually amazing results. There are many other possibilities to give incredible results. The fibre content of the yarn to be used does not need to be considered.

If you are stuck for inspiration, try some of the following suggestions, but then continue with combinations of your own choosing.

- A smooth DK-weight yarn and a DK-weight mohair yarn
- A short space-dyed DK-weight yarn and a dark single-colour DK-weight yarn
- A pale yarn shade of one colour combined with a dark yarn shade of the same colour
- A mercerized bedspread-weight yarn and a heavily textured yarn
- A sock-weight yarn and a tinsel chunky-weight yarn
- A shiny ribbon yarn and a DK-weight sequin yarn
- A sparkly craft yarn and a matching single-colour plain yarn

Increasing

It is essential to know the best ways of increasing for Tunisian crochet, especially as all four sides of a piece of Tunisian simple stitch are different. For this reason, whenever possible, it is advisable to avoid shaping at the very edge of the fabric.

Technically, Tunisian crochet is made up of a long series of connected crochet stitches. One side edge of the fabric resembles the top of a row of standard crochet stitches, whilst the other side edge resembles the bottom of the row, similar in appearance to that of the remaining single strand of a foundation chain that has been crocheted into by inserting the hook under two strands of yarn of each chain stitch. This is the reason for the edge of each side to have a dissimilar appearance. Once the difference in the edges of Tunisian crochet is understood, finding a variety of stitch patterns to use and having the ability to shape Tunisian crochet become both doable and fun.

Increasing is simple and is best done at the time that the loops are being picked up when working Stage 1 of a row.

Standard increase method

The following steps result in each row having two additional stitches, by working a single increase at the start of the row and one at the end of the row.

Step 1: At the beginning of the row, there is already a loop on the hook. Insert the hook under the top horizontal strand lying between the loop on the hook and the next vertical strand. (This top horizontal strand is often referred to as the top strand of the horizontal equals sign that is there as a result of removing the loops during Step 2 of the previous row, and it sits at the very top of the fabric.)

Step 2: yoh, pull the yarn through the top horizontal strand, and leave the loop on the hook. One increase has been made.

Step 3: Insert the hook under the next vertical strand not yet used, yoh, pull the yarn through the vertical strand, and leave the loop on the hook.

Step 4: Continue working along the row, picking up 1 loop from under each vertical strand remaining as for Tss, until 1 vertical strand is left to work.

Step 5: Insert the hook under the top horizontal strand lying between the loop on the hook and the last vertical strand.

Step 6: yoh, pull the yarn through the top horizontal strand, and leave the loop on the hook. One additional increase has been made.

Step 7: Insert the hook under the last vertical strand of the row, yoh, pull the yarn through, and leave the loop on the hook.

Step 8: Count the loops on the hook to check whether you have 2 loops more than for the previous row, and remove the loops on the hook as for Tss.

Alternative increase method

Work as above, but change the strand from which you pick up a loop to make the increase; instead of picking up a loop from under the top horizontal strand before the first vertical strand that would usually be worked under at the start of the row and before the last vertical strand of the row, pick up a loop by inserting the hook under the horizontal strand of yarn or protrusion at the back of the work lying directly behind the vertical strand that, when looked at from the other side of the fabric, resembles a purl stitch of the purl side of knitting.

This method gives the increase a different appearance. Having tried both ways of increasing, decide which method produces the best look for the project being made and which is the easiest to work.

This triangle is an example of an increase being made at the beginning and at the end of the rows.

A back view of the triangle with increases made at both edges.

It is worth the effort to spend a short time practising increasing. A useful way to practise is to make a series of triangles that can be used for bunting. Larger triangles can be converted into shawls, godets for movement and drape within a larger piece of fabric, asymmetrical fashion designs, patchwork blankets or other items, and much more.

Increase-method triangle

For a piece of crocheted fabric to be a triangle, it must have three straight sides and three points at the corners. Making straight sides and finishing with two sharp corners is not a problem to achieve. Unfortunately, beginning with a point can be a challenge.

Step 1: Make a slip knot that will slide into the finished fabric (*see* the section 'Principles of working Tunisian crochet' in Chapter 2), and place it on to a Tunisian crochet hook.

Step 2: Make 2ch.

Insert the hook under the next two vertical strands as shown.

The yarn has been pulled through the two vertical strands, resulting in a decrease of one stitch.

Continue working Tunisian simple stitch as normal.

Stop when there are three vertical strands remaining to be worked.

Step 3: Using the front loop only of the first chain made, yoh, pull yarn through, and leave the loop on the hook.
Step 4: Pick up the back loop only of the same chain, yoh, pull the yarn through, and leave the loop on the hook, to result in 3 loops in total on the hook.
Step 5: Remove all of the loops as for Tss (that is, work as for Tss Row 1, Stage 2 as given in Chapter 2). [3sts]
Work as for Tss and increase at both ends of the row, starting with the next row and continuing with each subsequent row. By adding 2 loops per row, the stitch count will go from 3 to 5, to 7, to 9, and so on.
Continue until the triangle is of the required size.
Last row: Beginning with 1 loop on the hook, finish the previous row by working double crochet across the row (that is, work as given for the 'Last row' of the section 'A quick trial run – producing the basic Tunisian simple stitch'– *see* Chapter 2), and check to see whether an additional chain or stitch is required to make both ends have a sharp point. Fasten off. Return to the start of the work, at the very tip of the triangle.
Finishing: Tighten the slip knot as necessary. With a fine crochet hook or a sewing needle, tease the stitches of the beginning of the triangle into a sharp point.

Decreasing

You can decrease for Tunisian crochet as you pick up the loops from under the vertical strands during Stage 1 of the row or as you remove the loops on the hook when working Stage 2. For even tension, remember to make sure that the hook is sitting on top of the stitches and not lying along the front of the work.

Again, it is worth practising both methods to see which is the one most suited to your project and which you find the easiest to work.

Decreasing when picking up loops (Stage 1 decreases)

Of the two methods presented here, this one is probably the simplest and least confusing.
Step 1: With 1 loop on the hook, insert the hook under the first 2 vertical strands of the previous row at the same time.
Step 2: yoh, pull the yarn through both vertical strands at once, and leave the resulting single loop on the hook. One decrease has been made.

Step 3: Continue working across the row as for Tss until 3 vertical strands are left to work.

Note: At the beginning of the row, 1 loop is already on the hook, therefore, by inserting the hook under the next 2 vertical strands available, the decrease occurs close to, but not quite at, the right-hand edge of the fabric. However, to have the decreases looking even on both sides of the work, it is necessary at the end of the row to work the decrease 1 stitch in from the edge, as follows.

Step 4: Insert the hook under the first 2 of the remaining 3 vertical strands.

Step 5: yoh, pull the yarn through both vertical strands at once, and leave the resulting single loop on the hook. One additional decrease has been made.

Step 6: Insert hook under the last vertical strand of the row.

Step 7: yoh, pull the yarn through, leave the loop on the hook.

In total, two decreases have been made, and both decreases are worked just inside the edge of the fabric.

Insert the hook under the next two vertical strands as shown.

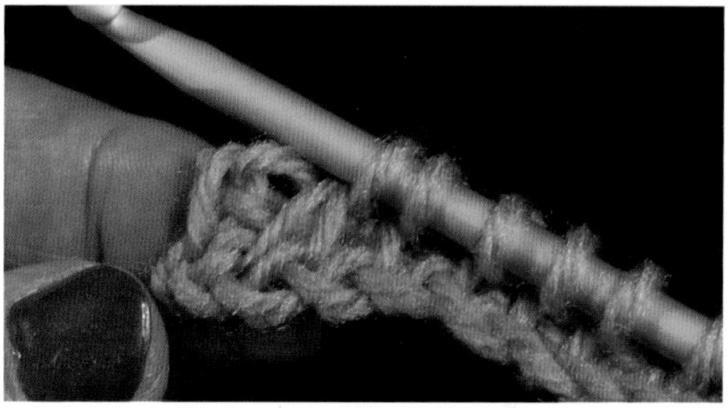

The yarn has been pulled through the two vertical strands, resulting in a decrease of one stitch.

Decreasing during the removal of loops (Stage 2 decreases)

As mentioned, decreasing can also be achieved when removing the loops on the hook, by pulling the yarn through three loops instead of the usual two when working Stage 2. On the surface, this method may seem the easier, but I personally find it more difficult to keep an accurate check of my stitches when decreasing using this method. Therefore, I tend to reserve this process for when working elaborate stitch patterns.First, work the fabric to the desired length or point in your design where you want to start to decrease.

Step 1: Work Stage 1 of the next row as for Tss.

Step 2: At the start of the next Stage 2, do not work a chain to lift the hook: instead, yoh.

Step 3: Pull the yarn through the first 3 loops on the hook (that is, the last loop made at the end of the previous Stage 1 step and the adjacent 2 loops). One decrease has been made.

Step 4: Continue working across the row as for Tss until 3 loops remain on the hook.

Step 5: yoh, and pull the yarn through all 3 loops at once. One additional decrease has been made.

Repeat Steps 1–5 until the desired fabric width or stitch count is reached, ending with Step 4.

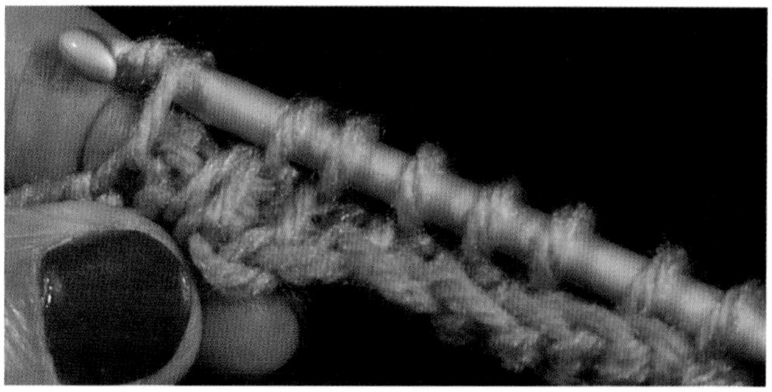

Work the remaining stitch as normal.

To decrease during the removal of the loops, no turning chain is worked.

Decreases have been completed at both ends of the row, causing the sides to slope inwards.

This triangle is an example of the decreases being made 1 stitch in from the edge and decreasing to a point.

Decrease method triangle

Work a foundation chain by first working a slip knot that will slide into the finished fabric (*see* the section 'Principles of working Tunisian crochet' in Chapter 2) and then a chain of the required number of chain stitches; next, pick up 1 loop from under the top strand of each chain in turn: there must be an odd number of loops on the hook after working this first row of Tss. An odd number of stitches is essential to obtain a sharp point at the end.

Step 1: Make one decrease at each end of the row by using your preferred method as described above. Continue decreasing until 5sts remain after Stage 2.

Step 2: With 1 loop on the hook, insert the hook under the next 3 vertical strands, yoh, pull the yarn through all 3 strands at once, leave the loop on the hook, insert the hook under the last vertical strand of the row, yoh, pull the yarn through, and leave the loop on the hook. [3 loops on hook]

Step 3: Work Stage 2 as for Tss.

Step 4: With 1 loop on the hook, finish by inserting the hook under the remaining 2 vertical strands of the row, yoh, and pull the yarn through all of the loops. Fasten off.

Joining Tunisian Crochet

Common joining methods

Pieces of Tunisian crochet can be joined by several methods:

- Sewing with the same colour and yarn as used for working the crochet and by using backstitch, whip stitch or mattress stitch to link the two opposite sides, ideally aligning the individual stitches of the pieces together.
- Oversewing the two pieces together evenly from the right side of the fabric with decorative embroidery threads.
- Working double crochet in a neutral colour from the wrong side of the fabric.
- Working double crochet and crab stitch with a contrasting colour from the right side of the fabric. The method for achieving this is described below.

Double crochet and crab stitch join

This is a favourite way of joining pieces of Tunisian simple stitch together, because it can hide minor irregularities along the edges. It also produces both texture and an eye-catching finish to the design. Remember to include the join as part of the overall design from the outset, particularly when working to a specified measurement.

Step 1: Encircle the Tunisian crochet pieces to be joined with double-crochet stitches prior to joining, making sure that the opposite sides of the different pieces to be joined contain the same number of stitches.

Step 2: With wrong sides together, place the two pieces to be connected in the correct orientation and position and temporarily secure them in place with a stitch holder, ties or basting stitches of yarn, so that they will not move.

Step 3: Double crochet through the two adjacent pieces, picking up two threads from each piece, matching the pieces stitch to stitch (this is why the opposite sides of the different pieces to be joined need to contain the same number of stitches).

Step 4: Finish the joining of the pieces by working crab stitch along the row of double crochet from the right side.

Joining garment pieces

Where possible, avoid having to join pieces of crochet together for forming a garment. Unless you are very skilled both in achieving a tension that never varies and in using the different methods of joining neatly, it is advisable to plan your design in such a way that it has a minimum number of seams and joins. The only exception to this is when the join is part of a decorative design.

Options for reducing the need for joins

1. Work the right front, back and left front of a cardigan in one piece to the armhole. Complete the rest of the garment in three pieces: right front, back and left front. These can be joined with any of the given methods or with an invisible join at the shoulders.
2. Have a drop or square armhole in a cardigan or sweater to avoid the need of inserting a complex shaped sleeve.
3. Start at the level of the shoulder and work the two or three pieces for the front and back or right front, back and left front down from the shoulder to the end of the armhole, then link these pieces together to form a seamless finish. Continue to work the garment in one piece as a waist-, hip-, calf- or full-length garment.
4. Cap sleeves can be incorporated seamlessly for pieces worked from the armhole to the shoulder.
5. Similarly, square sleeves can be worked seamlessly in the same way, by working up from the armhole to the shoulder.
6. Elbow-length, three-quarter-length and full-length sleeves can be started by picking up stitches at the armhole opening and working downwards, decreasing to the required size of the cuff, as necessary. This alleviates inserting the sleeve into the armhole at the end when working and assembling a garment.
7. It is possible to work a sleeve in the round so that there is no underarm seam.
8. Decorative joins can be included in the design, where colourful or textured borders are worked and joined as described for the joining of pieces of, for example, a patchwork blanket (*see* the section 'Modular designs'). When designing, allow room to accommodate the addition of the edging or border.

Line up the unfinished edges of the pieces of Tunisian simple stitch to be joined.

Pick up one vertical strand from the right side of each piece. The wrong side of the back piece is visible.

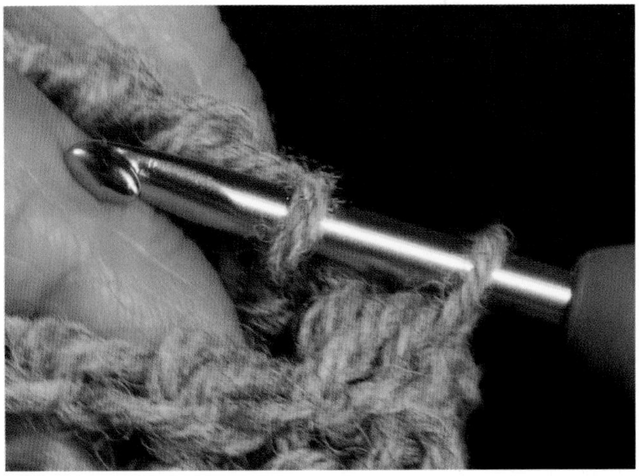

The finger between the front and back pieces maintains the small opening, ready for the next stitch to be worked.

Complete the double-crochet stitch, whilst the finger is still in place, holding the two pieces open.

A section of completed invisible joining.

A loop from the front collected after *the one from the back.*

Working an invisible join

This method is ideal to use when joining the front and back pieces of a garment to form a shoulder seam, but it is useful for seaming other pieces too.

Step 1: Leave the pieces to be joined without a double-crochet finish.

Step 2: Arrange the pieces with their right sides together and the wrong side of the front piece facing you.

Step 3: Line up the stitches of the two pieces to have one-to-one alignment (that is, the first stitch of the right-hand end of front piece sits directly in line with the first stitch of the right-hand end of the back piece, and so on to the last stitch at the left-hand end of each piece).

Step 4: Using the same colour of yarn as used to work the last row of stitches along the edges to be joined, or the colour deemed to give the best seaming result, and with either a crochet hook or a sewing needle (depending on whether the join will be crocheted or sewn), pick up the vertical strand from the front piece and then the vertical strand from the back piece for the first pair of stitches to be joined. Link these two strands together by pulling the yarn under both strands to work a double crochet or a whip stitch. Although the vertical strands are on the right sides of the pieces, the join is worked with the wrong sides facing.

Step 5: Ensuring that the join remains flat and even, continue by working 1dc for each pair of vertical strands to the end of the rows to be seamed. A finger of the free hand (the one not holding the hook or needle) keeps the opening ready for making the next stitch and, at the same time, helps to maintain good tension on both fabric pieces and the join.

Alternatively, place the right sides of the Tunisian crochet pieces together. Replace with place a sewn whip stitch in each pair of vertical strands to the end.

ALL-SQUARE SLEEVELESS JACKET

The first side of the reversible, unisex All-Square Sleeveless Jacket, inspired by a pattern of Maris Groter.

Materials

West Yorkshire Spinners ColourLab DK (225m/100g)
300(350,350)g in M
250(250,300)g in C
4.50mm crochet hook
5.00mm crochet hook
6.00mm double-ended Tunisian crochet hook
7(14) buttons

Tension

Measured over Tgs: 4 stitches and 5 rows to 2.5cm/1in

Size

To fit a wearer of UK clothing size 12–14(16,18) and with a bust/chest circumference of 91–96(101,108)cm/36–38(40,42½)in

Note that the garment design includes a 10cm/4in ease allowance.

Pattern note

With the exception of the final borders, the whole garment is constructed with Tgs.

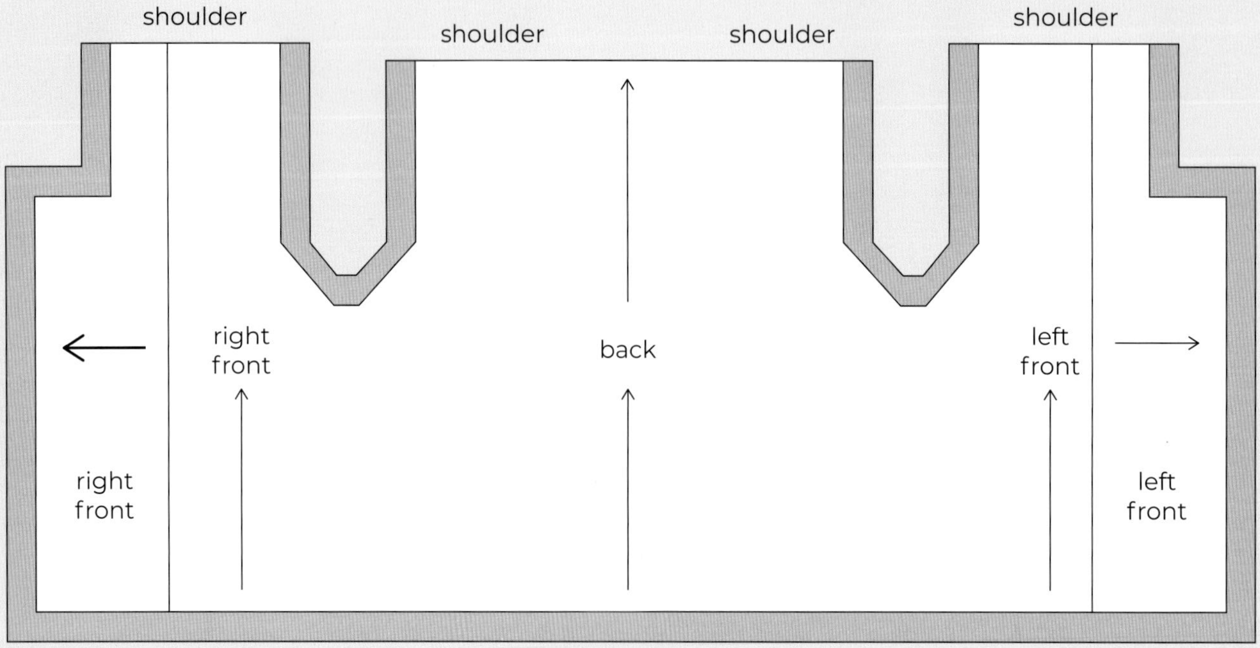

Schematic for the All-Square Sleeveless Jacket.

The buttons have been added to only one side, which is the left-hand side of one side of the reversible fabric of this jacket. To make this garment truly reversible, buttons would need to be on both sides of the fabric, making the other side suitable for a man to wear (with the buttons on the right-hand side).

Pattern instructions

Body

The garment is started as one body piece and then worked towards the shoulders. When the position of the start of the underarms is reached, the fronts and back of the garment are each worked in turn by using the specified stitches of the body piece.

Step 1: With M, make a slip knot and place it on to the 5.00mm crochet hook. With the same hook, make 141(149,157)ch. Place the last chain on to the 6.00mm double-ended Tunisian crochet hook.

Step 2: Work as follows:

Row 1, Stage 1: With the 6.00mm double-ended Tunisian crochet hook, pick up 1 loop and place on to the hook directly by working under the top strand only of each chain, starting from the 2nd chain from the hook (or, later, pick up 1 loop for each vertical strand in turn across the row). Slide these loops to the other end of the hook. Turn the work.

Row 1, Stage 2: Leaving M attached at the opposite end of the work, make 1ch with C by pulling the yarn through the first loop on the hook. Remove all of the remaining loops to the end of the row as for Tgs.

Row 2, Stage 1: With C, pick up 1 loop for each vertical strand across the row. Slide these loops to the other end of the hook. Turn the work.

Row 2, Stage 2: Change to using M instead of C. With M, remove all of the loops as for Tgs.

Continue working Tgs on these 141(149,157)sts until the work measures 30cm/12in or to the required length.

Right partial front

Step 3: Keeping the Tgs pattern consistent and the colour changes alternating correctly, pick up 1 loop for each vertical strand in turn until there are 25(26,28) loops on the hook. The place between the innermost stitch on the hook and the unworked stitches is the right underarm point.

Note: It is now necessary to break off the yarn from the other end of the row in order to continue in Tgs as follows:

Step 4: Reposition the broken-off yarn and use it to remove all of the loops picked up in Step 3 as for Tgs.

Step 5: With the relevant yarn to continue in Tgs, pick up 1 loop on and place to the hook from under the next 2 vertical strands [1 decrease made], then pick up 1 loop and place on to the hook from under each vertical strand in turn to the end of the row.

Step 6: Work a further 9 rows in Tgs, keeping the colour changes alternating and decreasing 1st at the armhole edge on every row during Stage 1 when picking up loops (that is, by picking up 1 loop from under the first 2 or the last 2 vertical strands of the row, as necessary).

Step 7: Continue working in Tgs on the remaining 15(16,18)sts until the work measures 22(24,24)cm/8½(9½,9½)in or to the required length from the underarm to the top of the shoulder. Fasten off both yarns.

The second side of the reversible, unisex All-Square Sleeveless Jacket.

Back

Step 8: Leave 5(5,6)sts adjacent to the right underarm point unworked, and, with the appropriate yarn, pick up 1 loop for each of the next 81(87,89) vertical strands. The position between the leftmost stitch on the hook and the unworked stitches is the left underarm point.

Step 9: Continue working in Tgs and decreasing 1st (by picking up 1 loop from under 2 vertical strands) at *each* end of the next 10 rows during Stage 1 when picking up loops. [61(67,69)sts]

Step 10: On these 61(67,69)sts, continue working in Tgs until the work measures 22(22,22)cm, working the final stage of the final row with the same colour as used to work the final row and stage for the Right Partial Front. Do not break the yarn.

Step 11: Place the wrong sides of the Right Partial Front and Back together, matching the top row of the two pieces stitch for stitch.

Step 12: With the yarn that is still attached, join each of the paired stitches of the Right Partial Front and the Back in turn with an invisible join (that is, pick up the vertical strand from the front piece *and* the vertical strand of the corresponding stitch from the back to work a double crochet – *see also* the section 'Working an invisible join').
Fasten off both yarns.

Left partial front

Step 13: Leave 5(5,6)sts adjacent to the left underarm point unworked.
Step 14: Work as for the Right Partial Front, starting with the appropriate yarn, to pick up 25(26,28) loops on to the hook (*see* Step 3).
Step 15: Continue working in Tgs, decreasing at the armhole edge only, to mirror the shaping of the Right Partial Front (*see* Steps 4–6).
Step 16: Continue working in Tgs on the remaining 15(16,18) sts until the work measures 22(24,24)cm/8½(9½,9½)in or to the required length from the underarm to the top of the shoulder. Do not break the yarn.
Step 17: Join the Left Partial Front and the Back together with an invisible join as described for the Back (*see* Steps 11–12).
Fasten off both yarns.

Right front

Note that this garment piece is worked from side to side, not bottom to top.
Step 18: Turn the work by 90 degrees.
Step 19: With WS facing and M, pick up 1 loop for every row along the edge of the Body and Right Partial Front. [89sts]
Step 20: Work straight in Tgs for 3(5,9)cm/1½(2½,3½)in.

Right-front neck

Step 21: On the next row worked from the bottom edge of the garment towards the shoulder, pick up 1 loop from each stitch in turn across the row, leaving 20sts unworked at the end of the row.
Step 22: Continue working in Tgs for 5cm/2in, ending by working the final stage of the final row with the predominant colour.
Step 23: Make 1ch, and work 1dc in each stitch to the end of the row.
Fasten off yarn.

Left front

Note that this garment piece is worked from side to side, not bottom to top.
Step 24: With RS facing and using the same yarn as used to start the Right Front, pick up 1 loop for every row along the edge of the Body and Left Partial Front. [89sts]
Step 25: Work straight in Tgs for 3(5,9)cm/1½(2½,3½)in.

Left-front neck

Step 26: Break off the yarn just used to remove all of the loops during the previous Stage 2 step.
Step 27: Miss the first 20sts of the row. Rejoin the yarn just used to the 21st stitch of the row by pulling the yarn through under the vertical strand of this stitch.
Step 28: Continue working in Tgs for 5cm/2in, ending by working the final stage of the final row with the predominant colour.
Step 29: Make 1ch, and work 1dc in each stitch to the end of the row.
Fasten off yarn.

Border

Join the short edges of the sides of the Right Front and Left Front to the Back at the shoulders with an invisible seam: select either a double-crochet stitch or a sewn whip stitch for working the seam (*see also* the section 'Working an invisible join').

With the 4.50mm crochet hook and RS facing, join M to the centre back of neck and make 1ch.
Step 30: Work as follows:
Round 1: Work 1dc in each stitch in turn to inner corner at shoulder of Left Front, dc2tog at inner corner between back neck and shoulder, 1dc in each stitch over shoulder to short extension of Left Front, dc2tog at inner corner between shoulder and short extension of Left Front, 1dc in each row end of short extension of Left Front, 3dc at top corner of Left Front, 1dc in each stitch down long edge of Left Front, 3dc at bottom corner of Left Front, 1dc in each row end or stitch along bottom edge of garment to bottom corner of Right Front, 3dc at bottom corner of Right Front, 1dc in each stitch up long edge of Right Front, 3dc at top corner of Right Front, 1dc in each row end of short extension of Right Front, dc2tog at inner corner between short extension and shoulder of Right Front, 1dc in each stitch over shoulder of Right Front, dc2tog at inner corner between shoulder of Left Front and back neck,

and 1dc in each stitch to centre back of neck. Join to the 1ch at the start of the round with 1 slip stitch (slst), make 1ch, and turn.

Round 2: Work 1dc in each stitch to inner corner between back neck and shoulder of Right Front, dc3tog at inner corner, 1dc in each stitch over shoulder of Right Front, dc3tog at inner corner between shoulder and short extension of Right Front, 1dc in each stitch to top corner of Right Front, 3dc at top corner, 1dc in each stitch down Right Front to bottom corner, 3dc at bottom corner, 1dc in each stitch along bottom edge to bottom corner of Left Front, 3dc at bottom corner of Left Front, 1dc in each stitch up Left Front, 3dc at top corner of Left Front, 1dc in each stitch to inner corner between short extension and shoulder of Left Front, dc3tog at inner corner, 1dc in each stitch over shoulder of Left Front, dc3tog at inner corner between shoulder of Left Front and back neck, and 1dc in each stitch to centre back of neck. Join to the 1ch at the start of the round with 1slst, make 1ch, and turn. Leave the remaining loop on a stitch marker.

Round 3: (contrast row): With WS facing, join C to bottom corner of Left Front and make 1ch, *work 1dc, 1dtr, 2dc in turn in the next 4sts along the Left Front; repeat from * by working up the Left Front, across the back neck and down the Right Front to bottom corner of Right Front. Do *not* continue across the bottom edge of the garment. Fasten off C.

Buttonhole row

Step 31: Mark the positions of 7 buttonholes spaced evenly along the Right Front.

Step 32: Work as follows:

Round 4: Place the loop from centre back of neck held on a stitch marker on to the 4.50mm crochet hook and pull the M yarn up behind the contrast row so that the yarn link between Round 2 and this round is as inconspicuous as possible. With RS facing and M, make 1ch, and *work as for Round 2 to the next buttonhole marker, miss 1st, make 2ch over the missed stitch; repeat from * until all of the buttonhole markers have been passed, and continue in double crochet as for Round 2 to the end of the round at centre back of neck. Join to the 1ch at the start of the round with 1slst, make 1ch, and turn.

Round 5: With WS facing, work as for Round 2 until the first buttonhole is reached, *work 1dc in the 2chsp, and 1dc in each stitch to the next buttonhole; repeat from * until all of the buttonholes have been worked over, and continue in double crochet as for Round 2 to the end of the round at centre back of neck. Join to the 1ch at the start of the round with 1slst, make 1ch, and turn.

Round 6: With RS facing, work as for Round 2. At the end of the round, make 1ch but do *not* turn work.

Round 7: Work crab stitch in each stitch to the end of the round. Join the loop on the hook to the 1ch at the start of the round with 1slst.

Fasten off.

Armhole bands

Step 33: Work as follows:

Round 1: With the 4.50mm crochet hook and RS facing, join M to the centre of the right underarm, make 1ch, and work 1dc in each stitch or row end evenly around the whole armhole. Join to the 1ch at the start of the round with 1slst, make 1ch, and turn.

Round 2: Work 1dc in each stitch to next inner corner of underarm, dc2tog at inner corner, 1dc in each stitch to top of armhole (at the shoulder seam), dc2tog at top of armhole, 1dc in each stitch to next inner corner of underarm, dc2tog at inner corner, and 1dc in each stitch to the end of the round. Join to the 1ch at the start of the round with 1slst, make 1ch, and turn.

Rounds 3–4: Repeat Round 2 twice.

Round 5: With RS facing, work 1 round of crab stitch.

Fasten off.

Finishing

For a woman to wear, sew on 7 equally spaced buttons to the Left Front of the garment, aligned with the positions of the corresponding buttonholes on the Right Front. To make this jacket completely reversible and suitable for a man to wear, sew 7 additional buttons to the Right Front behind those already attached. Sew in all yarn ends.

This photograph clearly shows both directions of Tunisian garter stitched work in the All Square Waistcoat.

CHAPTER 4

TUNISIAN CROCHET LACE

Although Tunisian crochet is commonly thought to produce a fairly dense fabric, the Tunisian crochet hook can be used to make beautiful open and lacy fabrics with an appearance of traditional crochet worked on a small crochet hook. Unlike working Tunisian simple stitch, making Tunisian crochet lace requires the foundation chain to contain an exact multiple of stitches for the chosen lace pattern, if the fabric is to have the correct result.

As Tunisian crochet lace is ostensibly about making holes, it is essential that the hook chosen to work the relevant collection of stitches and stitch patterns is sufficiently large to accommodate the yarn in use. If in doubt when selecting a hook, choose the larger size. Luxury mohair, angora or alpaca yarns worked in a Tunisian crochet lace stitch make ideal shrugs, stoles, shawls, and so on. When working with yarns produced from the coats of animals, it is vital that the size of the hook is large enough to allow the individual fibres to breathe. Also, it is important to work a trial tension piece to check whether the chosen pattern is not trapping the hairs or fibres of the yarn in the stitches too tightly or in an unsightly way during construction, as this would be undesirable.

OPPOSITE PAGE: Unadorned Tunisian cluster lace worked with a thick, smooth yarn. Both the cluster side and the knitted-look side of the fabric can be seen.

Not everyone enjoys working with hairy-fibre yarns such as those containing mohair and alpaca, but other yarns can easily be substituted. Fine, soft wools or acrylics are suitable for Tunisian crochet lace, as they drape well and keep their shape even after being crumpled up into a small space. However, be aware that the finer, smoother yarns emphasize the stitch structure. For these yarns, choose the size of the Tunisian crochet hook more in keeping with the one recognized as being standard for the thickness of yarn selected, that is, two to three sizes larger than the size of the crochet hook normally recommended for working general crochet when using the same yarn. Some cottons and firm, tightly twisted yarns may hold their shape more easily, but they often do not drape so well, making it particularly necessary to use a larger size of Tunisian crochet hook with these potentially unforgiving yarns.

One important point to remember about Tunisian crochet lace concerns measuring both the finished item and the initial tension trial piece. Making a trial piece gives an understanding of what can occur in the construction of the stitch design and in how the finished fabric will react. Because there is extra movement in Tunisian crochet lace fabrics than in the conventional, frequently worked solid Tunisian crochet fabrics, it is particularly important to understand how each stitch pattern reacts. Allowance has to be made for movement in a Tunisian crochet lace fabric. The measurement may be very different having first stroked the work from top to

The back side of a sample of Tunisian corded-look simple .stitch.

The front side of a sample of Tunisian corded-look simple stitch.

bottom compared to the measurement having stroked the fabric from side to side. I personally favour stroking the fabric in the direction that it will hang when the finished item is in use. In this way, realistic allowance can be made for the effect of gravity, which could distort the finished item.

Tunisian Corded-Look Simple Stitch

Inserting the Tunisian crochet hook in a different place to the vertical strand when working Tunisian simple stitch opens up the fabric. Therefore, the resulting fabric fits more into the category of Tunisian crochet lace, so this variant of Tunisian simple stitch is included here rather than being included in Chapter 2, covering exploration of Tunisian simple stitch. The final fabric has the appearance of being worked over another strand of yarn or cord.

Trial piece of Tunisian corded-look simple stitch

Set-up: With a crochet hook of an appropriate size for the yarn, make a length of chain stitches by starting with a slip knot that will slide into the finished fabric (*see* the section 'Principles of working Tunisian crochet' in Chapter 2).

The number of chain stitches must match the number of stitches required for the finished fabric. Change to using a Tunisian crochet hook of an appropriate size for the yarn.

Row 1: Work as for Tss (Row 1, Stages 1–2).

Pattern row, Stage 1: *Insert the Tunisian crochet hook from top to bottom under the horizontal strand of yarn or protrusion at the back of the work lying directly behind the next vertical strand, yoh, and pull the yarn through; repeat from * to the end of the row.

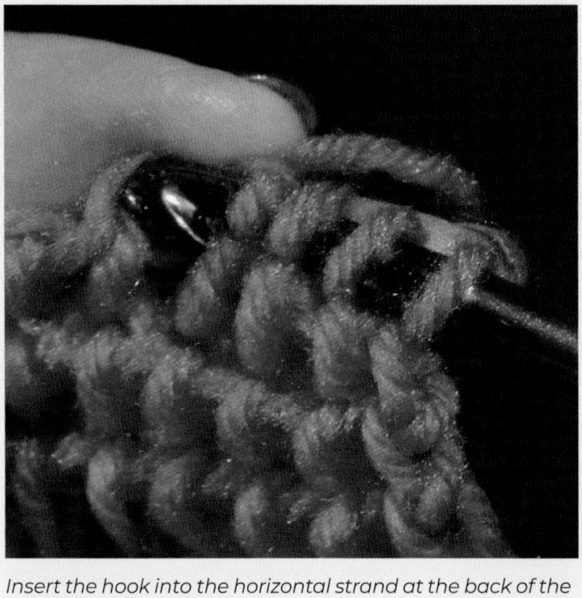

Insert the hook into the horizontal strand at the back of the work as shown.

Pattern row, Stage 2: Remove all of the loops as for Tss.

Repeat the pattern row, Stages 1–2, being careful that you insert the hook in the same place each time when you pick up the last stitch during Stage 2, until the fabric is of the desired length.

Basic Tunisian Lace Stitch

This sample is showing the possibility of a bias developing in a fabric.

Although the basic Tunisian lace stitch is an easy stitch to work, it unfortunately has a tendency to bias, that is, the nature of the stitch pattern results in a rectangle of fabric not having perpendicular vertical sides but sides that slant to the right if you are right-handed or slant to the left if you are left-handed. Although a noticeable bias is not always produced, it is a good idea before working a large item to try making the following stitch sample first. If the result is not a pleasing one, wastage of time and yarn has been avoided! Should a bias occur, try working the standard Tunisian lace stitch.

Working basic Tunisian lace stitch requires that you start by making a slip knot and then working a length of chain stitches, with the number of stitches being divisible by 2sts, plus 1st (so, there must be an odd number of stitches in total).

Note: The yarn that is pulled through 'the next 3 loops' when working Row 2, Stage 2 lies horizontally and forms a lookalike chain. The top part of this stitch plus the 1ch also made when working Row 2, Stage 2 are utilized for the picking up of the loops on to the hook for Row 3, Stage 1. In the following instructions, the relevant part of the stitch from which to pick up a loop is referred to as 'the top strand of each chain'. No vertical strands are used, except for the last one at the end of the row when working this Stage 1 step.

Trial piece of basic Tunisian lace stitch

Set-Up: With a 5.50mm crochet hook and a DK-weight yarn, work 11ch. Change to using an 8.00mm Tunisian crochet hook.

Row 1, Stage 1: Pick up 1 loop and place on to the hook for each chain, insert the hook under the top strand of each chain in turn and pull the yarn through. [11 loops on hook]

Row 1, Stage 2: Remove all of the loops as for Tss, until 1 loop remains on the hook.

Row 2, Stage 1: Pick up 1 loop for each vertical strand across the row as for Tss. [11 loops on hook]

Row 2, Stage 2: yoh, pull the yarn through 1 loop, yoh, pull the yarn through the next 2 loops, *make 1ch, yoh, pull the yarn through the next 3 loops; repeat from * until 1 loop remains to be worked at the end of the row, make 1ch, yoh, pull the yarn through 2 loops. [1 loop on the hook]

Row 3, Stage 1: Pick up 1 loop and place on to the hook by inserting the hook under the top strand of each chain in turn, yoh, pull yarn through repeating to the end of the row: *do not* insert the hook under any vertical strands, except that at the end of the row – *see* Note. [11 loops on hook]

Row 3, Stage 2: Remove all of the loops as for Row 2, Stage 2.

Repeat Row 3 until the fabric is of the desired length.

Pull the yarn through two loops as shown at the start of removing all of the loops.

Make one chain, yoh and then pull the yarn through the working loop on the hook and the next two loops.

Make one chain, yoh, then pull the yarn through the working loop on the hook and the last loop at the end of the row.

From Row 3 onwards, only the horizontal strands are used when picking up loops during Stage 1.

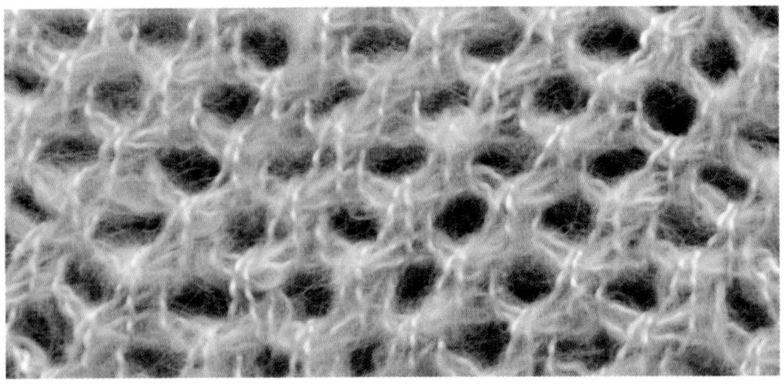
A close-up of basic Tunisian lace stitch worked with a mohair yarn.

A close-up of standard Tunisian lace stitch.

Once the basic Tunisian lace stitch has been mastered, and if mohair is a fibre you enjoy working with, the following Lightweight Mohair Stole is an ideal project, but the stitch pattern used here is the standard Tunisian Lace Stitch, as noted in the following section. The number of rows could be increased to make a luxurious throw. Similarly, fewer stitches and fewer rows could be worked to make a scarf, or the scarf ends could be joined into a ring, to turn it into a cowl. Alternatively, the basic Tunisian lace stitch can be used in a very similar way to produce a scarf or cowl, stole or throw.

Standard Tunisian Lace Stitch

With the basic Tunisian lace stitch featured in the previous section, the opening up of the fabric comes as the loops are removed from the hook, whereas, for standard Tunisian lace stitch, the holes are produced when the loops are picked up. Once again, it is necessary to have a number of chain stitches that is divisible by 2, plus 1 (so, once again, there must be an odd number of chain stitches).

Trial piece of standard Tunisian lace stitch

It is necessary to place yoh before inserting the hook into the work.

Insert the hook under the next two vertical strands of the previous row.

The yarn is being pulled through the working loop, the vertical strand and the wrapped yarn, to give a space.

Set-Up: With DK-weight yarn, make a slip knot and place it on to a 5.50mm crochet hook. With the same hook, work 11ch. Place the last chain on to an 8.00mm Tunisian crochet hook.

Row 1, Stage 1: With the 8.00mm Tunisian crochet hook, pick up 1 loop and place on to the hook for each chain, by inserting the hook under the top strand only of each chain, working yoh, and pulling the yarn through. [11 loops on hook]

Row 1, Stage 2: Remove all of the loops as for Tss, until 1 loop remains on the hook.

Row 2, Stage 1: *yoh, insert the hook under 2 vertical strands, yoh and pull the yarn through the 2 strands; repeat from * to the last stitch of the row, yoh, insert the hook under the last vertical strand, yoh, and pull the yarn through.

Row 2, Stage 2: yoh, pull the yarn through 1 loop, *yoh, pull the yarn through 3 loops; repeat from * to the end of the row.

Repeat Row 2, Stages 1–2, until the fabric is of the desired length.

LIGHTWEIGHT MOHAIR STOLE

The luxurious Lightweight Mohair Stole.

Materials

300g luxury 90-per-cent mohair DK-weight yarn
10.00mm crochet hook
15.00mm Tunisian crochet hook

Tension

It is not easy to measure tension for all lace stitches; therefore, check whether the tension is correct after a few rows of fabric have been produced.
Measured over standard Tunisian lace stitch: 8 stitches and 6 rows to 10cm
Note: The same pattern can be made with a lightweight and soft DK-weight yarn with an 8.00mm crochet hook and a 10.00mm Tunisian crochet hook. The result will not be as large as the size given below.

Size

Approximately 70cm/27½in wide × 200cm/79in long

Pattern instructions

Note: The yarn that is pulled through 'the next 3 loops' when working Row 3, Stage 2 lies horizontally and forms a lookalike chain. The top of this stitch plus the top of the 1ch also made when working Row 3, Stage 2 are utilized for the picking up of loops on to the hook for Row 4, Stage 1. In the following instructions, the relevant part of the stitch from which to pick up a loop is referred to as 'the top strand of each chain'. No vertical strands are used, except for the last one at the end of the row when working this Stage 1 step.

Stole body

Set-Up: Make a slip knot and place it on to the 10.00mm crochet hook. With the same hook, make 71ch. Place the last chain on to the 15.00mm Tunisian crochet hook.
Rows 1–2: Work 2 rows as for Tss.
Row 3, Stage 1: Pick up 1 loop and place on to the hook for each vertical strand across the row as for Tss.
Row 3, Stage 2: Make 1ch, yoh, pull the yarn through 2 loops, *make 1ch, yoh, pull the yarn through the next 3 loops; repeat from * to the end of the row.
Row 4, Stage 1: Pick up 1 loop and place on to the hook by inserting the hook under the top strand of each chain present across the row. The last loop is picked up from under the vertical strand at the end of the row (*see* Note). Check whether you have 71 loops on the hook.
Row 4, Stage 2: Make 1ch, (yoh, pull the yarn through the next 2 loops) twice, *make 1ch, yoh, pull the yarn through the next 3 loops; repeat from * until 2 loops remain on the hook, make 1ch, yoh, pull the yarn through 2 loops. [1 loop on hook]
Repeat Rows 3–4 until the fabric is of the desired length.
Complete the fabric with a row of double crochet, inserting the hook under each vertical strand across the row in turn to remove the unwanted holes, keeping the pattern holes present and in sequence.

Finishing

Fasten off, and sew in all yarn ends.

Optional finishing

Cuffs

Step 1: Fold the crocheted fabric in half lengthwise, to bring the two long sides together.
Step 2: At one end of the fabric, as an opening for the hand, sew a short seam of approximately 5cm in length along the edge of the long side of the doubled fabric, beginning from where two corners of the fabric meet.
Step 3: Join the yarn to the cuff edge of the opening, make 1ch, and, using every stitch around the cuff edge in turn, dc2tog, to edge the circle.
Step 4: Join the top of the last dc2tog worked to the top of the first dc2tog worked with 1slst, and turn the work.
Step 5: For the next and all subsequent rounds, make 1ch, work double crochet to the end of the round, join the start and end of the round with 1slst, and turn the work.
Step 6: Once the cuff is deep enough, complete the current row and fasten off. Work the cuff at the other end of the stole in the same way.
If preferred, the double-crochet cuff can be replace with a raised-treble rib cuff, which gives a little elasticity to the cuff.

Decorative curlicue closure

Step 1: Gather the edge of the short side of one end of the stole, and sew it into a tight bunch.
Step 2: Crochet a number of curlicues, ideally of different lengths. A curlicue is produced by making a short foundation chain and 2 turning chain, working 5 treble (tr) into each foun-

dation chain. Vary the number for stitches for the foundation chain from 5ch to 11ch, to obtain differing lengths of curlicue.
Step 3: Securely sew 3–7 curlicues to the gathered end of the stole.
Leave the other short side of the stole flat, that is, ungathered.
Note: The curlicues give a design detail and the weight of the curlicues holds the stole in place when worn over the shoulders, preventing it from flying away in the wind.

Pixie-style hood
Step 1: Find the centre of one long side of the stole.
Step 2: Place a marker on each side of the centre point, positioned 22cm away from it.
Step 3: With the Tunisian crochet hook and the same yarn as used for the body of the stole, starting at the right-hand marker, yoh and pull the yarn through to pick up 1 loop at evenly spaced intervals over this 44cm length until you reach the left-hand marker, approximately matching the stitch spacing of the fabric of the stole body. (The fabric between the markers should not pucker or undulate.)
Step 4: Count and check whether there is an odd number of stitches; if not, remove 1 loop or pick up an additional 1 loop.
Step 5: Work basic Tunisian lace stitch until the hood fabric measures 36cm in length from the edge of the stole body or until the required length is reached.
Step 6: Work 1 row of double crochet, to finish the top edge of the hood fabric.
Step 7: Fold this hood fabric in half, so that the fold line is centred over the centre point of the stole body, to form the hood.
Step 8: Join the top edges of the sides of the hood together with a whip stitch or your preferred joining method (an invisible join would be a good choice: *see* the section 'Working an invisible join' in Chapter 3).
Step 9: The hood is complete, but, if desired, to frame the face, the hood edge can be finished with one row of double crochet and one following row of crab stitch, to give it an appealing finish, depending on the chosen yarn.

Shaped hood
Step 1: Work Steps 1–5 as given for the pixie-style hood, but stopping once the work measures 15cm in length from the edge of the stole body.
Step 2: Decrease 2sts on the next and every following row, by working one decrease at the start and one decrease at the end of each row, until the length of the fabric is appropriate to fit the head of the intended wearer. These decreases shape the hood. For added shaping, you could also decrease 1 stitch at the centre of the hood (2 or 3 decreases per row, as preferred).
Step 3: Work 1 row of double crochet, to finish the top edge of the hood fabric.
Step 4. Fold this hood fabric in half to form a hood, so that the fold line is centred over the centre point of the stole body, to form the hood.
Step 5: Join the top edges of the sides of the hood together invisibly (*see* the section 'Working an invisible join' in Chapter 3).
Step 6: An optional finish could be used to add texture; join the sides of the top, doubled edge of the hood together on the right side of the fabric by working one row of double crochet and one finishing row of crab stitch. Alternatively, make the join with a whip stitch or your preferred joining method.
Step 7: The hood is complete, but, if desired, to frame the face, the hood edge can be finished with one row of double crochet and one finishing row of crab stitch, to give it an appealing finish, depending on the chosen yarn.

Bias-Free Basic Tunisian Lace Stitch

By working a modified version of the main pattern for basic Tunisian lace stitch over two rows instead of one, it is possible to remove the bias that basic Tunisian lace stitch can create.

A sample of basic Tunisian lace stitch with one row Tss worked on every other row, to remove bias.

Trial piece of bias-free basic Tunisian lace stitch

Note: The yarn that is pulled through 'the next 3 loops' when working Row 2, Stage 2 lies horizontally and forms a lookalike chain. The top of this stitch plus the top of the 1ch also made when working Row 2, Stage 2 are utilized for the picking up of the loops on to the hook for Row 3, Stage 1: in the following instructions, the relevant part of the stitch from which to pick up a loop is referred to as 'the top strand of each chain'. No vertical strands are used, except for the last one at the end of the row when working this Stage 1 step.

Set-Up: With a DK-weight yarn, make a slip knot and place it on to a 5.50mm crochet hook. With the same hook, work a length of chain stitches, with the number of stitches being divisible by 2sts, plus 1st (there must be an odd number of stitches in total). Place the last chain on to an 8.00mm Tunisian crochet hook.

Row 1: With the 8.00mm Tunisian crochet hook, work as for Tss.

Row 2, Stage 1: Pick up 1 loop and place on to the hook for each vertical strand across the row as for Tss.

Row 2, Stage 2: Make 1ch, yoh, pull the yarn through 2 loops, *make 1ch, yoh, pull the yarn through the next 3 loops; repeat from * to the last stitch, make 1ch, yoh, and pull the yarn through 2 loops.

Row 3, Stage 1: Pick up 1 loop and place on to the hook by inserting the hook under the top strand of each chain present across the row. Do not insert the hook under any vertical strands – *see* Note. Check whether you have the correct number of loops on the hook.

Row 3, Stage 2: Make 1ch, yoh, pull the yarn through 2 loops, *make 1ch, yoh, pull the yarn through 2 loops; repeat from * to the end of the row.

Row 4, Stage 1: Omit picking up a loop from under the top strand of the first chain only, and pick up 1 loop and place on to the hook for each vertical strand across the row.

Row 4, Stage 2: Remove all of the loops as for Row 2, Stage 2.

Repeat Rows 3–4 until the fabric is of the desired length.

The Eric Morecambe statue adorned with a colourful mohair neck warmer worked with Tunisian cluster lace.

Trial piece of open Tunisian lace stitch

Set-Up: With a DK-weight yarn, make a slip knot and place it on to a 5.50mm crochet hook. With the same hook, make 15ch. Place the last chain on to a 6.50mm Tunisian crochet hook.

Row 1: With the 6.50mm Tunisian crochet hook, work as for Tss.

Row 2, Stage 1: *Insert the hook under next 2 vertical strands, yoh, and pull the yarn through; repeat from * to the last stitch, yoh, insert the hook under the last vertical strand, yoh, and pull the yarn through.

Note: The number of stitches appears to have been halved, and it seems that there too few loops on the hook. [8 loops on hook]

Row 2, Stage 2: yoh, pull the yarn through 1 loop, *make 2ch, yoh, pull the yarn through the next 2 loops; repeat from * to the end of the row.

Row 3, Stage 1: Counting the loop pulled through the last 2 loops of the previous row as a chain, *pick up 1 loop and place on to the hook, by inserting the hook under the top strand of each of the 2ch worked during Row 2, Stage 2; repeat from * to the last stitch (14 loops currently on hook), pick up 1 loop from under the vertical strand at the end of the row. [15 loops on hook]

Row 3, Stage 2: Remove all of the loops as for Tss.

Repeat Rows 2–3 until the fabric is of the desired length.

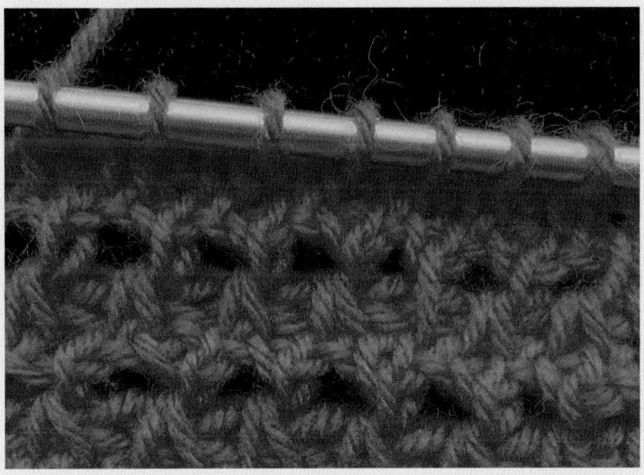

There appears to be too few loops on hook at this step of working open Tunisian lace.

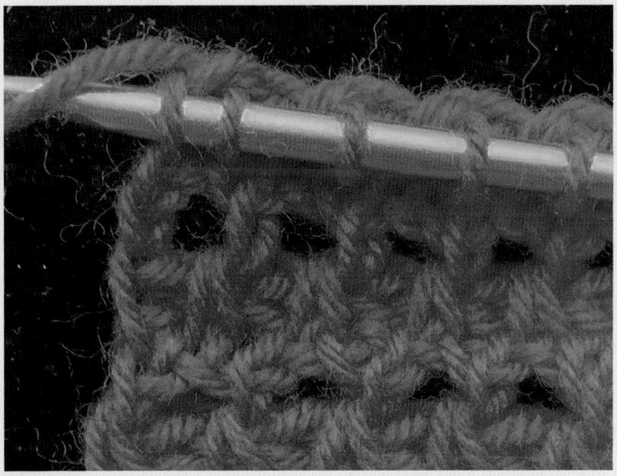

Picking up the final loop from the end of the row when working open Tunisian lace.

Open Tunisian Lace Stitch

The open Tunisian lace stitch is an extension of the standard Tunisian lace stitch and seems to go against all expectations, as it initially appears to have too few stitches on the hook after Stage 1 has been completed. All becomes clear once more rows are worked.

To become acquainted with this stitch, try working the trial piece. As for the other Tunisian crochet lace stitches, the foundation chain needs to begin with a slip knot and be of a number of chain stitches that is a multiple of 2sts, plus 1st (that is, an odd number of stitches in total).

Tunisian Cluster Lace

Tunisian cluster lace is both effective as lace and quickly produced. To understand the workings of Tunisian cluster lace, select a DK weight yarn and a 6.50 Tunisian crochet hook. Follow the body of the scarf instructions on page 73. A smooth yarn has been used for the Tunisian cluster lace the following Quick-And-Easy Scarf, as can be seen in the close-up photograph. However, the colourful Bernat Klein mohair neck warmer that is draped on the Eric Morecambe statue is worked in the same pattern, with the addition of a crocheted shell edging.

QUICK-AND-EASY SCARF

Unadorned Tunisian cluster lace worked with a thick, smooth yarn. Both the cluster side and the knitted-look side of the fabric can be seen.

Choose any yarn and an appropriate size of Tunisian crochet hook for that yarn. This scarf has no materials, size or tension given, as it is rather like a trial piece and all of these aspects can be determined according to personal preference. As usual, a crochet hook smaller than the Tunisian crochet hook to be used will be required for working the foundation chain.

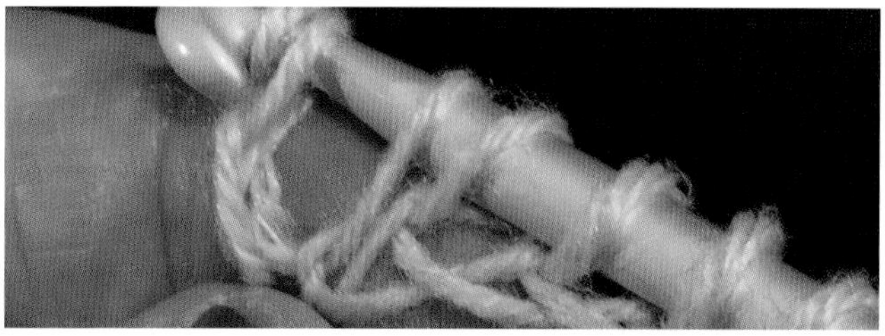

Work two chains at the start of removing all of the loops.

Pattern instructions

Scarf body

Set-Up: Make a slip knot and place it on to a crochet hook of an appropriate size for the yarn being used. With the same hook, work a length of chain stitches, with the number of stitches being divisible by 4. Place the last chain on to a Tunisian crochet hook of an appropriate size for the yarn being used.

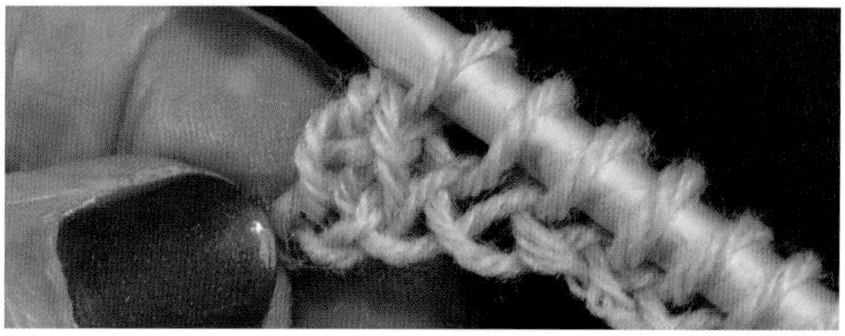

Here, the yarn has been pulled through the next two loops on the hook.

Row 1, Stage 1: With the Tunisian crochet hook, pick up 1 loop and place on to the hook for each chain in turn by inserting the hook under the top strand of the chain, working yoh, and pulling the yarn through.

Row 1, Stage 2: Make 2ch, yoh, pull the yarn through 2 loops, *make 4ch, yoh, and pull the yarn through the next 5 loops; repeat from * to the last 3 loops, make 3ch, yoh, and pull the yarn through all 3 loops.

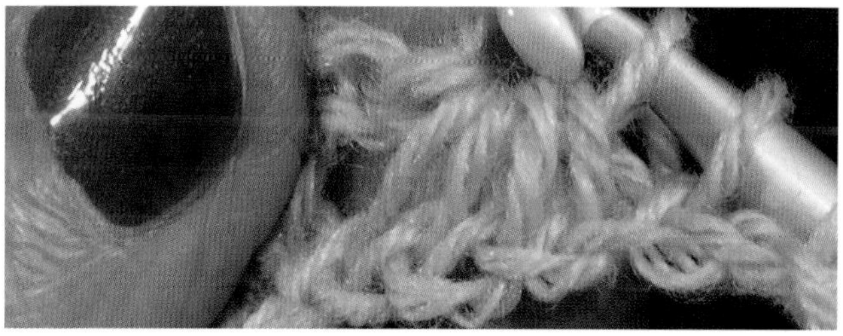

Now, the yarn has been pulled through the next five loops, to make a cluster.

Row 2, Stage 1: Omit picking up a loop from under the top strand of the first chain (that is, the last stitch made at the end of the previous row), pick up 1 loop and place on to the hook, by inserting the hook under the top strand of each chain across the row as for Row 1, Stage 1 – *do not* pick up a loop for any of the clusters!

Row 2, Stage 2: Work as for Row 1, Stage 2.

Repeat Row 2 until the fabric is of the desired length. Do not break the yarn if the fabric is to be converted into a shorter neck warmer with a border or a longer scarf. Break off the yarn only if the fabric is being made as a trial piece.

Insert the hook under the top strand of the chain as shown.

Finishing

Sew in all yarn ends.

Continue picking up one loop from under the top strand of each chain in turn across the row but missing the clusters.

Trial piece of Tunisian filet lace

Note: Because Txtr stitches have more height than Tss stitches, the making of 2ch is required at the start of each row, when working Stage 1, in order to lift the hook to the required level above the work.

Set-Up: Make a slip knot and place it on to a crochet hook of an appropriate size for the yarn being used. With the same hook, work a length of chain stitches, with the number of stitches being divisible by 2sts, plus 1st. Place the last chain on to a Tunisian crochet hook of an appropriate size for the yarn being used.

Row 1, Stage 1: With the Tunisian crochet hook, yoh twice, insert the hook into the 3rd chain from the hook, yoh, pull the yarn through the chain only (4 loops on hook), yoh, pull the yarn through 1 loop (still 4 loops on hook), yoh, pull the yarn through the first 2 loops (3 loops on hook), yoh, pull through the next 2 loops on the hook (= 1Txtr made), *yoh twice, miss 1ch, 1Txtr in next chain; repeat from * to the end of the row.

Note: The number of loops on the hook should equal the number of chain stitches of the foundation chain.

Row 1, Stage 2: Remove all of the loops as for Tss, remembering that some of the loops are simply yarn wrapped around the hook (from working yoh for the preceding Stage 1 step).

Row 2, Stage 1: Make 2ch, *yoh twice, insert the hook under both the topmost slightly sloping vertical strand of the next Txtr of the previous row and the next vertical strand at the front of the same Txtr of the previous row, yoh, pull the yarn through the 2 vertical strands only (1 loop added to hook), yoh, pull the yarn through 1 loop, yoh, pull the yarn through the next 2 loops on the hook (= 1Txtr); repeat from * to the end of the row.

Row 2, Stage 2: Remove all of the loops as for Row 1, Stage 2. Repeat Row 2, Stages 1–2, until the fabric is of the desired length.

The yarn is wrapped twice prior to the hook being inserted into the work.

Work yoh and pull the yarn through the first loop on the hook only.

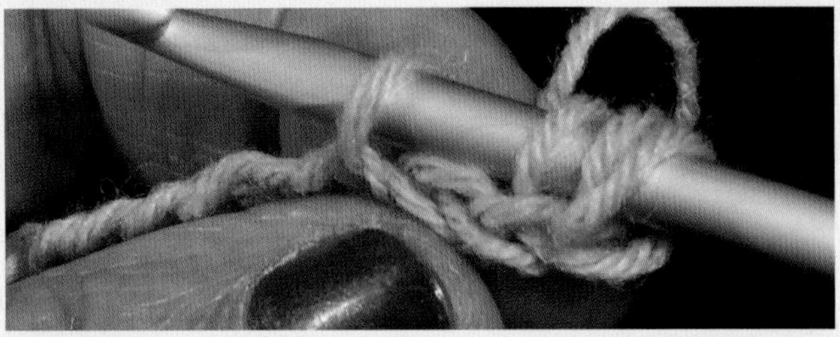

Next, the hook is inserted into the top of the third chain from the hook.

Next, the yarn is pulled through the first two loops on the hook – there will now be three loops on the hook. One Tunisian extended treble has been made.

There will now be four loops on hook.

Work yoh twice for working the next stitch.

One chain needs to be missed before working the next Tunisian extended treble.

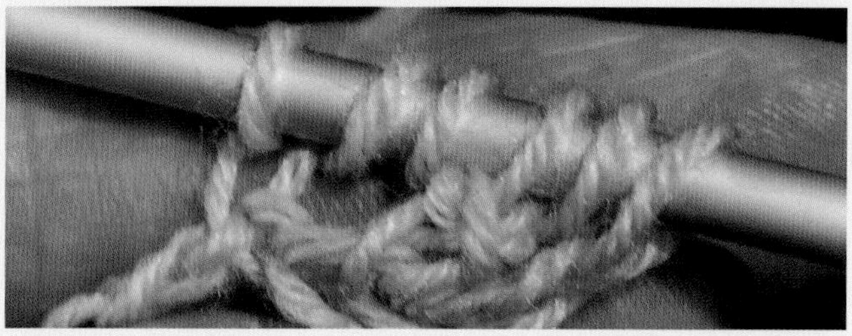

Continue to pick up only one strand of yarn, to result in another loop on the hook.

The unworked wrap of yarn remaining from working yoh twice replaces the missed chain.

At the end of each row, pick up one loop from under the top strand of the last chain.

Two chains need to be worked at the start of a new row.

After wrapping the yarn around the hook twice, insert the hook under both the slanting vertical strand and the vertical strand at the top of the Tunisian extended treble of the previous row to work the next Tunisian extended treble.

The Tunisian extended trebles appear more open during working but take on the correct tension as extra rows are completed.

An example of a piece of Tunisian crochet filet lace, viewed from the front.

An example of a piece of Tunisian crochet filet lace, viewed from the back.

Optional finishing for scarf

Change to using the crochet hook to add a crocheted shell edging around all four sides of the Tunisian cluster lace fabric just worked as follows:

Make 1ch, work 2tr in 3chsp, 1dc 3tr 1dc in each 4chsp to end of top edge, 1dc in corner, 1dc in chsp, 1dc in chain at edge of row, 1dc 3tr 1dc in each chsp in turn until bottom edge is reached, 1dc in last stitch, 1dc in corner, 1dc in first stitch at start of bottom edge, 1dc 3tr 1dc in each chsp in turn until last chsp is reached, 1dc 2tr 1dc in last chsp, 1dc in last stitch, 1dc in corner, 1dc in first stitch at start of remaining side edge, 1dc 3tr 1dc in each chsp to complete the shell edging, 1dc in last stitch, and 1slst to start of round.

Fasten off.

Sew in all yarn ends.

Alternative yarns

When a larger hook than usual is selected for use with a yarn containing a luxury fibre such as yarn from a long-haired goat, llama, alpaca, and so on, the effect achieved is very different, as the photograph of the scarf worked with a Bernat Klein mohair yarn and a 10.00mm Tunisian crochet hook over 24sts reveals. The finished dimensions of this mohair neck warmer are 90cm × 30cm.

The same Tunisian cluster lace stitch has been worked with a chunky yarn and a 12.00mm Tunisian crochet hook to produce the featured longer-length scarf shown on page 72. The optional crocheted finish was omitted. The result is a thicker textured look, and the spaces of the lace are almost hidden because of the type of yarn used. However, this yarn choice keeps the scarf lightweight and warm.

Tunisian Crochet Filet Lace

This Tunisian crochet stitch pattern combines a taller Tunisian crochet stitch in the form of a Tunisian extended treble (Txtr) and also spaces made by putting yarn over the hook (yoh) to create additional loops on the hook. Note that a Txtr is three times the height of a Tss. Producing the Txtr stitch works on the same principle as for producing the extended treble stitch of classic crochet, meaning that the yarn is pulled through only a single loop on the hook prior to the yarn being pulled through two loops. In order to make the spaces needed in Tunisian filet lace, during Stage 1, the hook is wrapped twice with yarn prior to working the Txtr. One of the two wrapped loops remains on the hook after the Txtr has been worked and is counted as a loop when working Stage 2. Tunisian filet lace still has the squared appearance that traditional filet lace is recognized by, but, this time, it is the holes that provide the square look.

Tunisian filet lace is a suitable fabric with which to quickly produce unshaped beachwear cover-ups. Two rectangles joined at the shoulders are ideal, particularly if worked with a cotton-fibre yarn. The finished crochet can be lined for use as a single-layer garment or added as an unlined extra to the top layer of an ensemble. Overlaying Tunisian filet lace on to a strong contrast colour as a background, by adding a lining to a garment, opens up endless design possibilities, whether for clothes or for accessories.

Combining the principles of Tunisian lace with those of decreasing can create a lovely shawl worked in Tunisian filet lace. The following shawl pattern is worked in Tunisian filet lace and in bands of colour, but, if preferred, only a single colour can be used – just add up the total number of balls of yarn required and proceed to make a monochromatic version. Decreasing when working Tunisian trebles requires particular attention to be paid to the edges, to prevent them from becoming ragged. Follow the detailed instructions provided for both the Stage 1 beginnings and ends of Row 5 and Row 6 for a pleasing result.

TUNISIAN CROCHET FILET-LACE SHAWL

This is the large, lightweight Tunisian Crochet Filet-Lace Shawl.

Materials

West Yorkshire Spinners Bo Peep luxury baby 4-ply (199m/50g)
3 × 50g balls in M
1 × 50g ball in four different colours: C1, C2, C3 and C4
5.00mm crochet hook
5.50mm crochet hook
7.00m Tunisian crochet hook

Tension

It is not easy to measure tension when working with lace stitches; therefore, check whether the tension is correct after a few rows of fabric have been produced.
Measured over Tunisian crochet filet lace: 18 stitches to 10cm (covering 9 filet-lace holes) and 5 rows to 7cm.

Size

Approximately 90cm/35½in × 150cm/59in (though, remember that measuring lace challenges accuracy!)

The yarn is wrapped around the hook (yoh), prior to the hook being inserted into the work.

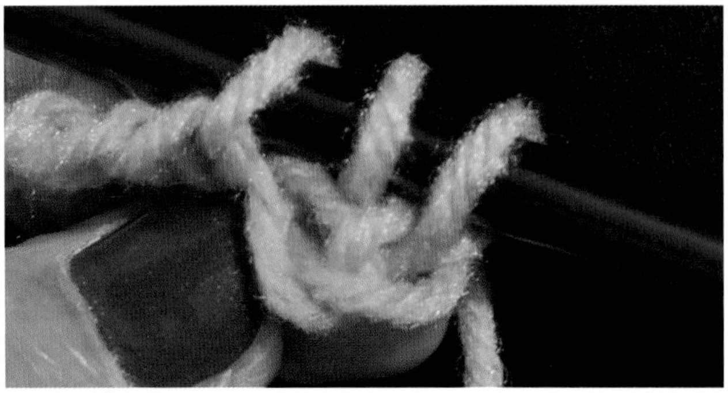

The yarn is pulled through under the top strand of the third chain from the hook (or under the next vertical strand or as otherwise directed in the pattern), giving three loops in total on the hook.

Pattern note

ALERT! The main stitch used for the Tunisian crochet filet lace of this project, the Tunisian crochet extended treble, is triple the height of Tss, requiring 4 stitches to be decreased on both Row 5 and Row 6, to result in the intended shaping of the shawl sides.

Read the points below before making the shawl:

1. For Row 6 of the pattern, picking up the two strands from the top of each Txtr of the previous row when working Stage 1 is technically correct, but it is a little difficult to achieve as, actually, the first of these two strands slopes and can easily be missed, because it has a tendency to slide under the more upright strand.
2. When working the Txtr stitches of the pattern, after wrapping the yarn around the hook twice ('yoh twice'), make sure that the following 'pull the yarn through the next 2 loops on the hook, leaving 2 loops to remain on the hook' is not missed.
3. It is necessary to take care when decreasing. At the beginning of Row 6, if the procedure given is followed, there will not be a problem; however, at the end of Row 6, it is essential that the intended complete decrease is made: take great care not to miss making the necessary decrease here, and check whether you have decreased by 4sts instead of only 2sts, by counting the loops on the hook after completing Stage 1.
4. It is advisable to count the loops on the hook after completing each Row 6, Stage 1.
5. The next colour is introduced once all but the last 3 loops on the hook have been worked, which avoids a noticeable change of colour at the edge of the shawl. Change to using a new colour as instructed before working Row 6, Stage 2 to completely remove all of the loops.
6. At the conclusion of the shawl, ensure that you remove the last loops as instructed, to form a neat point.
7. Check carefully during the working of the border that the first round is lying flat. Work only a little of the first round and then place the crocheted fabric on to a hard, flat surface to check whether the correct number of stitches is being used, to avoid the fabric being puckered or wavy along the edges.

Note: The Tunisian crochet treble (Ttr) is not the same as the Tunisian crochet extended treble (Txtr). Be sure to work the intended stitch when working through the row-by-row instructions, as both stitches are worked during both Row 5 and Row 6.

Tunisian crochet treble

The Tunisian Filet-Lace Shawl includes the Tunisian treble stitch, so, before beginning to work the shawl pattern, it is essential to understand how to form this stitch.

Step 1: To work a Tunisian treble, before the hook is inserted into the relevant part of the foundation chain or the previous row, first, put the yarn over the hook (yoh).

Step 2: Insert the hook under the top strand of the 3rd chain from the hook, yoh and pull the yarn through this chain only.

Step 3: yoh and pull the yarn through the next 2 loops on the hook.

The necessary steps of creating a Ttr have been completed: once the yarn has been pulled through the 2 loops on the hook during Step 3, just 1 loop of the Ttr is left on the hook. It is clear that a row of Ttr stitches is taller than a row of Tss stitches; as the Ttr stitches are taller, they produce a fabric that is less dense than is a Tss based fabric.

Note: Because Ttr stitches have more height than Tss stitches, the making of 1ch is required at the start of each row at Stage 1, to lift the hook to the required level above the work.

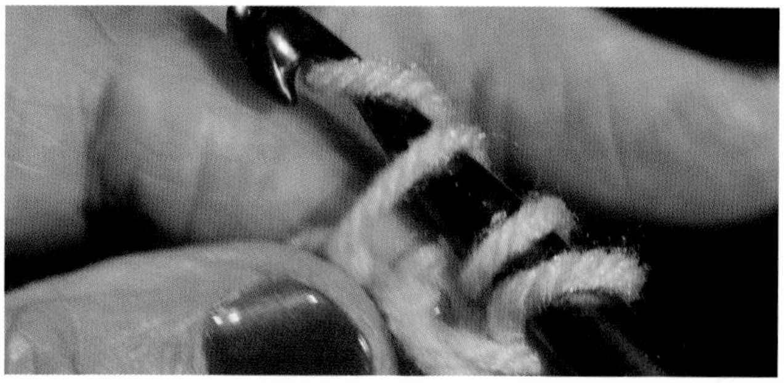

Again, yoh is worked and pulled through the next two loops of the Tunisian treble.

Having completed the Tunisian treble steps so far, one loop of the Tunisian treble remains, and it stays on the hook, to be worked during Stage 2.

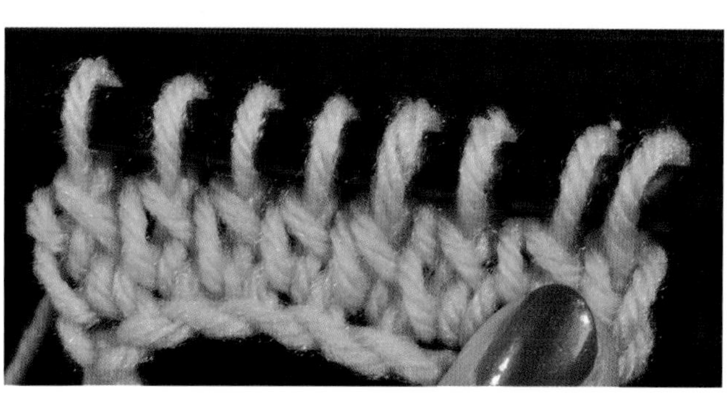

Tunisian treble stitches are taller than Tunisian simple stitch stitches.

Pattern instructions

Shawl body

Set-Up: With M, make a slip knot and place it on to the 5.50mm crochet hook. With the same hook, make 213ch. Place the last chain on to the 7.00mm Tunisian crochet hook.

Row 1, Stage 1: With the 7.00mm Tunisian crochet hook, pick up 1 loop and place on to the hook for each chain. [213 loops on hook]

Row 1, Stage 2: Remove all of the loops as for Tss.

Rows 2–4: Work as for Tss.

Row 5, Stage 1: Make 3ch, work 1Ttr as follows: yoh, insert the hook under the next 2 vertical strands of Tss, yoh, pull the yarn through the 2 vertical strands only, yoh, pull the yarn through the next 2 loops on the hook, leaving 1 loop to remain on the hook from the Ttr, *work 1Txtr as follows: yoh twice, insert the hook under the next 2 vertical strands of Tss, yoh, pull the yarn through the 2 vertical strands only, yoh, pull the yarn through the next loop on the hook, yoh, pull the yarn through the next 2 loops on the hook, leaving 2 loops to remain on the hook from the Txtr; repeat from * to the last 3 unworked vertical strands, work 1Ttr as at the start of the row by inserting the hook under the next 2 vertical strands of Tss, and work 1Ttr in the last stitch by inserting the hook under the last vertical strand of the row. [209sts; 2 double decreases made – double decrease at start and 1 at end of row]

Row 5, Stage 2: yoh, pull the yarn through 1 loop on the hook, *yoh, pull the yarn through the next 2 loops on the hook; repeat from * to the last 3 loops on the hook, yoh, pull the yarn through all 3 loops. [209sts as for Stage 1]

Row 6, Stage 1: Make 3ch (this counts as the first stitch of the row and lifts the hook to the right height for working the new row), yoh, ignoring the loops of the decrease made at the end of the previous row, insert the hook under the 2 strands from the top of the next stitch of the previous row, yoh, pull the yarn through the 2 strands only, yoh, pull the yarn through the next 2 loops on the hook, leaving 2 loops to remain on the hook, *yoh twice, insert the hook under the 2 strands from the top of the next stitch of the previous row, yoh, pull the yarn through the 2 strands only, yoh, pull the yarn through the next 2 loops on the hook, leaving 1 of the 2 original wrapped loops to remain on the hook; repeat from * to the last 4sts of the row (it is easier to think of them as the last stitches associated with the last 2 filet-lace holes), work 1Ttr under the 2 strands from the top of the next stitch of the previous row, and work 1Ttr in the last stitch of the row. [205sts; 2 double decreases made – 1 double decrease at start and 1 double decrease at end of row]

Row 6, Stage 2: *yoh, pull the yarn through the next 2 loops on the hook; repeat from * to the last 3 loops on the hook, yoh, pull the yarn through all 3 loops. [205sts as for Stage 1]

Rows 7–12: Repeat Row 6 six times. [181sts]

Row 13: Work as for Row 6, but change from using M to C1 at the end of Stage 1 by working with M to the last stitch and working the last Ttr with C1. [177sts]

Rows 14–17: With C1, repeat Row 6 four times. [161sts]

Row 18: Change from using C1 to M as described for Row 13. [157sts]

Row 19: Change from using M to C2 as described for Row 13. [153sts]

Rows 20–24: With C2, repeat Row 6 five times. [133sts]

Row 25: Change from using C2 to M as described for Row 13. [129sts]

Row 26: With M, repeat Row 6 once. [125sts]

Row 27: Change from using M to C3 as described for Row 13. [121sts]

Rows 28–33: With C3, repeat Row 6 six times. [97sts]

Row 34: Change from using C3 to M as described for Row 13. [93sts]

Rows 35–36: With M, repeat Row 6 twice. [85sts]

Row 37: Change from using M to C4 as described for Row 13. [81sts]

Rows 38–44: With C4, repeat Row 6 seven times. [53sts]

Row 45: Change from using C4 to M as described for Row 13. [49sts]

Rows 46–56: With M, repeat Row 6 eleven times. [5sts]

Row 57, Stage 1: Make 3ch, insert the hook under the next 2 strands, yoh, pull the yarn through, insert the hook under the next 2 strands, yoh, and pull the yarn through. [3 loops on hook]

Row 57, Stage 2: yoh, pull the yarn through all 3 loops on the hook to form a neat point.

Do not break off the yarn; continue with M attached to make the border.

Border

Worked with M throughout. *See* point 7 of Pattern Notes.

Round 1: With the 5.50mm crochet hook and the RS of the shawl fabric facing, make 2ch, and double crochet along the first diagonal edge of the Tunisian filet lace rows, checking frequently that the border is lying flat. I found that 5dc to 2 row ends worked, but everyone's tension is different, so do check! Work 2dc at the first corner, 1dc into each stitch of the long Tss row, 2dc at the second corner, double crochet along the second diagonal edge of the Tunisian filet-lace rows, again checking frequently that the border is lying flat, until you reach the bottom point of the shawl, work 1slst into top of the 2ch worked at the start of the round (however, note that it may be necessary to add 3dc at the end of this round before working the slst, to achieve a pleasing finish), make 1ch, and turn.

Round 2: With the WS of the shawl fabric facing, double crochet around all 3 sides of the shawl, checking frequently that the border is lying flat, and adding extra stitches at the 3 corners as desired to keep the points sharp. At the end of the round, work 1slst into the 1ch worked at the end of the previous round, make 1ch, and turn.

Round 3: With RS facing, double crochet around all 3 sides of the shawl, checking frequently that the border is lying flat, and adding extra stitches at the 3 corners as desired to keep the points sharp. At the end of the round, work 1slst into the 1ch worked at the end of the previous round. Break the yarn.

Round 4: With RS facing and the 5.50mm crochet hook, join M to the point, leaving a yarn end of enough length for possible adjustment of the shape later (to work a few extra stitches to achieve a pleasing finish, if needed). Make 1ch, work 1dc in each stitch to the end of the round, and add extra stitches at the corners where necessary. Work 1slst into the 1ch worked at the start of the round. *Do not* turn the work.

Round 5: Change to using the 5.00mm crochet hook. Work 1 round of crab stitch into the double-crochet stitches of the previous round, beginning by working 1ch and ending by working 1slst into the 1ch at the start of the round, and fasten off.

Finishing

With a fine crochet hook or a sewing needle, adjust the point if necessary by teasing the stitches. Sew in all yarn ends.

Tunisian Cobweb Lace

Tunisian cobweb lace is very delicate. It is totally impractical to produce a project worked wholly with the single row of the cobweb-lace pattern, unless it is to be protected against wear and tear with a lining or by some other means. However, when combined with an additional row of more substantial Tunisian simple stitch, to work a fabric of alternating rows of Tunisian cobweb lace and Tunisian simple stitch, it is possible to use Tunisian cobweb lace to produce ethereal designs.

As this is a lace, it can be a challenge to measure accurately for tension. Unless a pattern is being written for someone else to follow, it may not be necessary to measure for tension, but it is vital that, after a few rows of working the fabric, you check and evaluate your work at the point when there is only 1 loop on the hook, to ensure that the resulting fabric will be fit for the purpose and of appropriate dimensions for the use in mind.

A front-side view of Tunisian cobweb lace.

A back-side view of Tunisian cobweb lace.

Trial piece of Tunisian cobweb lace

Tunisian cobweb lace is worked with a multiple of 3sts, plus 2sts. It is easier to count the stitches when all of the loops have been placed on to the hook. Work with a 4-ply yarn to keep the ethereal character.

Set-Up: With a 5.00mm crochet hook, make a foundation chain of 17ch in length, or any other length that is a multiple of 3, plus 2. Place the last chain on to a 6.00mm Tunisian crochet hook.

Row 1: Work as for Tss. This Tss row is necessary to provide some vertical strands to allow for the insertion of the Tunisian crochet hook when beginning to work the 1 row lace pattern.

Row 2, Stage 1: Make 2ch (used only to lift the hook), *insert the hook through the next 3 vertical strands of Tss, yoh, pull the yarn through all 3 strands, make 2ch; repeat from * to the last stitch, pick up 1 loop from the last stitch of the row and place on the hook, make 2ch. [7 loops on hook – 1 for each pulled-through loop from each group of 3 vertical strands used, plus the start and end loops]

Row 2, Stage 2: yoh, pull the yarn through 1 loop, make 1ch, *yoh, pull the yarn through 2 loops, make 2ch; repeat from * until 3 loops remain on the hook, yoh, pull the yarn through 2 loops, make 1ch, yoh, pull the yarn through 2 loops. [1 loop on hook]

Row 3, Stage 1: Make 2ch (used only to lift the hook), *work 3Ttr in the last of the next 2ch made during Row 2, Stage 1; repeat from * to the last stitch of the row, work 1Ttr in the second (top) chain of the 2ch made for turning at the very end of Row 2, Stage 1. [17 loops on hook]

Row 3, Stage 2: Remove all of the loops as for Tss.

Repeat Rows 2–3 until the fabric is of the desired length.

Final row: Work a row of double crochet to complete this test piece; however, it will be necessary to reduce the number of stitches in order to keep the final row the same width as that of the Tunisian cobweb lace. As a guide, *work 1dc under each of the next 4 vertical strands in turn, and work dc2tog over the next 2 vertical strands; repeat from * to the end of the row.

COBWEB COWL

The Cobweb Cowl, with one twist introduced into the fabric before seaming the two short ends.

Materials

1 × 50g ball West Yorkshire Spinners Bo Peep luxury baby 4-ply (199m/50g)
5.00mm crochet hook
6.00mm Tunisian crochet hook

Tension

Measured over Tunisian cobweb lace: approximately 9sts to 5cm/2in and 12 rows to 17.5cm/7in
Preferably measure the fabric with only 1 loop on the hook after working 6–9 rows of fabric, to check whether there is sufficient width to produce a cowl of the desired dimensions.

Size

18cm/7in wide × 80cm/31½in long, before the two ends of the cowl fabric are joined.

An effective yarn that is difficult to work with can produce beautiful cowls where tension and size is not of paramount importance.

Flattening the curl of the cowl to show the lacy fabric of a cowl worked in a difficult yarn.

Pattern instructions

Cowl body

Set-Up: Make a slip knot and place it on to the 5.00mm crochet hook. With the same hook, make 29ch. Place the last chain on to the 6.00mm Tunisian crochet hook.
Row 1: Work as for Tss.
Work Rows 2–3 as given for the trial piece of Tunisian cobweb lace until the fabric is of the desired length.
Next row: Pick up 1 loop on to the hook from each of the next 2 vertical strands, *insert the hook under the next 2 vertical strands and pick up 1 loop, pick up 1 loop from each of the next 4 vertical strands; repeat from * 3 times, pick up 1 loop from each of the remaining 2 vertical strands. (This should keep the last row the same width as the open lacy rows.)
Next row: Remove all of the loops as for Tss.
Work 1 row in Tss.
With the 5.00mm crochet hook, make 1ch, work double crochet by working into each stitch in turn to the end of the row, but do not break off the yarn. Continue by working in double crochet along the first side of the rectangle, across the bottom edge and along the second side, working 2dc at each corner. How many double crochet stitches are placed along the side edges depends on your tension; usually 3dc to 2 pattern rows works well. Work 1slst into the 1ch at the start of the row, to join into a round. Do not turn the work.
Work 1 round of crab stitch into the double crochet stitches of the previous round. Fasten off.

Finishing

Optional: Before joining the two short ends of the fabric, turn over one short end only of the rectangle so that the other side of the fabric is uppermost. This introduces a single twist to create a Möbius strip, so enhancing the design.

Arrange the two ends with the wrong sides together, to form a tube. Join the ends by sewing them together, just below the crab stitch finish. Using your preferred stitch and with the right side facing, the sewing stitches are hidden. One side of the cowl fabric will have a decorative ridge whilst the other will have a flat seam.

CHAPTER 5

TANTALIZING TEXTURE

To reiterate, Tunisian crochet is traditionally a smooth fabric, with one side having a flat pattern of squares and the reverse side resembling the rough purl side of knitted stocking stitch. Initially, it is important to understand that the word 'texture' for crochet means that either the yarn or the fabric is not smooth. This is different to the use of the word 'texture' within the field of art and design, where it is used for everything that can be touched including paper, shiny ceramic tiles, highly polished non-tooled wood and many other materials and surfaces – not so for crochet.

Tunisian crochet can combine any yarn of any fibre that is smooth with any yarn of any fibre that contains a characteristic that removes the smooth look. The texture may be introduced to the yarn through plying or by injection. Yarns that have knobbly lumps, long hairs protruding, or move from thick to thin at regular or irregular intervals can be classed as textured in the context of crochet.

To prevent repeating myself, *see* the section on yarns in Chapter 2. Chapter 3, covering Tunisian simple stitch, contains many examples of the use of textured yarns to change the look of the fabric. This is particularly noticeable when working Tunisian tweed stitch with a single-ended Tunisian crochet hook or Tunisian garter stitch with a double-ended Tunisian crochet hook. The variety of yarn combinations when working either of these stitches is endless.

OPPOSITE PAGE: The Casual-Extra Top, combining Tunisian raised trebles and Tunisian puff stitches for textural patterns.

Likewise, fabrics made of any stitch pattern that introduces lumps and bumps, overlays raised stitches during the construction of a Tunisian crochet fabric or incorporates a variety of stitch heights within one row in such a way that the stitches cannot lie flat are referred to as textured Tunisian fabrics.

Creating texture within a Tunisian fabric using a smooth yarn can be a lot of fun. As mentioned previously, it helps to understand that a row of Tunisian crochet is simply a lot of unfinished ordinary crochet stitches. With this realization, it is possible to design numerous Tunisian stitch patterns. For example, a row of Tunisian simple stitch is only a series of unfinished double-crochet stitches until the loops are worked off to close and finish the linked double crochet stitches.

Initially, when placing the loops on to a Tunisian crochet hook during Stage 1 of working Tunisian simple stitch, the process resembles that of making a multi-wrapped treble. Stage 2 removes these loops, to allow the hook to get back to holding only one loop – a point that all crochet stitches eventually reach. By turning the work 90 degrees anticlockwise, the edge where the Tunisian crochet rows start at the top shows an obvious similarity to the top of normal crochet stitches. Similarly, the opposite side of the row (now lying at the base of the turned work) is not unlike that of ordinary crochet after the foundation chain has been worked, when two loops of the chain have been picked up and the yarn pulled through to make the stitches.

A circle, seen from the back.

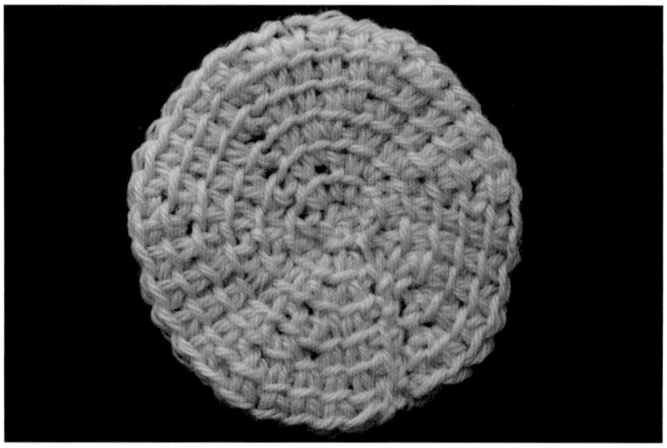

A circle, seen from the front.

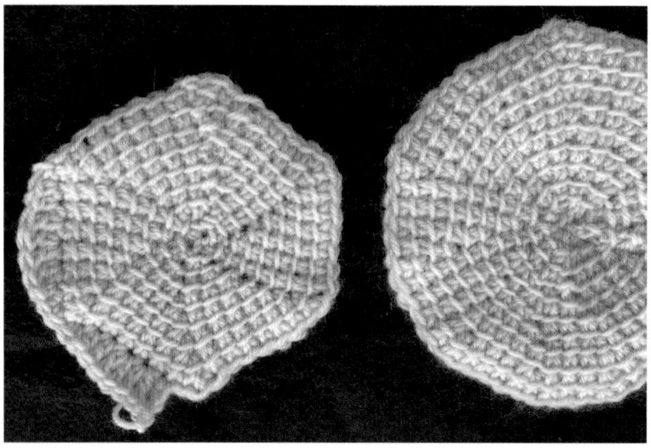

The six wedges of a hexagon have the start of a traditional crochet edge being applied, sitting alongside an unedged circle of twelve wedges.

There are many and various Tunisian stitch patterns included in these pages to allow for experimentation. However, once the structure of a Tunisian crochet stitch is understood, the door to limitless numbers of patterns and designs becomes wide open, and a whole new world of fun-filled investigation is available.

Prior to explaining and exploring textured Tunisian crochet, it would be advantageous to know how to execute a circle, hexagon, octagon, etc.

Circles and Hexagons

The use of partial rows is what makes it possible for circles to be produced. Circles are made by working partial rows either by starting from the centre of the circle or from the edge of the circle's circumference. The number of chains you begin with determines the size of circle. The length of the foundation chain should equal the radius of the circle that you are planning to complete. Whether you start with only 7ch, as I am suggesting here as a trial piece, or with, say, 38ch, to give a finished diameter suitable for a round cushion, the procedure is the same.

Initially, the trial circle will appear quite round, but, as it grows, it will turn into a hexagon. The interesting characteristic of working the circle/hexagon in Tunisian crochet, is the need for a choice to be made by the designer. Once the required size has been reached, the final row or border row is what will determine the final shape of the piece. The border row(s) enhance the shape, either as a circle or as a hexagon.

For a hexagon, the simplest of finishes will suffice, with just an additional stitch being added to each of the outer points of the wedges.

For a true circle, one or two rows will need to be worked by using crochet stitches of varying heights to turn the straight lines between the outer points of the wedges into curves. To ensure a true curve, the number of double crochet on each side of the central stitches of treble must be the same. It helps on large pieces to place a marker at the central point of each wedge around the circumference. Begin by working a crochet slip stitch on the point at the edges of the straight lines running between the wedges. Work two or three double crochet followed by three to five treble. How many stitches are required depends on how large the hexagon has become. Continue with double crochet followed by one slip stitch to complete the wedge. Repeat the same process on each wedge.

Trial piece of a small circle

Try working this small circle with a DK weight yarn with a 5.50mm crochet hook and 6.50mm Tunisian crochet hook. Note that the whole circle is worked with Tss.

Set-Up: Make a slip knot and place it on to the 5.50mm crochet hook. With the same hook, make 11ch, and place the last chain on to the 6.50mm Tunisian crochet hook.

Row 1, Step 1: Counting the loop on the hook as the first stitch, insert the hook into the top strand only of the second chain from the hook, yoh, and pull through leaving the loop on the hook. Rep for the next 9ch leaving the last chain unworked. [10 loops on hook]

Row 1, Step 2: *yoh, and pull the yarn through 2 loops; repeat from * to the end of the row: note that the yarn is pulled through 2 loops immediately, without making a turning chain and continue by removing all of the loops as for Tss.

Row 1, Step 3: Counting the loop on the hook as 1 stitch, pick up 1 loop and place on to the hook for each of the first 8 vertical strands of the row, leaving the rest of the vertical strands of the row unworked. [8 loops on hook]

Row 1, Step 4: Work as for Row 1, Step 2.

Row 1, Step 5: Counting the loop on the hook as 1 stitch, pick up 1 loop and place on to the hook for each of the first 6 vertical strands of the row, leaving the rest of the vertical strands of the row unworked. [6 loops on hook]

Row 1, Step 6: Work as for Row 1, Step 2.

Row 1, Step 7: Counting the loop on the hook as 1 stitch, pick up 1 loop and place on to the hook for each of the first 4 vertical strands of the row, leaving the rest of the vertical strands of the row unworked. [4 loops on hook]

Row 1, Step 8: Work as for Row 1, Step 2.

Row 1, Step 9: Counting the loop on the hook as 1 stitch, pick up 1 loop and place on to the hook from the first 2 vertical strands of the row, leaving the rest of the vertical strands of the row unworked. [2 loops on hook]

Row 1, Step 10: yoh, and pull the yarn through 2 loops: there is only 1 loop on the hook, as for the end of a typical Tss Stage 2 step.

By working Row 1, Stages 1–10, the first wedge has been completed.

When all but the last of the foundation chains have been used, and a wedge formed, work the next wedge as follows.

Row 2, Step 1: Counting the loop on the hook as 1 stitch, pick up 1 loop and place on to the hook for each of the first 10 vertical strands of the row.

Row 2, Step 2: Work as for Step 1, Stage 2.

Continue to make the second wedge as for the first, by working as for Row 1, Steps 3–10.

Make 4 additional wedges in the same way as for the second wedge.

Join the last loop of the last wedge to the foundation chain of the first wedge by working slip stitches or whip stitches to join together the sides to form a circle, with the last crochet or sewn stitch being worked into the one remaining foundation chain at the centre of the circle.

The work should lie flat and, from only 11sts, form a circle.

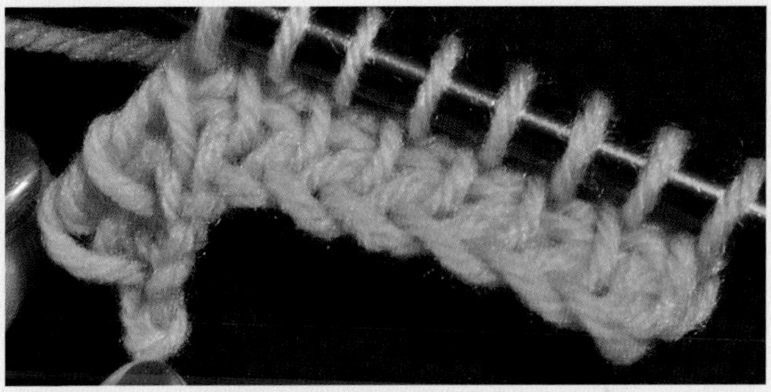

Here, the last chain of the foundation chain and the last two vertical strands of the previous row are not worked.

Work yoh and pull the yarn through the next two loops on the hook.

At the end of Step 5, there will be six loops on the hook.

Trial piece of a small circle *(cont'd)*

At the end of Step 7, there will be four loops on the hook.

Pick up one loop from under the next vertical strand to start the next wedge of the circle.

At the end of Step 9, there will be two loops on the hook.

Continue by picking up one loop from under the rest of the ten vertical strands.

At the end of Step 10, there will again be only one loop on the hook.

All ten loops are now on the hook at the end of Row 2, Step 1.

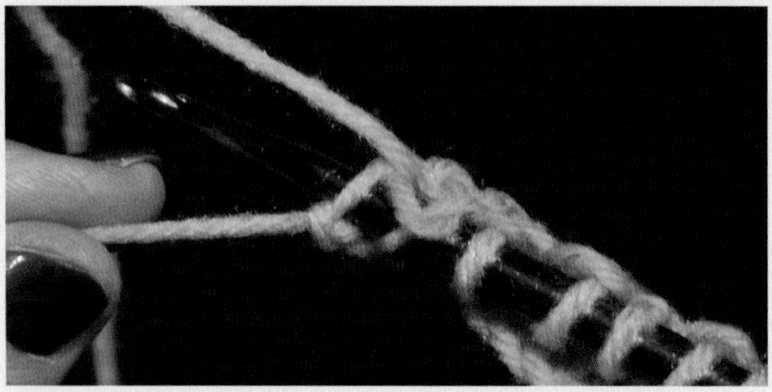

The missed chain of the foundation chain – here highlighted by being temporarily picked up on to the hook – is worked into only when all of the wedges have been completed.

Again all of the loops have been removed; the first wedge is completed and the second wedge is underway.

CHILD'S BEANIE

The Child's Beanie starts with a circle at the crown.

Materials

1 × 100g ball West Yorkshire Spinners DK-weight yarn (approximately 225m/100g); a space-dyed yarn works well for this design
5.50mm crochet hook
6.50mm Tunisian crochet hook

Tension

Measured over Tss: 6 stitches and 8 rows to 5cm

Size

One size, to fit the head of a 3–5-year-old child
Circumference when unstretched 44cm/17½in; depth before edge turnback and below crown circle 15cm/6in

Pattern note

Raised treble back and front

Instructions to work the traditional-crochet stitches raised treble back (RtrB) and raised treble front (RtrF) can be found on pp. 104–106 of *Crochet for the Absolute Beginner* (*see* Bibliography and Further Reading for more details.)

Also, these traditional crochet stitches are similar to the Tunisian crochet raised treble stitches (TRtrB and TRtrF), which are explained and illustrated in the section 'Tunisian crochet raised treble stitch' that appears in 'Monochromatic textured patterns'.

Pattern instructions

Crown

Step 1: Make a slip knot and place it on to the 5.50mm crochet hook. With the same hook, make 9ch. Place the last chain on to the 6.50mm Tunisian crochet hook.
Step 2: With these 9sts, work a circle as given for the trial piece of a circle, stopping when all 6 wedges have been completed: the crown ends at the circumference edge. Do not close the circle by working 1slst. Change to using the 5.50mm crochet hook.

Side

Step 3: Continue working around the circumference of the circle by placing 1dc in each row end (54sts). Change to using the 6.50mm Tunisian crochet hook.
Step 4: Continue by working Tss for 12 rows. Change to using the 5.50mm crochet hook.

Band

Step 5: Work as follows:
Row 1: Work 1dc in each stitch to the end of the row, make 2ch, and turn.
Row 2: Work 1 half treble (htr) in each stitch to the end of the row, make 2ch, and turn.
Row 3: *Work 1RtrF in the next stitch and 1RtrB in the following stitch; repeat from * to the end of the row, make 2ch, and turn.
Rows 4–7: Repeat Row 3 four times.

Finishing

Step 6: Join the sides of the fabric on each side of the slit running from the crown to the band either by sewing or crocheting along the length of the seam.
Step 7: Make 3 curlicues as given in the instructions for the Lightweight Mohair Stole in Chapter 4 (*see* the section 'Decorative curlicue closure').
Step 8: Attach the curlicues to the centre of the crown.
Step 10: Sew in all yarn ends.

Monochromatic Textured Patterns

Having covered textured yarns and Tunisian garter stitch, it is time to add heavy texture into the mix of Tunisian crochet fabrics presented in this book. The solid appearance of Tunisian crochet is what it is best known for, and adding various embossed looks adds more appeal to this incredibly special style of crochet.

Introducing texture is often as simple as adding a tall stitch in a row of short stitches. In Chapter 4 on Tunisian crochet lace, it was necessary to wrap the yarn over the hook before inserting it into the work, so this technique should have become very familiar to you. The Tunisian crochet treble (Ttr) and Tunisian crochet extended treble (Txtr) are two Tunisian crochet stitches used to make lace; these stitches can also be used to create dense and textured fabrics.

Tunisian pebble stitch

This pebble stitch is produced over two rows and made by working Tunisian double trebles (Tdtr) alternately with stitches of Tunisian simple stitch. On the second row, the Tunisian crochet double treble will sit over the Tunisian simple stitch of the previous row. The bumps – or pebbles – that the Tunisian double-treble stitches make sit at the front of the fabric, whilst the back of the fabric retains the appearance of the reverse side of knitted stocking stitch, as with Tunisian simple stitch.

The Tunisian double treble is used in the trial piece that follows, but that stitch can be changed to a Tunisian treble, to make the pebbles less prominent, or to a Tunisian triple treble (Ttrtr), for an even more prominent embossed effect. The Ttrtr is worked as follows: yoh 3 times, insert the hook under next vertical strand, yoh, pull the yarn through, (yoh, pull the yarn through the next 2 loops on the hook) 3 times.

A close-up of Tunisian pebble stitch.

Tunisian bobbles are made with a cluster of three Tunisian trebles.

Application suggestions

A long enough strip of pebble stitch worked with cotton makes a good sweatband or, with a different yarn, can make a hair tidy. This pattern adds interest when used for a cuff on a garment instead of the more common treble rib cuff or band of double crochet design. It can also be used for the yoke area of a garment or as an added feature in the form of a pocket.

Tunisian bobbles

Looking through any source of stitch patterns, you will see the word 'bobble' used for any protuberance incorporated within a Tunisian crochet fabric or indeed any other needlecraft. Such lumps and bumps, referred to as bobbles, include the pebble stitch, puff stitch and many others. Unfortunately, this only adds to the confusion in understanding what is trying to be communicated in magazines, books and single-leaflet patterns on Tunisian crochet.

The Tunisian bobble should not be confused with the Tunisian puff stitch, which from a distance can look the same as the bobble, because these two stitches are constructed very differently.

Continuing the principle of Tunisian stitches initially being a line of unfinished crochet stitches that are then closed during a second stage, the Tunisian bobble is made of three

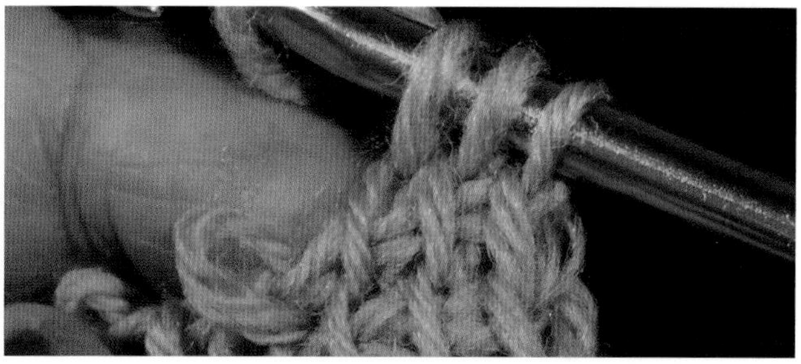
With three loops already on the hook, work yoh before inserting the hook under the next vertical strand, the position for making the bobble showing position not the making of the bobble that comes below.

Once one Tunisian treble has been made, as shown here, work yoh, to be ready to work the next Tunisian treble in the same place.

Trial piece of Tunisian pebble stitch

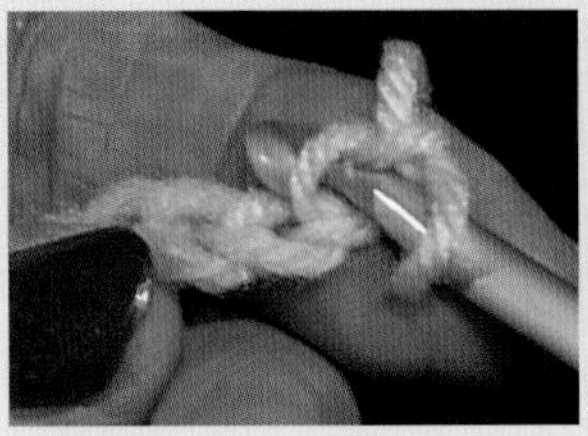

Always pick up from under the top strand of a chain when working Tunisian crochet.

When picking up loops on to the hook as for Tunisian simple stitch, make sure that the tall Tunisian double treble stitches sit at the front of the work.

Tunisian double trebles and Tunisian simple stitch stitches are worked alternately across the row.

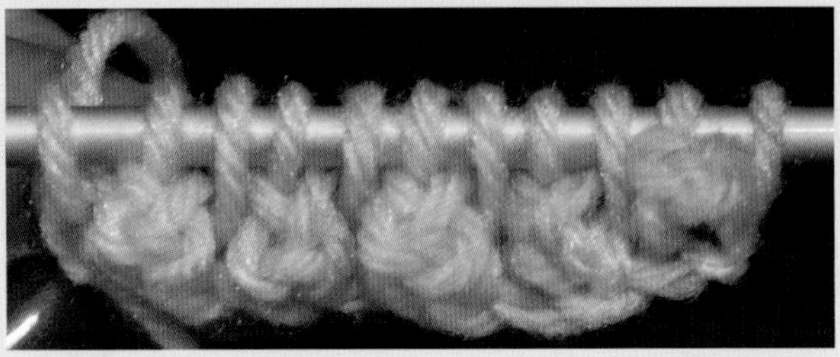

Regardless of where the last Tunisian double treble of the row lies, the last stitch is always worked as a Tunisian simple stitch.

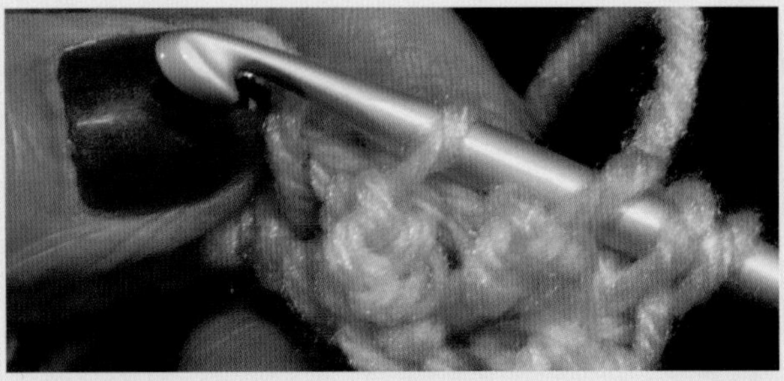

On subsequent rows, the Tunisian simple stitch stitches sit on top of the Tunisian double treble stitches of the previous row, and vice versa.

Set-Up: With a DK-weight yarn, make a slip knot, and place it on to a 5.50mm crochet hook. With the same hook, make 11ch. Place the last chain on to a 6.50mm Tunisian crochet hook. (This size of hook keeps the taller stitches sitting neatly as part of the fabric.) The pattern begins immediately; there is no need for a starting or base row.

Row 1, Stage 1: Insert the hook under the top strand only of the next chain, yoh, and pull the yarn through, *yoh twice, insert the hook under the top strand only of the next chain, yoh, pull the yarn through to the front of the work [5 loops on hook], (yoh, and pull the yarn through 2 loops on the hook) twice [3 loops on hook = 1Tdtr made], insert the hook under the top strand of the next chain whilst bending the long Tdtr just made forwards, yoh and pull the yarn through; repeat from * to the end of the row.

Row 1, Stage 2: Remove all of the loops as for Tss.

Row 2, Stage 1: Throughout the working of this row, pick up loops and place on to the hook by using each vertical strand in turn, as follows: *work 1Tdtr, bend the Tdtr's additional height forwards as the hook is inserted under the next vertical strand to make 1Tss; repeat from * to the last stitch, 1Tss under the last vertical strand of the row.

Row 2, Stage 2: Remove all of the loops as for Tss.

Row 3, Stage 1: Throughout the working of this row, pick up loops and place on to the hook by using each vertical strand in turn, as follows: *work 1Tss, 1Tdtr, bend the Tdtr's additional height forwards as the hook is inserted under the next vertical strand; repeat from * to the last stitch, 1Tss under the last vertical strand of the row.

Row 3, Stage 2: Remove all of the loops as for Tss.

Repeat Rows 2–3 until the fabric is of the desired length.

Once all of the loops of the Stage 1 are on the hook, work Stage 2 until the fabric is back to having only one loop on the hook.

Tunisian trebles worked under the same vertical strand. When these stitches are closed, an embossed bump appears on the surface.

Tunisian crochet bobbles can be incorporated into a pattern in a similar way as that of the pebble stitch, but it does use a lot of yarn and can look overly heavy. Alternatively, randomly inject the bobbles for added interest in a design. My personal preference is to space them at regular intervals within a pattern and not have them too close together.

Here the yarn is about to be pulled through for making the second Tunisian treble of the bobble.

Making a Tunisian bobble

Begin by making sure that there is an available vertical strand for use belonging to a stitch of the row below where you want to place a bobble.

Having a row of Tunisian simple stitch to work from will do the trick. Using the chosen stitch, proceed to make a bobble as follows.

Step 1: yoh before inserting the hook into the work.
Step 2: Insert the hook under the vertical strand of the stitch to be used for the working of the bobble.
Step 3: yoh.
Step 4: Pull the yarn through the vertical strand.
Step 5: yoh, and pull the yarn through 2 loops on the hook. [1Ttr made, leaving 1 bobble loop on the hook]
Step 6: yoh, and insert the hook under the same vertical strand just used.
Step 7: Work as for Step 5.
Repeat Steps 6–7 once.
Step 8: yoh, and pull the yarn through 3 loops, leaving the resulting loop on the hook to complete the stitch.

This remaining loop is the equivalent to a loop placed on to the hook during Stage 1 in readiness for removal during Stage 2 of Tss.

Here three Tunisian trebles have been worked under the same vertical strand.

The yarn has been pulled through the three loops at the top of the three trebles, leaving one loop at the top of the bobble to remain on the hook.

Tunisian puff stitch

The Tunisian puff stitch (Tpuff) is similar to the Tunisian bobble but without the working off of any of the wraps to make the stitch. Once all of the wraps have been made, they are reduced to one loop. Once again, it is necessary to have a stitch of the previous row available with a vertical strand in order to make a Tunisian puff stitch.

A close-up of a finished piece of Tunisian puff stitch.

Making a Tunisian puff stitch

Work yoh before inserting the hook under the next vertical strand for making the puff stitch.

Yarn has been wrapped and pulled through the vertical strand twice showing five of the puff stitch loops on the hook.

Eight puff-stitch loops are now on the hook, plus the wrap of yarn of a yoh lying over the hook and the finger.

Using the chosen stitch, proceed to make a Tunisian crochet puff stitch as follows:

Step 1: yoh before inserting the hook into the work.
Step 2: Insert the hook under the vertical strand of the stitch to be used for working the puff stitch.
Step 3: yoh.
Step 4: Pull the yarn through the vertical strand.
Step 5: yoh, and insert the hook under the same vertical strand just used.
Step 6: yoh, and pull the yarn through the vertical strand. Repeat Steps 5–6 twice.
Step 7: Close to the head of the hook, pinch all eight of the yarn wraps and loops of the puff stitch between the index finger and thumb of the hand holding the yarn.
Step 8: yoh, and pull the yarn through all of the wraps and loops of the puff stitch, leaving the resulting loop on the hook to complete the stitch.
This remaining loop is the equivalent to a loop placed on the hook during Stage 1 in readiness for removal during Stage 2 of Tss.

It is difficult to work Tunisian crochet puff stitches side by side, as they want to push against each other. Ideally, pick up 1 loop from at least the next stitch as for Tss before making another Tunisian crochet puff stitch, but several vertical loops can be worked as for Tss before the next puff stitch needs to be made.

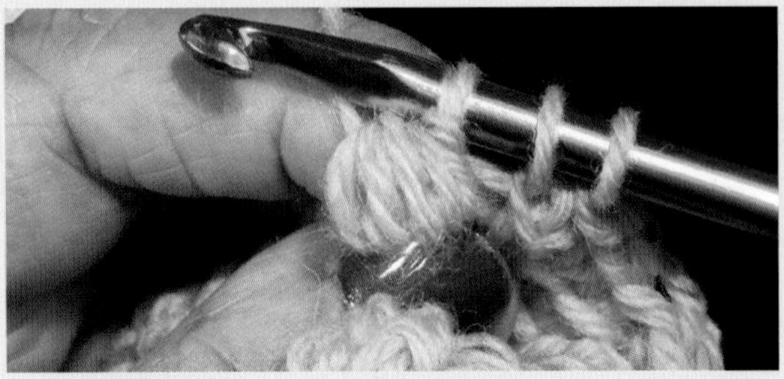

One completed Tunisian puff stitch.

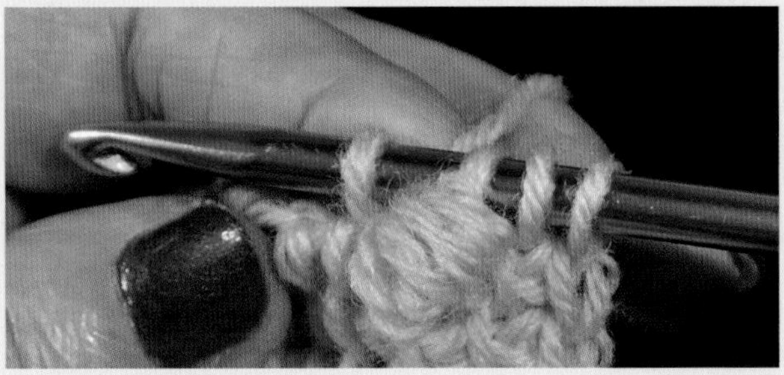

Now, the completed Tunisian puff stitch is being framed by another stitch, separating it from the next puff stitch to be made further along the row.

Tunisian raised treble stitch

A raised treble worked with Tunisian crochet has not got the elasticity that can be obtained with a traditional crochet raised treble, because the Tunisian crochet raised treble is (almost always) worked with the right side of the fabric facing. Its embossed look has a similar appearance to that of surface crochet, making it ideal for introducing strong lines into a design, as can be seen in the Casual-Extra Top. For this reason, the Tunisian raised-treble abbreviation (TRtrF) includes an F, and 'front' is added to the stitch's description. In reality, it is possible to experiment with working the Tunisian raised treble at the back of the work, in which case the abbreviation would be TRtrB, with a B for 'back'.

A Tunisian raised treble lies over and covers a stitch or stitches of the previous row. The hook is inserted into the work or under the stem of a previously made TRtr to anchor the base of the Ttr. This requires two rows of stitches to be made prior to the working of any Tunisian raised trebles. The trial piece suggests working two rows of Tunisian simple stitch, but the Tunisian raised treble can be worked over any crochet or Tunisian crochet fabric.

Trial piece of Tunisian raised-treble stitch

Set-Up: With DK-weight yarn, make a slip knot and place it on to a 5.00mm crochet hook. With the same hook, work 11ch. Place the last chain on to a 6.50mm Tunisian crochet hook.
Rows 1–2: Work 2 rows as for Tss.
Row 3, Stage 1, Step 1: *Insert the hook under the next vertical strand of the previous row (that is, as for picking up a loop for working Stage 1 as normal in Tss), yoh, and pull the yarn through. [2 loops on hook]
Row 3, Stage 1, Step 2: yoh.
Row 3, Stage 1, Step 3: Insert the hook under the vertical strand that sits below the next vertical strand of the previous row (that is, the vertical strand 2 rows below the row currently being worked).
Row 3, Stage 1, Step 4: yoh, and pull the yarn through the vertical strand.
Row 3, Stage 1, Step 5: yoh, and pull the yarn through the next 2 loops on the hook to complete the TRtrF.
Row 3, Stage 1, Step 6: *Insert the hook under the next vertical strand of the previous row, yoh, and pull the yarn through; repeat from * once.
Row 3, Stage 1, Step 7: Continue working by making 1TRtrF as every 3rd stitch of the current row and repeating Steps 2–6 twice.
Row 3, Stage 2: Remove all of the loops as for Tss.
Row 4, Stage 1, Step 1: Work as for Row 3, Stage 1, Step 1.
Row 4, Stage 1, Step 2: yoh, and insert hook under the stem of the TRtrF of the previous row without catching the vertical strand lying behind it.
Row 4, Stage 1, Step 3: yoh, and pull the yarn through from behind the previously worked TRtrF stitch.
Row 4, Stage 1, Step 4: yoh, and pull the yarn through 2 loops on the hook to complete the TRtrF.
Row 4, Stage 1, Step 5: *Insert the hook under the next vertical strand, yoh, and pull the yarn through; repeat from * once.
Row 4, Stage 1, Step 6: Continue working by making 1TRtrF as every 3rd stitch of the current row and repeating Steps 2–5 twice.
Row 4, Stage 2: Remove all of the loops as for Tss.
Repeat Row 4 until the fabric is of the desired length.

Working the yoh before inserting the hook under the vertical strand two rows below the row currently being worked.

Work yoh and pull the yarn through the next two loops on the hook to complete the Tunisian crochet raised-treble front stitch.

After Row 3, the hook is inserted under the stem of the TRrF and not into the fabric.

In the process of completing the next Tunisian crochet raised treble front.

CASUAL-EXTRA TOP

The Casual-Extra Top, combining Tunisian raised trebles and Tunisian puff stitches for a textural pattern design.

This pattern is for an easy-to-wear casual top made in two pieces and joined at the shoulders to make a slash-neck opening. The sides have a short join to enable the top to be worn over many outfits. The textured panels are central, permitting the two side parts to be made smaller or larger depending on the garment's intended purpose and the size of the person it is being made for. It is a perfect design to practise adding textured Tunisian crochet as it combines Tunisian puff stitches and Tunisian raised trebles.

A close-up of one shoulder and the back of the Casual-Extra top.

Materials

5 × 100g balls West Yorkshire Spinners DK-weight yarn (approximately 225m/100g)
7.00mm crochet hook
10.00mm Tunisian crochet hook

Tension

Measured over Tss: 5 stitches and 5 rows to 5cm

Size

One size, to fit a wide range of bodies
Length 63cm/25in; width (including the 2 borders of 2.5cm/1in in width) 75cm/29½in; bottom-border depth 4cm/1½in; neckband depth 5cm/2in; armhole depth (easily adjustable) 40cm/15½in; neck-opening width (easily adjustable) 28cm/11in

Pattern note

Three-treble cluster

A three treble bobble cluster (3trcl) worked in traditional crochet is included in the neck and hip borders of this top. Before beginning to work the panels of this top, it is essential to understand how to form this stitch.

When reaching the stitch position of the row in which to work a 3trcl, proceed as follows:

yoh, insert the hook into the next stitch, yoh, pull the yarn through the stitch, yoh, pull the yarn through the next 2 loops on the hook, yoh, insert the hook into the same stitch, yoh, pull the yarn through the stitch, yoh, pull the yarn through the next 2 loops on the hook (3 loops on hook), yoh, insert the hook into the same stitch, yoh, pull the yarn through the stitch, yoh, pull the yarn through the next 2 loops on the hook (4 loops on hook), yoh, pull the yarn through all 4 loops (= one 3trcl).

It is worth noting that in traditional crochet bobbles, such as clusters and puff stitches, and long stitches forming texture, and so on, become more prominent on the finished piece when worked from the back of the fabric.

Pattern instructions

Panels – two made alike

Set-Up: Make a slip knot and place it on to the 7.00mm crochet hook. With the same hook, make 83ch (to provide 83sts). Place the last chain on to the 10.00mm Tunisian crochet hook.

Row 1: Work as for Tss, using each chain and counting the loop already on the hook as one stitch.

Row 2, Stage 1: Using vertical strands throughout, pick up 24 loops on to the hook from each of the next 24 vertical strands in turn from the previous row (25 loops on hook), work 1Ttr by inserting the hook under the next vertical strand of the previous row, *pick up 7 loops in turn from each of the next 7 vertical strands of the previous row, work 1Ttr under the next vertical strand of the previous row; repeat from * 3 times, pick up 25 loops in turn from each of the next 25 vertical strands of the previous row to the end of the row. [83 loops on hook]

Row 2, Stage 2: Remove all of the loops as for Tss.

Row 3, Stage 1: Pick up 1 loop and place on to the hook from each of the next 24 vertical strands, insert the hook under the stem of the Ttr of the previous row to make 1TRtrF, *pick up 1 loop and place on to the hook from each of the next 7 vertical strands, work 1TRtrF with the Ttr of the previous row; repeat from * 3 times, pick up 1 loop and place on to the hook from each vertical strand to the end of the row. [83 loops on hook]

Row 3, Stage 2: Remove all of the loops as for Tss.

Row 4, Stage 1: Pick up 1 loop and place on to the hook from each of the next 24 vertical strands, insert the hook under the stem of the TRtrF of the previous row to make 1TRtrF, *pick up 1 loop and place on to the hook from each of the next 7 vertical strands, work 1TRtrF with the TRtrF of the previous row; repeat from * 3 times, pick up 1 loop and place on to the hook from each vertical strand to the end of the row. [83 loops on hook]

Row 4, Stage 2: Remove all of the loops as for Tss.

Row 5, Stage 1: Pick up 1 loop and place on to the hook from each of the next 24 vertical strands, work 1TRtrF with the TRtrF of the previous row, *pick up 1 loop and place on to the hook from each of the next 3 vertical strands, work 1Tpuff, pick up 1 loop and place on to the hook from each of the next 3 vertical strands, work 1TRtrF with the TRtrF of the previous row; repeat from * 3 times, pick up 1 loop and place on to the hook from each of the vertical strands to the end of the row. [83 loops on hook]

Row 5, Stage 2: Remove all of the loops as for Tss.

Rows 6–8: Repeat Row 4 three times.

Row 9: Repeat Row 5 once.

Rows 10–49: Repeat Rows 6–9 ten times.

Row 50–52: Work as for Tss.

Row 53: Change to using the 7.00mm crochet hook. By inserting the hook under each vertical strand in turn, work 1dc in each stitch to the end of the row, make 1ch, and turn.

Row 54: With WS facing, work 1dc in each dc in turn to the end of the row, make 1ch, and turn.

Row 55: With RS facing, work 1dc in each dc in turn to the end of the row, make 1ch, and turn.

Row 56 (3trcl bobble row): For the central textured section of the panel, the bobble stitches should align with each column of TRtrF stitches and each column of Tpuff stitches and be evenly spaced throughout the row: with WS facing, *not* counting the 1ch made at the end of the previous row as one stitch, and working into each stitch in turn, proceed by working 1dc in the same place as the 1ch (turning chain), *work 3dc, 3trcl (= 1 bobble); repeat from * to the last 4sts, work 1dc in each of the next 4sts, make 1ch, and turn.

Row 57: Work as for Row 55.

Row 58: Work as for Row 54.

Row 59: Work as for Row 55, but do not turn the work at the end of the row.

Row 60: With RS facing, work crab stitch in each stitch in turn to the end of the row. Fasten off.

Bottom border

With RS facing, connect the yarn to the foundation chain, make 1ch, work 1dc in each stitch to the end of the row, make 1ch, and turn.

Work Rows 54 to 60 once. Fasten off.

Shoulder join

When both panels have been worked, arrange them with their wrong sides and top edges together with the right side of the topmost panel facing you. Working from the aligned corners of the panels towards the neck edges, connect the top edges of the untextured sides of the panels, by sewing from the right side of the fabric and using the same yarn as that used for working the crocheted fabric. Do this first for the left-hand side of the top and then for the right-hand side. A backstitch worked very close to the crab stitch edge makes an invisible join.

Side border

Keeping the two panels joined only at the two shoulders, crochet the side borders as follows, by working up one side of one panel and then down one side of the other panel.

Step 1: With RS facing, join the yarn to edge of the last row worked for the bottom border.

Step 2: Make 1ch, work 3dc over the double crochet rows of the first bottom border, work 1dc in each Tunisian crochet row to the start of the crocheted rows at the top of the first panel using the technique that prevent holes appearing (*see* the section 'Working an Edging or Border' in Chapter 3), work 6dc over the crocheted rows at the top of the first panel, shoulder join and crocheted rows at the top of the second panel, work 1dc in each Tunisian crochet row to the bottom border again by using the techniques that prevent holes appearing, work 3dc over the double crochet rows of the second bottom border, work 1dc in the corner stitch, make 1ch, and turn.

Step 3: With WS facing, work 1 row of double crochet, make 1ch, and turn.

Step 4: With RS facing, work 1 row of double crochet, but do not turn the work.

Step 5: Work 1 row of crab stitch. Fasten off.

Step 6: Repeat Steps 1–5 for other side of the top.

Finishing

Fold the top at the shoulder join so that the bottom rows are with wrong sides together and aligned at the bottom edges. With RS facing, sew through the two sides of the top to connect 14–16 stitches of the fabric, working from the aligned corners of the panels towards the underarm, by using backstitch as described for the shoulder join.

Sew in all yarn ends.

Tunisian Cross Stitch

Before moving on to incorporating colour with texture, there is one untextured and single-colour technique that needs to be in your library of stitches. This technique is Tunisian cross stitch, which is useful but can create unexpected difficulties if included without understanding what happens when cross stitch is combined with other Tunisian crochet stitches.

An occasional Tunisian cross stitch worked within a pattern design will not affect the final outcome, as utilized for the Colourful Textured Car Coat featured later in this chapter. However, when Tunisian cross stitch is worked as a band within a fabric of other Tunisian stitches, it contracts the work. The best way to understand this would be to work the following trial piece. The abbreviation 'Tx' refer to both the crossing of the Tunisian crochet stitches when collecting the loops for Stage 1 and the removal of these loops as for Tss, as well as the completed Tunisian crochet cross stitches themselves.

Trial piece of Tunisian cross stitch

With DK-weight yarn, make a slip knot and place it on to a crochet hook of an appropriate size for the yarn. Make a length of chain stitches with a number of chains that can be divided by 2, and place the last chain on to a Tunisian crochet hook of an appropriate size for the yarn.

Rows 1–3: Work as for Tss.

Row 4, Stage 1: Count the single loop on the hook at the start of the row as the first stitch, *miss the next stitch, insert the hook under the next vertical strand, yoh, pull the yarn through this vertical strand, insert the hook under the vertical strand of the stitch just missed, yoh, and pull the yarn through this vertical strand (= 1Tx made); repeat from * to the last stitch, insert the hook under the last vertical strand, yoh, and pull the yarn through.

Row 4, Stage 2: Remove all of the loops as for Tss.

Rows 5–12: Repeat Row 4 eight times.

Row 13: Work 1 row as for Tss.

Because the crossed stitches will first appear on Row 3 and no crosses will show on Row 12, only 1 row of Tss is required to make the sample piece symmetrical at the top and bottom, with what looks like 2 rows of Tss. These starting and finishing rows will be wider than the rows of Tunisian cross stitch.

Tunisian cross stitch contracts the row and so reduces its width.

A close-up of Tunisian cross stitches.

Introducing Colour

Before combining colours and stitches in a more challenging way, the following sleeveless-coat pattern includes Tunisian cluster stitch and features uncluttered bands of colour, making it a useful project to start with. Just by adding colour to Tunisian crochet textured stitches expands the range of possible designs available and increases the possibilities to be explored.

Worked with a wool yarn for warmth, this coat looks heavy but in fact is surprisingly light in weight. This is because the stitches that result in the textured look belong to the lace pattern used throughout the coat, and lace patterns by their very nature are airier and lighter. The spaces are not visible because they are hidden by the heavier texture. The invisible spaces between the textured columns reduce the physical weight of the fabric. It is a well-known fact that trapped air acts as an insulator, even in some unlikely instances, for example, for a string vest. For the coat, the textured columns close up the spaces, trapping the air for additional warmth.

ACCENT-ON-AUTUMN COAT

The front and back of the Accent–On-Autumn Sleeveless Coat.

The coat is worked from the shoulders down to the hem, making it easy to adjust the length. However, if working in coloured bands, do ensure the bands of colour form an overall balance!

Materials

West Yorkshire Spinners Re:Treat chunky roving (140m/100g)
2 × 100g balls in Serene (olive)
2(2,3) × 100g balls in Mellow (yellow)
3(4,4) × 100g balls in Tranquil (terracotta)
6.00mm crochet hook
6.50mm crochet hook
10.00mm Tunisian crochet hook (straight or with a wire extension)

Tension

Measured over textured pattern (*see* Back Rows 1–2): 10 stitches and 5 raised columns to 10cm

Size

One size, to fit a range of bodies
Bust circumference 97cm/38in; length (including 3cm/1¼in border) 90cm/35½in; armhole depth (excluding border) 30cm/12in

Pattern instructions

Back

With olive, make a slip knot and place it on to the 6.50mm crochet hook. With the same hook, make 60ch. Place the last chain on to the 10.00mm Tunisian crochet hook.

Row 1, Stage 1: Pick up 1 loop from under the top strand of each chain in turn as for Tss.

Row 1, Stage 2: Make 2ch, *yoh, pull the yarn through 4 loops, make 1ch; repeat from * until 2 loops remain on the hook, yoh, and pull the yarn through the remaining 2 loops.

Row 2, Stage 1: *Insert the hook into the next 1chsp, yoh, pull the yarn through the 1chsp, insert the hook under the top strand of the same 1ch, yoh, pull the yarn through, insert the hook under all 4 strands to form a cluster, yoh, pull the yarn through [4 loops on hook]; repeat from * to the end of the row, insert the hook into the remaining 1chsp, yoh, pull the yarn through the 1chsp, insert the hook into the centre of the top of the chain from Row 1, Stage 2, yoh, and pull the yarn through.

A close-up of the textured pattern for the Accent-On-Autumn Sleeveless Coat.

Row 2, Stage 2: Work as for Row 1, Stage 2.

Rows 3–14: Repeat Row 2 twelve times, joining in yellow while there are still 2 loops left on the hook when working Stage 2 of the last row, to avoid a colour drag. Fasten off olive.

Rows 15–24: Work Row 2 ten times with yellow. Fasten off.

Note: The shoulders and fronts are worked directly from the first row of the Back.

Before working the fronts, with yellow make two chains each of 12 chains in length, for the underarms, and keep them safe.

Right front

With olive, make a slip knot and place it on to the 6.50mm crochet hook. With the same hook, make a length of 12 loose chain stitches, for the front-of-body extension for this front piece. Fasten off, and keep the chain safe.

Row 1, Stage 1: With RS of the Back facing and the 10.00mm Tunisian crochet hook, join in olive with 1slst to the right-hand corner of the right-hand side of the Back [1 loop on hook], *insert the hook into the next space from the foundation chain at the first row of the Back, yoh, pull the yarn through, insert the hook under the first long strand of the next group of gathered stitches of the first row of the Back, yoh, pull the yarn through, insert the hook under all 3 remaining strands of this group, yoh, and pull the yarn through [4 loops on hook]; repeat from * until there are 19 loops on the hook.

Row 1, Stage 2: Work as for Row 1, Stage 2 of the Back.

Check whether the stitches of the Right Front are continuing the patterning columns of the Back (although the column stitches of the Back will now appear to be upside down).

Rows 2–6: Work Row 2 of the Back five times on these 19sts.

Row 7, Stage 1: Continuing in pattern, pick up loops as for

Back Row 2, Stage 1 until 2sts remain to be worked, insert the hook into the space below the next 1ch of the previous row, yoh, pull the yarn through the space, insert the hook under the top strand of the 1ch, yoh, and pull the yarn through. Connect a length of 12ch previously made by picking up 1 loop from under the top strand of each chain in turn. [30 loops on hook]
Row 7, Stage 2: Work as for Row 1, Stage 2 of the Back.
Rows 8–18: Work Row 2 of the Back eleven times, joining in yellow when there are still 2 loops left on the hook when working Stage 2 of the last row, to avoid a colour drag. Fasten off olive.
Rows 19–28: With yellow, work Row 2 of the Back ten times. Fasten off.

Left front

With olive, make a slip knot and place it on to the 6.50mm crochet hook. With the same hook, make a length of 12 loose chain stitches, for the front-of-body extension for this front piece. Fasten off, and keep the chain safe.
Row 1, Stage 1: With RS of the Back facing, insert the 10.00mm Tunisian crochet hook into the 19th chain from the left-hand corner of the left-hand side of the Back, and join in olive with 1slst [1 loop on hook], *insert the hook into the first lace space of the first row of the Back, yoh, pull the yarn through the space, insert the hook under the first long strand of the next group of gathered stitches of the first row of the Back, yoh, pull the yarn through, insert the hook under all 3 remaining strands of this group, yoh, pull the yarn through; repeat from * until there are 19 loops on the hook.
Row 1, Stage 2: Work as for Row 1, Stage 2 of the Back.
Check whether the stitches of the Left Front are continuing the patterning columns of the Back (remembering that the column stitches of the Back will now appear to be upside down).
Rows 2–6: Work Row 2 of the Back five times on these 19sts, attaching the length of 12ch previously made by picking up 1 loop from under the top strand of each chain in turn when working Stage 2 of the last row.
Row 7, Stage 1: Using the loops picked up from the extended chain first and continuing in pattern, pick up loops across the row. [30 loops on hook]
Row 7, Stage 2: Work as for Row 1, Stage 2 of the Back.
Rows 8–18: Work Row 2 of the Back eleven times, joining in yellow when there are still 2 loops left on the hook when working Stage 2 of the last row, to avoid a colour drag. Fasten off olive.
Rows 19–28: With yellow, work Row 2 of the Back ten times. Do not fasten off.

Body

The body is worked by first joining the Left Front, Back and Right Front in turn, with the addition of the two chains previously made for the underarms, and the fabric then being worked as one piece to the bottom edge, as follows:
Row 1, Stage 1: With yellow, continue to pick up loops in pattern across the 30sts of the Left Front, attach one of the prepared 12ch lengths with 1slst, pick up 12 loops across this chain length by picking up 1 loop from under the top strand of each chain in turn, continue to pick up loops in pattern across the 60sts of the Back [102 loops], attach the second prepared 12ch length with 1slst, pick up 12 loops across this chain length by picking up 1 loop from under the top strand of each chain in turn, and continue to pick up loops in pattern across the 30sts of the Right Front. [144 loops on hook].
Row 1, Stage 2: Remove all of the loops as for Row 2 of the Back.
Rows 2–12: Work 11 rows in pattern on these 144sts, joining in terracotta when there are still 2 loops left on the hook when working Stage 2 of the last row, to avoid a colour drag. Fasten off yellow.
Rows 13–44: With terracotta, work 32 rows in pattern.
Last row: With the 6.50mm crochet hook, make 2ch, *work 1tr in next 1ch of previous row, 1tr through next 4-loop group, 1tr under next 1chsp of previous row, 1tr in same 1ch, 1tr through next 4-loop group; repeat from * to the last 2sts (the 2ch made for turning for Stage 2 of the previous row), 1tr under next 1chsp, and 1tr in same 1ch. Fasten off.

Armhole bands – two made alike

The armhole bands are to be worked in rows over 48sts. Begin by marking where the central 8sts lie over the shoulder. This will leave 20sts from each marker to where the underarm extension chain is, on each side. Each set of 20sts needs to be divided evenly for the back and the front. On the first row, decreases will be made over the shoulder stitches to give 48sts in total for the band.
Row 1: With RS facing and the 6.50mm crochet hook, join olive to the left-hand underarm edge at the end of the extension with 1slst, work 1dc into each row end in turn to first shoulder marker, dc2tog over the next pair of row ends twice, for start of shoulder shaping, 4 dc over next 4 row ends, dc2tog over the next pair of row ends twice, to second marker (8sts in total for shoulder), 1dc into each row end in turn to

the other underarm edge and link the last stitch made into the opposite end of the extension chain with 1slst. Fasten off olive.
Row 2: Turn the work. With WS facing, join in yellow with 1slst to the end of the previous row, make 1ch, work 1dc in each stitch in turn to the end of the row, and link the last stitch to the work with 1slst. Fasten off yellow.
Row 3: Turn the work. With RS facing, join in terracotta with 1slst to the end of the previous row, make 1ch, work 1dc in each stitch in turn to the end of the row.
Row 4: Keeping RS facing, work 1 row of crab stitch. Fasten off.
Complete the first armhole band by sewing in all yarn ends by attaching them to the extension chain to firmly anchor the band to the underarm.
Work the second armhole band as for the first.

Front bands and neckband

Row 1: With RS facing and the 6.50mm crochet hook, join in olive to the right-hand corner of the bottom edge with 1slst, make 1ch, work 1dc into each row end (without introducing holes) by working up the right-hand side of the fabric, work 2dc in the corner at the top of the Right Front, work 1dc into each stitch or row end around the neck (working dc2tog as required at the concave curves of the neck to avoid frilling or fullness), work 2dc into the corner at the top of the Left Front, work 1dc into each row end (without introducing holes) by working down the left-hand side of the fabric to the left-hand corner of the bottom edge.
Row 2: Make 1ch, turn the work, and work 1dc in the same place as the 1ch to maintain a straight bottom edge. Work 1dc in each stitch of the previous row, increasing by working 2dc at each of the two corners and decreasing by working dc2tog at the concave curves of the neck as required; change to using yellow when pulling the yarn through the last 2 loops on the hook when working the last stitch. Fasten off olive.
Rows 3–4: Work Row 2 twice with yellow; change to using terracotta to work off the last 2 loops on the hook at the end of Row 4.
Row 5: Work Row 2 once, ending by working 2dc into the corner at the end of the row, working 4dc along the edge of the front band at the bottom left of the coat, and linking into the last stitch of the final treble row of the coat body with 1slst.Neaten the edges of front band when sewing in all yarn ends.

A close-up of borders at the neck and armhole edges.

Bottom border

With RS facing and the 6.50mm crochet hook, starting at the bottom right corner of the coat, join in terracotta to the last stitch of the final treble row of the coat body with 1slst. Work 5dc along the end of the front band.
Row 1: Make 2ch, turn the work so that the WS is facing, work 1htr in each stitch of the bottom edge to the end of the row, and turn.
Row 2: Make 1ch, work 1dc in each stitch to the end of the row (if you feel that the edge is getting too loose, change to using the 6.00mm crochet hook for working this row onwards, otherwise change to using a smaller hook on Row 5).
Rows 3–4: Work 2 rows of double crochet. Do not turn.
Row 5: With RS facing, change to using the 6.00mm crochet hook (if not already being used). Work crab stitch to the end of the row; do not fasten off but continue working in crab stitch up the Left Front band, around the neck band, and down the Right Front band. Fasten off.

Finishing

Sew in all yarn ends.

Texture and Colour Combinations

As already indicated, there are numerous names given to Tunisian crochet, but these other names are rarely used today. Unfortunately, this is not so when searching for the name of a stitch pattern. I have tried to give the most frequently used name for a stitch pattern, but I am the first to accept that it may not be the name that you know it by.

Because these are stitch patterns, the size of the crochet hook and Tunisian crochet hook are not given, because any hook size will be suitable as long as it works well with the yarn selected and for the end purpose of the project. It is those two aspects that should determine the hook sizes used. To remove any challenges that might be created by the yarn, for all of the techniques and stitch patterns given, a smooth DK-weight yarn has been used. Remember that all of the stitch patterns shown will change their look if different yarn combinations are used.

Tunisian box stitch

Trial piece of Tunisian box stitch

Work with two contrasting colours: the primary colour (M) is the background colour, whilst C, although prominent, forms the contrast.

Set-Up: With C, make a slip knot, place it on to a crochet hook of an appropriate size for the yarn, and make a chain containing a number of stitches that is divisible by 4, plus 1. Place the last chain on to a Tunisian crochet hook of an appropriate size for the yarn.

Row 1: With C, work 1 row as for Tss, changing to M when 2 loops remain on the hook when working Stage 2.

Rows 2–4: With M, work 3 rows as for Tss, changing to using C when 2 loops remain on the hook when working Stage 2 of the last row.

Row 5, Stage 1: With C, pick up 1 loop and place on to the hook from under the next vertical strand of the previous row, *at the next stitch position across of the fabric, work 1Tdtr under the vertical strand of Row 1 (the contrast-colour row – that is, yoh twice before inserting the hook under the relevant vertical strand and remove the loops in sets of 2, to leave 1 loop on the hook for the Tdtr at the end of this stitch), pick up 1 loop on to the hook from under each of the next 3 vertical strands of the previous row – *do not use the strand behind the just-made Tdtr*; repeat from * to the last 3sts, work 1Tdtr, pick up 1 loop on to the hook from under the vertical strands of each of the remaining 2sts.

Row 5, Stage 2: Remove all of the loops as for Tss; change to M when 2 loops remain on the hook when working Stage 2.

Rows 6–8: With M, work 3 rows as for Tss, changing to C when 2 loops remain on the hook when working Stage 2.

Row 9, Stage 1: With C, pick up 1 loop on to the hook from under the next vertical strand of the previous row, *work 1Tdtr under the stem of the Tdtr of Row 5, pick up 1 loop on to the hook from under each of the next 3 vertical strands; repeat from * to the last 3sts, work 1Tdtr, pick up 1 loop on to the hook from under each of the remaining 2sts.

Row 9, Stage 2: Remove all of the loops as for Tss; change to using M when 2 loops remain on the hook when working Stage 2.

The last four rows (Rows 6–9) form the box-stitch pattern.

Alternative sized boxes

Smaller box squares can be worked with a chain of a number of stitches that is divisible by 3, to leave one Tss stitch at each end of the fabric to frame the boxes. This is a three-row pattern worked as opposite, but by using Ttr stitches instead of Tdtr stitches and having only 2 rows worked with M between the contrast-colour rows.

Larger box squares can be worked with a chain of a number of stitches that is divisible by 5sts, to leave two Tss stitches at each end of the fabric to frame the boxes. This is a five-row pattern worked as opposite, but by using Ttrtr stitches instead of Tdtr stitches and having 4 rows worked with M between the contrast-colour rows.

Tunisian crochet drop stitch

Once mastered, drop stitches can create many patterns, as seen for the alternatives of the box stitch. It is an ideal stitch to use in colour camouflage or to break up a straight line as when working the first row of a border in a symmetrically repetitive way, or it can be introduced as a single drop stitch randomly, to add interest.

This example of Tunisian box stitch includes Tunisian double trebles.

These Tunisian drop stitches produce a flatter finish for the fabric.

Trial piece of Tunisian drop stitch

Work with two contrasting colours: the primary colour (M) is the background colour, whilst C, although prominent, forms the contrast.

Set-Up: With C, make a slip knot, place it on to a crochet hook of an appropriate size for the yarn, and make a chain of a number of stitches that is divisible by 4sts, plus 1st. Place the last chain on to a Tunisian crochet hook of an appropriate size for the yarn.

Row 1: With C, work 1 row as for Tss, changing to M when 2 loops remain on the hook when working Stage 2.

Rows 2–4: With M, work 3 rows as for Tss, changing to C when 2 loops remain on the hook when working Stage 2 of the last row.

Row 5, Stage 1: With C, pick up 1 loop on to the hook from under the next vertical strand of the previous row, *over the next stitch, insert the hook through the vertical strand of Row 1 (the contrast-colour row) yoh, and lift the yarn to form an extended upside-down vertical V to cover the 3 subsequently worked rows of Tss, yoh, pull the yarn through this vertical-V drop-stitch loop, checking whether the strands of the stitch are lying flat against the fabric (= 1 drop stitch worked), pick up 1 loop on to the hook from under each of the next 3 vertical strands of the previous row – *do not use the strand behind the just-made drop stitch*; repeat from * to the last 3sts, work 1 drop stitch, pick up 1 loop on to the hook from under each of the vertical strands of the remaining 2sts.

Row 5, Stage 2: Remove all of the loops as for Tss; change to M when 2 loops remain on the hook when working Stage 2.

The last 4 rows (Rows 2–5) form a symmetrical square pattern by using drop stitches.

Inserting the hook as necessary to work Row 5, Stage 1 of drop stitch.

The long loop is extended and left on hook unworked.

Tunisian raised stitches can form an interesting repeat pattern by being worked into different rows.

The raised treble rib of the jerkin is not worked in Tunisian, but ordinary crochet.

The back neck of the jerkin has the heavier embossed look of the contrast stitch on the inside.

Note: If the drop stitch is not pulled up to the correct tension, it can cause the rows of Tss lying behind it to clump up, so the work will not lie flat and eventually shorten the length of the crocheted fabric. Aim to make the loop of the drop stitch to lie flat over the previously worked rows of the crocheted fabric. It is also essential that the pulled-up loop does not twist, which would change the look and be unsightly.

The fabric of drop stitch is worked with two colours. For simplicity, try working a drop-stitch pattern similar to that of the box stitch, but, in this case, you will see that there is a flat vertical V lying on top of the work instead of a cord-like embossed stitch made with a Ttr, Tdtr or Ttrtr.

Modifications

For camouflage:

Placing the drop stitch at different levels, by inserting the hook into different rows when pulling the yarn through to the front of the fabric, is a perfect way to change the look of a straight stripe or to work over a section of crochet to camouflage the background.

Camouflage of geometric shapes

Whether using the Tunisian crochet drop stitch or any of the Tunisian crochet raised stitches, any colour that is worked over rows of another colour will change the look of the base fabric. Just by using either an individual drop stitch or a raised stitch, straight stripes will disappear and can become geometric shapes of triangles, boxes, chevrons or castellated designs, or alternatively they can be used randomly for breaking up a colour that appears too dominant.

Small amounts of colour worked in this way can be used to add interest to a design, in a similar way to that shown for the Tunisian crochet raised stitches (TRtrF and TRdtrF) used for the following Junior Jerkin pattern. If the border is to be the interest point of a design, consider including drop stitches at regular intervals when working the first row of the border. This stops the border having an added-on look and helps it to become part of the design instead.

To create pattern repeats:

Inserting the hook deliberately and intentionally into different rows is a way of reproducing colour patterns as seen in the patchwork designs of quilters. A limitless number of pattern repeats can be designed in this way. One example could be to replace the contrasting raised stitches of the Junior Jerkin with drop stitches.

JUNIOR JERKIN

A front view of the Junior Jerkin.

Materials

West Yorkshire Spinners ColourLab DK-weight yarn (225m/100g)
2 × 100g balls in M
1 × 100g ball in C
5.50mm crochet hook
6.50mm Tunisian crochet hook

Tension

Measured over Tss: 7 stitches and 7 rows to 5cm

Size

One size, to fit a 6–8-year-old child
Chest circumference 70cm/27½in; back length 25cm/10in

Pattern instruction

Body

Set-Up: With M, make a slip knot and place it on to the 5.50mm crochet hook. With the same hook, make 100ch, to provide 100sts. Place the last chain on to the 6.50mm Tunisian crochet hook, and work 25 rows as for Tss.
Next, divide for armhole as follows.

Right front

Rows 1–7: Work 7 rows as for Tss on the first 22sts, joining in C to work off the last 2 loops on the hook when working Stage 2 of the last row; there is no need to break off M.
Row 8, Stage 1: Counting the loop on the hook in C as the first stitch, work 1TRtrF under the vertical strand 2 rows below the next stitch, work 1TRdtrF under the vertical strand 3 rows below the next stitch, *work 1Tss (that is, pick up 1 loop from under the next vertical strand), 1TRtrF under the vertical strand 2 rows below the next stitch, and 1TRdtrF in the vertical strand 3 rows below the next stitch; repeat from * to the last stitch, and work 1Tss. [22 loops on hook]
Row 8, Stage 2: Remove *all* of the loops as for Tss, changing to M to work off the last 2 loops on the hook. To avoid creating a float with the C yarn, you may wish to cut off this contrast yarn each time that a row with Tunisian raised stitches has been worked.
Rows 9–11: With M, work 3 rows as for Tss, joining in C to work off the last 2 loops on the hook when working Stage 2 of the last row; there is no need to break off M.
Row 12, Stage 1: With C, work 1Tss, *work 1Tss, 1TRtrF under the vertical strand 2 rows below the next stitch, and 1TRdtrF under the vertical strand 3 rows below the next stitch; repeat from * to the last 2sts, and work 2Tss.
Row 12, Stage 2: Remove all of the loops as for Tss, changing to M to work off the last 2 loops on the hook.
Rows 13–15: With M, work 3 rows as for Tss, joining in C to work off the last 2 loops on the hook when working Stage 2 of the last row; there is no need to break off M.
Row 16, Stage 1: With C, *work 1Tss, 1TRtrF in the vertical strand 2 rows below the next stitch, and 1TRdtrF in the vertical strand 3 rows below the next stitch; repeat from * to the end of the row.
Row 16, Stage 2: Remove all of the loops as for Tss, changing to M to work off the last 2 loops on the hook. Fasten off C.
Row 17, Stage 1: Still using the 6.50mm Tunisian crochet hook and M, work 1dc into each of the next 7sts by inserting the hook under the vertical strand to pull up a loop for working each dc (that is, work in double crochet until 14sts remain to be worked for the Right Front), and pick up 1 loop for each vertical strand to the end of the row as for Tss. [15 loops on hook]
Row 17, Stage 2: Remove all of the loops as for Tss for the 15sts of Tss only.
Rows 18–22: With M, work 5 rows as for Tss.
Change to using the 5.50mm crochet hook; work 1dc in each stitch to the end of the row. Fasten off M.

Back

Miss the next 6sts adjacent to the Right Front for the right-side armhole. With the 6.50mm Tunisian crochet hook, join in M to next stitch of the body with 1slst.
Row 1, Stage 1: Pick up 1 loop and place on to the hook by inserting the hook under each of the next 43 vertical strands as for Tss, leaving 28sts unworked (for the Left Front, to be worked later). [44 loops on hook]
Row 1, Stage 2: Remove all of the loops as for Tss.
Rows 2–18: Work 17 rows as for Tss.
Change to using the 5.50mm crochet hook; work 1dc in each stitch to the end of the row. Fasten off M.

Left front

Miss the next 6sts adjacent to the Back for the left-side armhole. With the 6.50mm Tunisian crochet hook, join in M to the next stitch of the body with 1slst.

Rows 1–7: Work 7 rows as for Tss on the last 22sts remaining for the body, joining in C to work off the last 2 loops on the hook when working Stage 2 of the last row; there is no need to break off M.

Row 8, Stage 1: With C, *work 1TRdtrF under the vertical strand 3 rows below the next stitch, 1TRtrF under the vertical strand 2 rows below the next stitch, and 1Tss (that is, pick up 1 loop from under the next vertical strand); repeat from * to the end of the row. [22 loops on hook]

Row 8, Stage 2: Remove all of the loops as for Tss, changing to M to work off the last 2 loops on the hook. To avoid creating a float with the C yarn, you may wish to cut off this contrast yarn each time that a row with Tunisian raised stitches has been worked.

Rows 9–11: With C, work 3 rows as for Tss, joining in C to work off the last 2 loops on the hook when working Stage 2 of the last row; there is no need to break off M.

Row 12, Stage 1: With C, work 1Tss, *work 1TRdtrF under the vertical strand 3 rows below the next stitch, 1TRtrF under the vertical strand 2 rows below the next stitch, and 1Tss; repeat from * to the last 2sts, and work 2Tss.

Row 12, Stage 2: Remove all of the loops as for Tss, changing to M to work off the last 2 loops on the hook.

Rows 13–15: With M, work 3 rows as for Tss, joining in C to work off the last 2 loops on the hook when working Stage 2 of the last row; there is no need to break off M.

Row 16, Stage 1: With C, work 2Tss, *work 1TRdtrF under the vertical strand 3 rows below the next stitch, 1TRtrF under the vertical strand 2 rows below the next stitch, and 1Tss; repeat from * to the last stitch, and work 1Tss.

Row 16, Stage 2: Remove all of the loops as for Tss, changing to M to work off the last 2 loops on the hook. Fasten off C.

Rows 17–22: With M, work 6 rows as for Tss on the first 15sts only.

Change to using the 5.50mm crochet hook; work 1dc in each stitch to the end of the row. Fasten off M.

Join the Left Front and Right Front to the Back at the shoulders, as necessary, with an invisible seam (*see* the section 'Working an invisible join' in Chapter 3).

Armhole borders

With RS facing and the 5.50mm crochet hook, join in M with 1slst to the Right Front at the right-hand end (towards the Back) of the underarm.

Row 1: With M, work 1dc into each row end around the armhole using the technique that avoids holes appearing (*see* the section 'Working an Edging or Border' in Chapter 3), ending at the left-hand end (towards the Right Front) of the underarm (*do not* work into the unworked stitches at the base of the armhole), make 1ch, and turn the work.

Row 2: With WS facing and M, work 1dc in each stitch in turn to the last stitch of the row, and join in C to complete the last 1dc (by pulling C through the last 2 loops on the hook, to avoid a colour drag when incorporating C), but do not break off M. Turn the work.

Row 3: With RS facing and C, work 1dc in each stitch around the armhole border. Fasten off C.

Row 4: Keep the RS facing and move the hook to the opposite end of the row, where M is still connected. With M, make 1ch, and work 1 dc in each stitch to the end of the row.

Row 5: With RS facing, work crab stitch to the end of the row. Fasten off M.

Work the other armhole border to match by joining in M with 1slst to the Left Front at the right-hand end (towards the Left Front) of the underarm and ending Row 1 at the left-hand end (towards the Back) of the underarm.

Bottom border

With RS facing and the 5.50mm crochet hook, join in M with 1slst to the bottom corner of the Left Front.

Row 1: Make 2ch, work 1htr in each stitch to the end of the row by inserting the hook under each vertical strand of Row 1 of the Body, missing the last vertical strand (as it is advisable to have an odd number of sts at this point). [99sts]

Row 2: Make 2ch, turn the work, *work 1RtrF in the next stitch, and 1RtrB in the next stitch; repeat from * to the end of the row, including the top of the 1ch at the start of the previous row.

Row 3: Work as for Row 2, changing to C when pulling the yarn through the last 2 loops of the final RtrB.

Row 4: With C, work as for Row 2.

Row 5: With C, work as for Row 2, changing to M when pulling the yarn through the last 2 loops of the final RtrB. Fasten off C.

Row 6: With M, work as for Row 2.

Row 7: With M, work as for Row 2; keep M attached at the end of the row.

Fronts-and-neck border

Row 1: Continuing with M, make 1ch, work 1dc in last stitch worked of last row of bottom border. Work 1dc in each row end of the bottom border. Continue up side of the Right Front by working 1dc in each row end (as for the armhole border), work 2dc in the corner, work 1dc in each stitch across the Right Front extension, work 1dc in each row end of the right side of the neck, work dc2tog at the concave curve between the right side of the neck and the back neck, work 1dc in each stitch of the back neck to the corner, work dc2tog at the concave curve between the back neck and the left side of the neck, work 1dc in each row end of the left side of the neck to the start of the Left Front extension, work 1dc in each stitch across the Left Front extension by inserting the hook under each vertical strand of the Tss row below to pull up a loop for working the dc (as for when working Row 17, Stage 1 of the Right Front), work 2dc in the upper corner of the Left Front, and continue down the side of the Left Front working 1dc in each row end to the end of the bottom border.

Row 2: Make 1ch, and turn the work. With WS facing and M, work 1dc in each stitch to the Left Front corner, work 2dc in the corner, work 1dc in each stitch to Right Front corner, work 2dc in the corner, work 1dc on each stitch to the end of the row (at the bottom corner of the Right Front). Fasten off M.

Row 3: With RS facing, join in C, and work as for Row 2, changing to M to work off the last 2 loops on the hook. Fasten off C.

Row 4: With RS facing, attach M to the turning chain worked in C at the beginning of Row 3. With M, make 1ch, and work 1dc in each stitch to the upper corner of the Right Front, work 2dc in the corner, work 1dc in each stitch to the concave curve between the Right Front extension and the right side of the neck, dc2tog at the concave curve, work 1dc in each stitch of the right side of the neck, back neck and left side of the neck to the concave curve between the left side of the neck and the Left Front extension, dc2tog in the concave curve, work 1dc in each stitch to the upper corner of the Left Front, work 2dc in the corner, and work 1dc in each stitch down the Left Front to the end of the row (at the bottom corner of the Left Front). Do not turn the work.

Row 5: With RS facing, work crab stitch to the end of the row (no increasing or decreasing is needed on this row). Fasten off M.

Finishing

The edges of each armhole band will butt together with the underarm fabric. For each band, use the yarn ends to attach the edges to the adjacent unworked stitches of the underarm. Sew in all other yarn ends.

A close-up of a piece of Tunisian claw stitch.

Tunisian claw stitch

This stitch gathers three unfinished long Tunisian raised treble stitches together so that only 1 loop remains on the hook after completing the Stage 1 actions of working this stitch. At least three rows worked with the main colour need to be present before working the claw-stitch row. The claw-stitch row is given twice in the trial piece to allow the claws to lie between each other, in a staggered fashion, as the work progresses. Two colours are required, to enable the claws to be visible against the background fabric. At least one Tss is needed to the right of the position of a claw stitch, to provide fabric into which to work the first long stitch of the claw. With 1 loop on the hook from the preceding Tss make the claw stitch by working 1TRtrF under the vertical strand that is three rows below the previous stitch position of the row currently being worked (this Tunisian raised treble stitch leans backwards, rather than being vertical, and temporarily leaves 3 loops on the hook), 1TRdtrF under the vertical strand that is four rows below the current stitch position being worked (this Tunisian raised double-treble stitch is vertical and temporarily leaves 4 loops on the hook) and 1TRtrF under the vertical strand that is three rows below the next stitch to be worked for the current row (this Tunisian raised treble leans forwards and temporarily leaves 5 loops on the hook) with the 3 Tunisian raised trebles worked, yoh and pull the yarn through the next 3 loops on the hook, to leave 1 loop remaining for the claw stitch – 1 claw stitch has been made.

Modifications

The claw stitches can be separated by additional Tss stitches and additional rows of Tss worked with the background colour, which

Trial piece of Tunisian claw stitch

Set-Up: With M, make a slip knot, place it on to a crochet hook of an appropriate size for the yarn, and work 17ch. Place the last chain on to a Tunisian crochet hook of an appropriate size for the yarn.

Rows 1–4: With M, work 4 rows in Tss, changing to C to work off the last 2 loops on the hook when working Stage 2 of the last row.

The staggered claw-stitch pattern begins on the next row and is worked over 10 rows in total.

Row 5, Stage 1 (first claw-stitch row): With C, pick up 1 loop and place on to the hook from under the next vertical strand (2 loops on hook), *make 1 claw stitch as follows: yoh, insert the hook under the vertical strand that is 3 rows below the previous stitch of the row currently being worked, yoh, and pull the yarn through the vertical strand, yoh and pull the yarn through 2 loops on the hook (= 1TRtrF made), yoh twice, insert the hook under the vertical strand that is 4 rows below the current stitch being worked, yoh and pull the yarn through the vertical strand, (yoh and pull the yarn through 2 loops on the hook) twice (= 1TRdtrF), yoh, insert the hook under the vertical strand that is 3 rows below the next stitch to be worked for the current row, yoh, and pull the yarn through the vertical strand, yoh and pull the yarn through 2 loops on the hook (= 1TRtrF made), yoh and pull the yarn through the next 3 loops on the hook (= 1 claw stitch made; 3 loops on hook), pick up 1 loop and place on to the hook from under each of the next 3 vertical strands; repeat from * to the last 3sts, make 1 claw stitch, pick up 1 loop on to the hook from under each of the remaining 2 vertical strands.

Row 5, Stage 2 (first claw-stitch row): Work as for Stage 2 of Tss, changing to M to work off the last 2 loops of the row.

Rows 6–9: With M, work 4 rows as for Tss, changing to C to work off the last 2 loops of the last row.

Row 10, Stage 1 (second claw-stitch row): With C *pick up 1 loop and place on to the hook from under each of the next 3 vertical strands (4 loops on hook), make 1 claw stitch; repeat from * to the last 4sts, pick up 1 loop and place on to the hook from under each vertical strand.

Row 10, Stage 2 (second claw-stitch row): Remove all of the loops as for Tss, changing to using M to work off the last 2 loops on the hook.

Rows 11–14: With M, work 4 rows as for Tss, changing to using C to work off the last 2 loops of the last row.

The last 10 rows (Rows 5–14) form the pattern that is to be repeated until the fabric is of the desired length.

opens up the pattern and reduces the density of the contrast colour. It is always advisable to have an odd number of Tss stitches between neighbouring claw stitches, for example, 5, 7, 9, and so on, to allow the staggered claw stitches of subsequent rows to sit symmetrically between the claw stitches made previously.

Colour Combinations Without Texture

Chevron stitch

A fabric of Tunisian simple stitch can include increases and decreases, to form peaks and dips in the rows, as for the classic chevron pattern of knitting and traditional crochet. Although the work can look beautiful when worked with only one colour, it is more effective with the introduction of another colour. Changing colour on each row is attractive but can look busy; therefore, either work two rows with a main colour that is kept throughout and introduce one row of another colour after each set of two rows of the main colour has been worked or work the chevron shape with Tunisian trebles, instead of Tunisian simple stitch stitches, to give more height to the rows, resulting in wider stripes of colour.

One pattern increase is divided between the beginning and the end of the row. For the trial piece, use one main colour that is kept throughout, but introduce different colours for the single-row contrast. Working the chevron pattern in this way is ideal for using up any oddments of yarn. A multiple of 12sts plus 1st is required to work the chevron shape as given for the trial piece. The vertical strand at the centre of an increase forming the chevron peaks needs to sit on top of the vertical strand at the centre of the chevron peak of the previous row, to successfully maintain the form of the chevron peaks throughout the fabric.

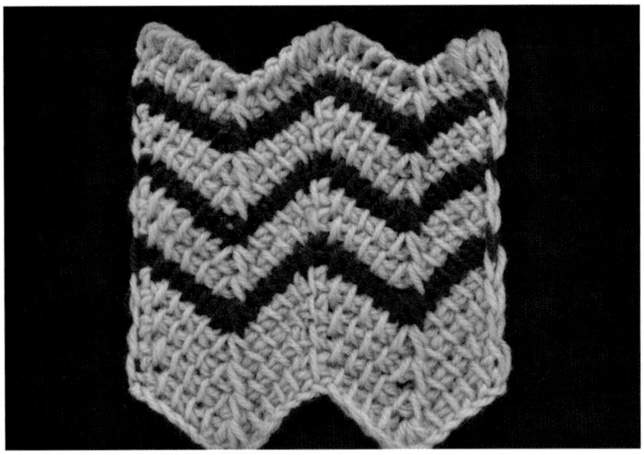

Chevrons are the result of including increases and decreases in sequence within a row.

Connecting-waves stitch

This pattern introduces the use of Tunisian slip stitch (Tslst) as a pattern stitch, which is worked by inserting the hook under the next vertical strand but then leaving the vertical strand on the hook, unworked. For the stitches between Tunisian slip stitches, pick up the vertical strand as normal, that is as for Tunisian simple stitch. The appearance of and applications for slip stitches become clearer when worked in a stitch pattern using two colours.

For the connecting-waves pattern, the first colour worked becomes the main yarn. This particular stitch pattern shows how the Tunisian slip stitch has the effect of bending one row to form waves. Tunisian slip stitch can also be useful for camouflage, and, in certain instances, it can replace the Tunisian drop stitch or the Tunisian raised treble. Always count the loop on the hook at the start of a row as a stitch.

If you have been following the book from the beginning, you will have realized how different a stitch pattern can look by changing either the size of the hook or the type of yarn used. To emphasize this, I have included two examples of this connecting-waves stitch, one with both yarns being of the same standard DK-weight thickness and one example using a thicker smooth yarn combined with a textured yarn.

Interlocking rows

Whenever a Tunisian slip stitch is to be included in a pattern, it is important to select the correct size of Tunisian crochet hook to be used for working the fabric. In this stitch pattern, the Tunisian slip stitch is being used frequently, on every row; therefore; it is essential to use a Tunisian crochet hook two or even three sizes larger than the Tunisian crochet hook that would normally be selected for the yarn. Refer to the

Trial piece of chevron stitch

Set-Up: With M, make a slip knot, place it on to a crochet hook of an appropriate size for the yarn, and make 25ch. Place the last chain on to a Tunisian crochet hook of an appropriate size for the yarn.

Row 1: Work as for Tss, changing to C to work off the last 2 loops of the row.

Row 2, Stage 1: With 1 loop on the hook, insert the hook under the topmost horizontal strand preceding the next vertical strand, yoh, and pull the yarn through this strand (1 increase made), *pick up 1 loop from under each of the next 4 vertical strands, insert the hook under the next 3 vertical strands, yoh and pull the yarn through all 3 vertical strands at once, pick up 1 loop from under each of the next 4 vertical strands, insert the hook under the topmost horizontal strand preceding the next vertical strand, yoh and pull the yarn through this strand (1 increase made), pick up 1 loop from under the next vertical strand, insert the hook under the topmost horizontal strand immediately following the preceding vertical strand, yoh and pull the yarn through this strand (1 increase made) (that is, there are 3 loops associated with the central vertical strand – the loop picked up from the strand and the two increase loops, one on each side of the vertical strand); repeat from * to the last stitch, pick up 1 loop from under the topmost horizontal strand preceding the last vertical strand of the row (1 increase made), and pick up 1 loop from under the remaining vertical strand. [25 loops on the hook]

Row 2, Stage 2: Remove all of the loops as for Tss.

Repeat Row 2 until the fabric is of the desired length, remembering to change colour when required using the last 2 loops on the row preceding the contrast-colour row.

connecting-waves pattern below for how to work Tunisian slip stitch.

Two contrasting colours of yarn are needed for the patterning to be visible. The first colour used is classed as the main colour (M). All of the slip stitches of one colour sit on top of stitches of the same colour, giving this pattern its distinctive look. It is a pleasing pattern to use in garments and for accessories.

A sample of connecting-waves stitch worked with a smooth DK-weight yarn; this stitch pattern introduces the Tunisian slip stitch.

Trial piece of connecting-waves stitch

With M, make a slip knot, place it on to a crochet hook of an appropriate size for the yarn, and make 15ch. Place the last chain on to a Tunisian crochet hook of an appropriate size.

Row 1: Work as for Tss, changing to C to work off the last 2 loops of the row.

Row 2, Stage 1: With C, *work 1Tslst with the next vertical strand, and 1Tss with each of the next 3 vertical strands; repeat from * to the last 2sts, work 1Tslst with the next vertical strand, and 1Tss with the remaining vertical strand.

Row 2, Stage 2: Remove all of the loops as for Tss, changing to M to work off the last 2 loops on the hook.

Row 3: With M, work as for Tss, changing to C to work of the last 2 loops of the row.

Row 4, Stage 1: With C, work 1Tss with each of the next 2 vertical strands, *work 1Tslst with the next vertical strand, 1Tss with the next 3 vertical strands; repeat from * to the last 3sts, work 1Tslst with the next vertical strand, and work 1Tss with each of the remaining 2 vertical strands.

Row 4, Stage 2: Remove all of the loops as for Tss, changing to C to work off the last 2 loops on the hook.

Row 5: Work as for Row 3.

The last 4 rows (Rows 2–5) form the pattern that is to be repeated until the fabric is of the desired length.

Using a chunky yarn and a brushed acrylic yarn can transform the look of the connecting-waves stitch.

Use of the Tunisian slip stitch forms vertical lines interlocking the two colours in this interesting stitch pattern.

The loose lining of the tote bag appearing from beneath the top edge.

A section of the tote bag fabric worked in Tunisian interlocking rows.

The gusset continues for the handle, ensuring added strength particularly if a cord is inserted.

Trial piece of interlocking rows

Set-Up: With M, make a slip knot, place it on to a crochet hook of an appropriate size for the yarn, and make 15ch. Place the last chain on to a Tunisian crochet hook of an appropriate size for the yarn and for working Tslst.
Row 1: Work as for Tss, changing to C to work off the last 2 loops of the row.
Row 2, Stage 1: With C, *work 1Tslst with the next vertical strand, and 1Tss with the next vertical strand; repeat from * to the end of the row.
Row 2, Stage 2: Remove all of the loops as for Tss, changing to M to work off the last 2 loops on the hook.
Row 3, Stage 1: With M, *work 1Tss with the next vertical strand, 1Tslst with the next vertical strand; repeat from * to the last 2sts, and work 1Tss with each of the remaining 2 vertical strands.
Row 3, Stage 2: Remove all of the loops as for Tss, changing to C to work off the last 2 loops on the hook.
Repeat Rows 2–3 until the fabric is of the desired length.

TOTE BAG

The Tote Bag fabric is worked with the interlocking-rows pattern and has a reinforced handle.

This bag can be of any size, by simply adding (or removing) stitches in multiples of 2sts for the numbers given in the pattern. A narrow gusset allows the bag's contents to sit safely. The gusset is continued to form a handle, for extra durability. Depending on the purpose of the bag, it can be lined with fabric. Attaching the lining only at the top edge enables it to be pulled out for cleaning if there is a spill within, without it being necessary to wash the whole bag.

Materials

West Yorkshire Spinners ColourLab DK-weight yarn (225m/100g)
1 × 100g ball in M
1 × 100g ball in C
6.00mm crochet hook
6.50mm Tunisian crochet hook
8.00mm Tunisian crochet hook
Optional:
Length of thick cord or rope, for reinforcing the handle
Sharp sewing needle and thread, suitable for attaching the cord or rope
Lining fabric of roughly 50cm (length) × 25cm (width)
Sharp sewing needle and thread, suitable for attaching the lining

Tension

Measured over interlocking-rows pattern (see Rows 4–5 of the following 'Bag' section): 13 stitches and 16 rows to 10cm

Size

Bag-panel width and length (excluding gusset and borders) approximately 22cm/8½in; gusset width 2.5cm/1in

Pattern instructions

Bag body

With M, make a slip knot, place it on to the 6.00mm crochet hook, and make 29ch. Place the last chain on to the 8.00mm Tunisian crochet hook.

Rows 1–3: With M, work 3 rows as for Tss, changing to C to work off the last 2 loops of the last row. [29sts]

Row 4, Stage 1: With C, *work 1Tslst with the next vertical strand, and 1Tss with the next vertical strand; repeat from * to the end of the row.

Row 4, Stage 2: Remove all of the loops as for Tss, changing to M to work off the last 2 loops on the hook.

Row 5, Stage 1: With M, *work 1Tss with the next vertical strand, 1Tslst with the next vertical strand; repeat from * to the last 2sts, and work 1Tss with each of the remaining 2 vertical strands.

Row 5, Stage 2: Remove all of the loops as for Tss, changing to C to work off the last 2 loops on the hook.

The last 2 rows (Rows 4–5) form the interlocking-rows pattern that is to be repeated for the main part of the fabric for this bag.

Repeat Rows 4–5 fourteen times.

Do not change colour from M to C on the last row, but continue working with M.

With M, work 3 rows as for Tss, for the base of the bag, changing to C to work off the last 2 loops of the last row.

Repeat Rows 4–5 fifteen times. Fasten off C.

With M, work 2 rows as for Tss.

With M and a 6.00mm crochet hook, make 1ch, and work 1dc in each stitch across the row; this double-crochet row will equal the height of 1 row of Tss (therefore, this double-crochet row and the preceding two rows of Tss will match the height of the first three rows of Tss worked at the start of the bag). Fasten off M.

Gusset and handle

With M, make a slip knot, place it on to the 6.00mm crochet hook, and make 5ch. Place the last chain on to the 6.50mm Tunisian crochet hook. As there are only 5sts to be worked, it is possible to work on a small crochet hook, but ensure that all of the loops go on to the thickest part of the shaft of the hook, to ensure that they are of an appropriate and consistent size.

Work as for Tss until the length of the strip equals twice the length of the height of the bag sides plus the full length required for the handle.

Finishing

Sew in all yarn ends.

Step 1: Attach one short end of the long gusset-and-handle strip to the ends of the 3 rows of Tss worked with M for the base of the bag on one side of the base.

Step 2: Ensuring that the strip isn't twisted, attach the other short end of the strip to the ends of the 3 rows of Tss for the base on the opposite side of the bag.

Step 3: Turn the bag fabric to have wrong sides facing outwards (that is, with the right sides together within the inside-out bag).
Step 4: Using M or a sewing thread of a matching colour, sew both edges of the start of one end of the long strip to the adjacent edges of the sides of the bag, to form the gusset on one side of the bag.
Step 5: Repeat Step 4 for the other end of the long strip, to form the gusset on the opposite side of the bag.

Optional finishing

Handle reinforcement
Step 6: Sew together the edges of the part of the long Tss strip that forms the handle over a length of cord or rope, for added strength.
Step 7: Secure each end of the cord or rope with firm sewing stitches and ending by passing the needle and thread through the cord or rope in several places, if possible, to prevent the ends of this handle support from pulling out with use.

Lining
Add a lining, as follows.
Step 1: Fold the lining fabric in half so that the short ends of the fabric align, with right sides together (that is, with the wrong sides of the fabric facing outwards), and sew a seam from the fold to the edge of the fabric for each side of the folded fabric (by hand or by using a sewing machine).
Step 2: Turn over the uppermost couple of centimetres at the top of the lining pocket, to form a tidier and more stable edge with which to attach the lining to the inside of the bag, and to hide the raw fabric edges behind the lining pocket once it is sewn into the bag.
Step 3: Turn the bag the right way out, that is with its right sides facing outwards, position the lining pocket within the bag, so that the wrong sides of the bag and lining are together. Sew the top edge of the lining to the inside of the bag fabric, using a whip stitch, back stitch or slip stitch, ensuring that the stitching does not show through to the right sides of the bag. Sew in all thread ends.

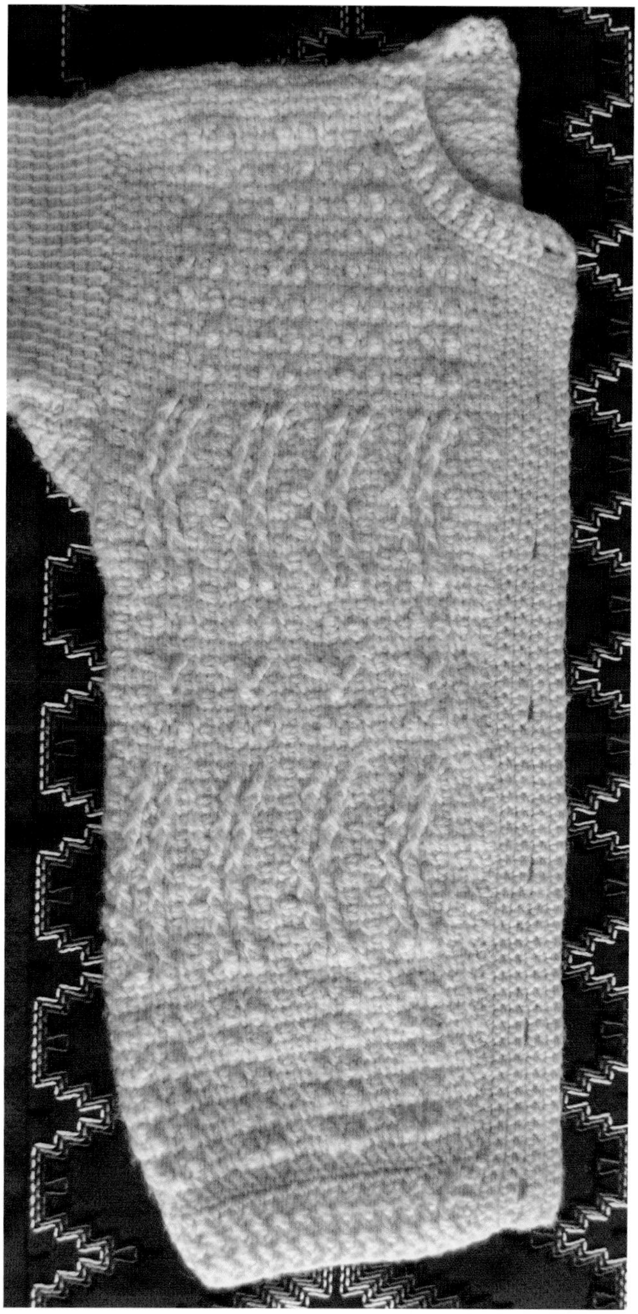

The Colourful Textured Car Coat (shown overleaf) can be worked in a single colour. Here we see one half of a monochromatic version.

COLOURFUL TEXTURED CAR COAT

Student Elsa at the seaside wearing the Colourful Textured Car Coat.

Gentleman David giving the Colourful Textured Car Coat a thumbs up for town wear.

Many of the designs featured in this book are suitable for both sexes and individuals of any age. This pattern is no exception: I think you will agree that this car coat looks equally good on Elsa, a university student, and David, a retired gentleman.

This design incorporates many of the techniques already studied and gives an opportunity for allowing the imagination to explore different colour combinations and stitches. The design can be safely used as a template or starting point when expanding your Tunisian crochet experience.

The car coat includes a variety of texture stitches that have been combined in such a way that the jacket has been prevented from becoming too heavy. When changing a stitch pattern or altering the thickness of the yarn to be used, it is necessary to take the physical weight of the end result into account!

The pattern is written for one size and a DK-weight yarn, but a smaller size can be obtained by using a 6.00mm Tunisian crochet hook and 4-ply yarn, whilst a larger size can be obtained by using an 8.00mm Tunisian crochet hook and aran-weight yarn.

Possible alterations to the existing design include the following, but use your imagination to come up with other changes:

- Make this coat without sleeves; because there are decorative bands at the sides of the garment, this coat can easily be made sleeveless. The lack of sleeves does not affect the overall usability of the garment.
- Increase the length by working more rows of the pattern before Row 53 of the back and the same number of additional rows before Row 15 of the front.
- Play with colour combinations to suit your personality or that of a friend, and the coat looks equally stunning worked in different shades of ivory, giving it a more classic look.
- Make the coat exactly as written, but substitute an unwashed oily natural pure wool of an Aran weight. By keeping the stated 7.00mm Tunisian crochet hook as the main hook, the jacket fabric becomes denser, so the coat becomes almost wind- and waterproof. Naturally oiled aran-weight wool is heavier than processed wool and therefore requires more yarn to produce a garment of the same size.

Materials

3 × 100g balls DK-weight yarn in M
2 × 100g balls DK-weight yarn in C1
2 × 100g balls DK-weight yarn in C2
1 × 100g ball DK-weight yarn in C3
5.00mm crochet hook
6.00mm crochet hook
7.00mm Tunisian crochet hook

Tension

Measured over Tss: 15 stitches and 11 rows to 10cm

Size

One size, to fit a bust/chest circumference of 102cm/40in
Length (including welt) 57cm/22½in; sleeve seam (including cuff) 50cm/19½in; armhole depth (with border) 27cm/10½in

Pattern instructions

Back

Set-Up: With M, make a slip knot, place it on to the 6.00mm crochet hook, and make 81ch. Place the last chain on to the 7.00mm Tunisian crochet hook.

Row 1: Work as for Tss, beginning by picking up 1 loop from under the top strand of each chain in turn.

Row 2: Work as for Tss.

Row 3: Work as for Tss. (Visually, this row will appear to be a row of Tunisian crochet cross stitch once Row 4 is completed.)

Row 4, Stage 1: Counting the first loop on the hook as the first stitch of the row, *work Tx over 2sts (*see* the section 'Tunisian crochet cross stitch' earlier in this chapter for step-by-step instructions for how to work Tx); repeat from * to the end of the row.

Row 4, Stage 2: Remove all of the loops as for Tss.

Rows 5–42: Repeat Rows 2–4 twelve times and Row 2 twice, changing to C1 to work off the last 2 loops of the last row.

Row 43, Stage 1: With C1, *work 1Tss with each of the next 2 vertical strands, and 1Tdtr under the next vertical strand; repeat from * to the last 3sts, and work 1Tss with each of the next 3 vertical strands. (This row is worked so that the two colours used so far will fuse and therefore the appearance of a harsh straight line resulting from the colour change is avoided.)

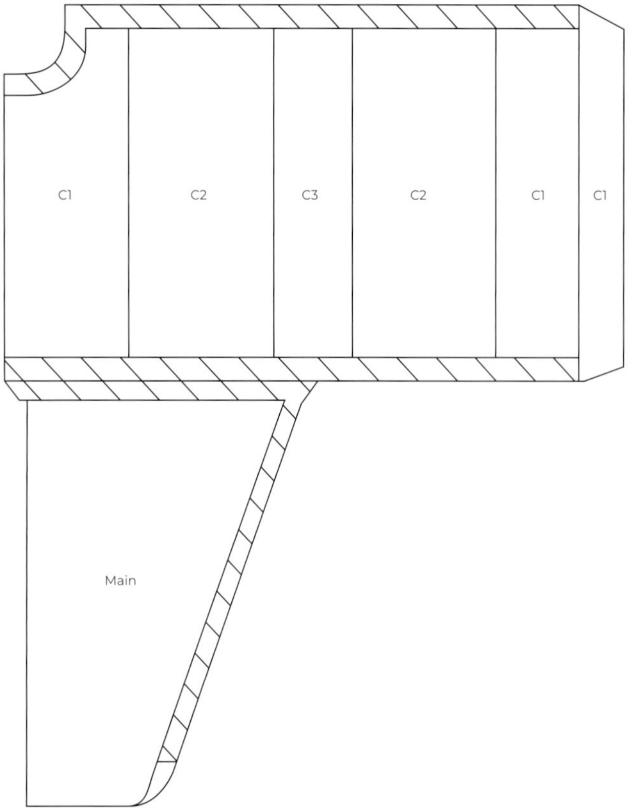

Schematic for the front of the Colourful Textured Car Coat.

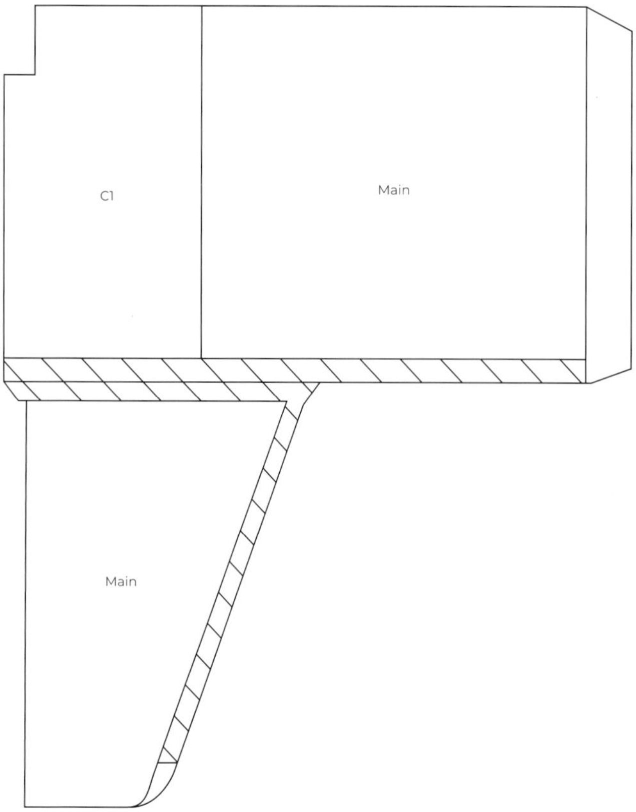

Schematic for the back of the Colourful Textured Car Coat.

Row 43, Stage 2: Remove all of the loops as for Tss.
Row 44: Work as for Tss.
Row 45, Stage 1: Work 1Tss under the next vertical strand, and 1Tdtr under the next vertical strand, *work 1Tss with each of the next 2 vertical strands, and 1Tdtr under the next vertical strand; repeat from * to the last stitch, and work 1Tss with the remaining vertical strand.
Row 45, Stage 2: Remove all of the loops as for Tss.
Row 46: Work as for Tss.
Row 47, Stage 1: *Work 1Tdtr under the next vertical strand, and 1Tss with each of the next 2 vertical strands; repeat from * to the last 2sts, and work 1Tss with each of the remaining 2 vertical strands.
Row 47, Stage 2: Remove all of the loops as for Tss.
Row 48: Work as for Tss.
Rows 49–62: Repeat Rows 43–48 twice and then Rows 43–44 once.

Right shoulder extension
Row 63: With the first 28sts of the row only, work as for Row 45.
Row 64: Work as for Row 46; break off yarn. Note: a double crochet row is not now worked, because the vertical strands will be required for working an invisible shoulder join.

Left shoulder extension
Miss the next 25sts adjacent to the Right Front (these missed stitches are for the back neck). Join in C1 to the next stitch with 1slst.
Row 63: Keeping the Tdtr in the correct place for the established sequence, work the remaining 28sts to the end of the row as for Row 45.
Row 64: Work as for Row 46.
Row 65: Make 1ch, and work 1dc by working under each vertical strand to the end of the row. Break off yarn.

Right front
With C1 and the 6.00mm crochet hook, make 41ch. Place the last chain on to the 7.00mm Tunisian crochet hook.
Row 1: Work as for Tss, by picking up 1 loop from under the top strand of each chain in turn.
Rows 2–3: Work as for Tss.
Row 4, Stage 1: With 1 loop on the hook, work 1Tss with the next vertical strand, *work 1Tdtr under the next vertical strand, and 1Tss with each of the next 3 vertical strands; repeat from * to the last 2sts, and work 1Tss with each of the remaining 2 vertical strands.
Row 4, Stage 2: Remove all of the loops as for Tss.
Rows 5–6: Work as for Tss.
Row 7, Stage 1: With 1 loop on the hook, work 1Tss in each of the next 3 vertical strands, *work 1Tdtr under the next vertical strand, and 1Tss in each of the next 3 vertical strands; repeat from * to the last 2sts, work 1Tdtr under the next vertical strand, and 1Tss in the remaining vertical strand.
Row 7, Stage 2: Remove all of the loops as for Tss.
Rows 8–12: Repeat Rows 3–7 once.
Rows 13–14: Work 2 rows as for Tss, changing to C2 to work off the last 2 loops of the last row. Break off C1.
Row 15: With C2, work as for Tss.
Row 16, Stage 1: With 1 loop on hook, work 1Tss in each of the next 4 vertical loops, *work 1TRdtr under the vertical strand 1 row below the current stitch position, 1Tss in the next vertical strand, 1TRdtr under the vertical strand 1 row below the current stitch position, and 1Tss in each of the next 4 vertical strands; repeat from * to the last stitch, and work 1Tss in the remaining vertical strand.
Row 16, Stage 2: Remove all of the loops as for Tss.
Note: Row 17 and all odd-numbered rows up to and including Row 29 are worked as for Tss.
Row 18, Stage 1: With 1 loop on the hook, work 1Tss in each of the next 3 vertical strands, *work 1TRdtrF under the next TRdtr of Row 16, 1Tss in the vertical strand behind the TRdtrF just worked, 1TRdtrF under the next TRdtr of Row 16, 1Tss in the vertical strand behind the TRdtrF just worked, and 1Tss in each of the next 4 vertical strands; repeat from * to the last 2sts, and work 1Tss in each of the remaining 2 vertical loops.
Row 18, Stage 2: Remove all of the loops as for Tss.
Row 20, Stage 1: With 1 loop on the hook, work 1Tss in each of the next 2 vertical strands, *work 1TRdtrF under the next TRdtrF of Row 18, 1Tss in the vertical strand behind the TRdtrF just worked, 1TRdtrF under the next TRdtrF of Row 18, 1Tss in the vertical strand behind the TRdtrF just worked, and 1Tss in each of the next 4 vertical strands; repeat from * to the last 3sts, and work 1Tss in each of the remaining 3 vertical strands.
Row 20, Stage 2: Remove all of the loops as for Tss.
Row 22: Work as for Row 20, using the TRdtrF stitches of Row 20 for working the TRdtrF stitches of the current row.
Row 24: Work as for Row 18, using the TRdtrF stitches of Row 22 for working the TRdtrF stitches of the current row.
Row 26: Work as for Row 16, using the TRdtrF stitches of Row 24 for working the TRdtrF stitches of the current row.
Row 28, Stage 1: With 1 loop on the hook, work 1Tss in each of the next 5 vertical strands, *work 1TRdtrF under the next TRdtrF of Row 26, 1Tss in the vertical strand behind the TRdtrF just worked, 1TRdtrF under the TRdtrF of Row 26, 1Tss in the vertical strand behind the TRdtrF just worked, and 1Tss in each of the next 4 vertical strands; repeat from * to the end of the row.
Row 28, Stage 2: Remove all of the loops as for Tss.
Row 30, Stage 1: With C2, work as for Tss, by picking up 1 loop for each stitch across the row.
Row 30, Stage 2: With C3, remove all of the loops as for Tss. Break off C2.
Rows 31–32: With C3, work as for Tss.
Row 33, Stage 1: *Work 1Tss in each of the next 3 vertical strands, and 1Tdtr under the next vertical strand; repeat from * to the last 4sts, and work 1Tss in each of the remaining 4 vertical strands.
Row 33, Stage 2: Remove all of the loops as for Tss.
Row 34, Stage 1: Work 1Tss in the next vertical strand, *work 1Tdtr under the next vertical strand, and 1Tss in each of the next 4 vertical strands; repeat from * to the last 3sts, and work 1Tdtr under the next vertical strand, and 1Tss in each of the remaining 2 vertical strands.
Row 34, Stage 2: Remove all of the loops as for Tss.
Rows 35–36: Repeat Rows 33–34 once.
Row 37–38: Work as for Tss.
Row 39, Stage 1: With C3, work as for Tss.
Row 39, Stage 2: With C2, remove all of the loops as for Tss. Break off C3.
Row 40: With C2, work as for Tss.
Row 41: Work as for row 18, by working under the C3 vertical strands of Row 39 for working the TRdtrF stitches of the current row.
Rows 42–50: With C2, repeat Rows 19–27 once.
Row 51: With C2, work as for Tss, changing to C1 to work off the last 2 loops on the hook. Break off C2.
Rows 52–53: With C1, work 2 rows as for Tss.
Row 54, Stage 1: Work 1Tss in the next vertical strand,

*work 1Tdtr under the next vertical strand, and 1Tss in each of the next 3 vertical strands; repeat from * to the last 3sts, work 1Tdtr with the next vertical strand, and work 1Tss in each of the remaining 2 vertical strands.

Row 54, Stage 2: Remove all of the loops as for Tss.

Rows 55–56: Work 2 rows as for Tss.

Row 57, Stage 1: Work 1dc in each of the next 4sts by inserting the hook under each vertical strand in turn to pull up a loop for working the dc, work 1Tss with the next vertical strand, *work 1Tdtr under the next vertical strand, 1Tss in each of the next 3 vertical strands; repeat from * to the end of the row.

Row 57, Stage 2: Remove all of the loops as for Tss. [37sts; 1 loop on hook]

Row 58, Stage 1: Insert the hook under the next 3 vertical strands, yoh, and pull the yarn through (to make 2 decreases at once), and work as for Tss to the end of the row.

Row 58, Stage 2: Remove all of the loops as for Tss. [35sts; 1 loop on hook]

Row 59, Stage 1: Insert the hook under the next 2 vertical strands, yoh, and pull the yarn through (to make 1 decrease), and work as for Tss to the end of the row.

Row 59, Stage 2: Remove all of the loops as for Tss. [34sts; 1 loop on hook]

Row 60: Insert the hook under the next 2 vertical strands, yoh, and pull the yarn through (to make 1 decrease), and work to the end of the row as for Row 54, keeping the Tdtr stitches correctly positioned to continue the established sequence. [33sts; 1 loop on hook]

Rows 61–62: Insert the hook under the next 2 vertical strands, yoh, and pull the yarn through (to make 1 decrease), and work as for Tss to the end of the row. [31sts when Row 62 is completed; 1 loop on the hook]

Row 63: Work to the end of the row as for Row 57, keeping the Tdtr stitches correctly positioned to continue the established sequence, but *do not* work any double-crochet stitches or decrease any stitches. [31sts; 1 loop on the hook]

Rows 64–65: Work as for Tss.

Row 66: Work to the end of the row as for Row 54, keeping the Tdtr stitches correctly positioned to continue the established sequence.

Rows 67–68: Work as for Tss.

Row 69: Work to the end of the row as for Row 57, keeping the Tdtr stitches correctly positioned to continue the established sequence, but *do not* work any double-crochet stitches or decrease any stitches.

Row 70: Work 1dc in each stitch to the end of the row. Break off C1.

Left front

Rows 1–56: Work as for Right Front Rows 1–56.

Row 57, Stage 1: Work 1Tss with each of the next vertical strands, *work 1Tdtr under the next vertical strand, and 1Tss in each of the next 3 verticals strands; repeat from * to the last 4sts, and leave the remaining 4sts unworked.

Row 57, Stage 2: Remove all of the loops as for Tss. [37sts; 1 loop on hook]

Row 58, Stage 1: Work as for Tss to the last 3sts, insert the hook under all 3 vertical strands, yoh, and pull the yarn through (to make 2 decreases at once).

Row 58, Stage 2: Remove all of the loops as for Tss. [35sts; 1 loop on hook]

Row 59, Stage 1: Work as for Tss to the last 2sts, insert the hook under both vertical strands, yoh, and pull the yarn through (to make 1 decrease).

Row 59, Stage 2: Remove all of the loops as for Tss. [34sts; 1 loop on hook]

Row 60: Work to the last 2sts as for Row 54, keeping the Tdtr stitches correctly positioned to continue the established sequence, insert the hook under both vertical strands, yoh, and pull the yarn through (to make 1 decrease). [33sts; 1 loop on hook]

Rows 61–62: Work as for Tss to the last 2sts, insert the hook under both vertical strands, yoh, and pull the yarn through (to make 1 decrease). [31sts when Row 62 is completed; 1 loop on the hook]

Row 63: Work to the end of the row as for Row 57, keeping the Tdtr stitches correctly positioned to continue the established sequence, but *do not* leave any stitches unworked. [31sts; 1 loop on the hook]

Rows 64–65: Work as for Tss.

Row 66: Work to the end of the row as for Row 54, keeping the Tdtr stitches correctly positioned to continue the established sequence.

Rows 67–68: Work as for Tss.

Row 69: Work to the end of the row as for Row 57, keeping the Tdtr stitches correctly positioned to continue the established sequence, but *do not* leave any stitches unworked.

Row 70: Work 1dc in each stitch to the end of the row. Break off C1.

For each shoulder, with right sides together, seam the shoulder with an invisible join, matching the stitches of the Left Front or Right Front, as relevant, to the stitches of the Back to avoid bulk, or alternatively work a joining row of double-crochet stitches from the wrong side of the fabric.

Side bands

These bands are made as long lengths, with each band running along the whole length of the front and back of one side of the garment.

Note: Always keep the RS facing.

Row 1: With the 6.00mm crochet hook, attach M to the bottom corner of the Right Front with 1slst. Make 1ch, work 1dc in same place (to create a sharp corner), work 1dc in each row end up the side of the Right Front and down the side of the Back, ensuring that no holes appear, and work 1dc in the 1ch (turning chain) at the bottom corner of the Back. Fasten off M.

Row 2: With the 6.00mm crochet hook, attach C1 to the bottom corner of the Right Front with 1slst. Make 1ch, and work 1dc in each stitch to the end of the row. Fasten off C1.

Row 3: Work as for Row 2, using C2 in place of C1. At the end of the row, fasten off C2.

Repeat these 3 rows (Rows 1–3) for the left side of the coat; for Row 1, attach M to the bottom corner of the Back, work 1dc in each row end up the side of the Back and down the side of the Left Front and end the row at the bottom corner of the Left Front for Row 1, and, for Row 2, attach C1 to the bottom corner of the Back.

Fronts-and-neck band

This band runs along the Right Front, around the neck of the garment and then along the Left Front.

Note: Always keep the RS facing.

Row 1: With the 6.00mm crochet hook, attach M to the bottom corner of the Right Front with 1slst. Make 1ch, work 1dc in same place (to create a sharp corner), work 1dc in each row end up the side of the Right Front to end at the upper corner (ensuring that no holes appear by inserting the hook under both the vertical strand closest to the edge of the fabric and the adjacent topmost horizontal strand lying next to it to pull up a loop for working the dc), work 2dc in the corner, work 1dc in each stitch or row end to the concave curve between the Right Front and the Back, work dc2tog at the curve, work 1dc in each stitch across the back neck to the concave curve between the Back and Left Front, work dc2tog at the curve, work 1dc in each row end or stitch to the upper corner of the Left Front, work 2dc in the corner, work 1dc in each row end down the side of the Left Front and work 1dc in the 1ch (turning chain) at the bottom corner of the Left Front (to create a sharp corner). Fasten off M.

Row 2: With the 6.00mm crochet hook, attach C1 to the bottom corner of the Right Front, make 1ch, and work 1dc in each stitch to the end of the row, placing 2dc at each of the upper corners of the fronts and decreasing at each concave curve at the back neck as for Row 1. Fasten off C1.

Row 3: Work as for Row 2, using C2 in place of C1. At the end of the row, fasten off C2.

Row 4: Work as for Row 2, using C3 in place of C1. At the end of the row, do not fasten off C3.

Row 5: Still with RS facing, continue with C3 to work a crab stitch to the end of the row. Fasten off C3.

Seaming for a sleeveless coat only

Place a stitch marker on both the Right Front and Back edge of the right side of the coat at the point where the underarm will be. The ideal position is at the centre of the band worked with C3. Ensure that the edges and bottom corners of the front and back pieces are properly aligned.

With RS facing, attach C3 with 1slst to the bottom corner of the side of the Right Front, and work the right side seam by working 1dc through each pair of aligned stitches of the Right Front and Back in turn, to connect both sides together, finishing at the underarm markers.

Still with RS facing, make 1ch, and continue round the armhole with crab stitch. 1slst to join. Fasten off yarn.

Work the left side seam as for the right side seam, placing stitch markers in an equivalent manner, attaching C3 beside the underarm markers, and working from the underarm to the bottom corner of the side of the Left Front.

Proceed by working the welt.

Welt

Sew in the yarn ends of the garment body and of all of the bands and seams.

Row 1: With RS facing and the 6.00mm crochet hook, join C1 to the bottom corner of the Left Front front band, make 2ch (to count as a stitch), work 2htr in the row ends of the band, work 1htr under each vertical strand in turn of the first row of the Left Front, work 6htr across the row ends of the front side of the left side band and the back side of the left side band, work 1htr under each vertical strand of the first row of the Back, work 6htr across the row ends of the back side of the right side band and the front side of the right side band, work 1htr under each vertical strand of the Right Front, work 3htr in the row ends of the Right Front band, make 2ch, and turn. (181sts)

Row 2: Counting the 2ch turning chain as the first stitch of the row, *work 1RtrF under the htr of the next stitch position, and 1RtrB under the htr of the next stitch position; repeat from * to the end of the row, make 2ch, and turn.

Row 3: Counting the 2ch turning chain as the first stitch of the row, *work 1RtrB under the next stitch of the previous row, and 1RtrF under the next stitch of the previous row; repeat from * to the end of the row, make 2ch, and turn.

Check whether the RtrF and RtrB stitches are producing columns, to provide an elastic finish.

Rows 4–7: Change to using the 5.00mm crochet hook. Work Rows 2–3 twice.

Row 8: Work as for Row 2, omitting the last 2ch. Fasten off C1.

Sew in all yarn ends. *Sleeves – two made alike*

Set-Up: With M and the 6.00mm crochet hook, work 66ch. Place the last chain on to the 7.00mm Tunisian crochet hook.

Row 1: Work as for Tss. [66sts]

Row 2, Stage 1: Pick up 1 loop from under the next 2 vertical strands (1 decrease made), pick up 1 loop and place on to the hook from under each vertical strand in turn to the last 3sts, pick up 1 loop from under the next 2 vertical strands (1 decrease made), and pick up 1 loop from under the remaining stitch.

Row 2, Stage 2: Remove all of the loops as for Tss. [64sts, with 1 loop on hook]

Repeat Row 2 twice. [60sts]

Row 5: Work as for Tss.

Row 6: Work as for Row 2.

Repeat Rows 5–6 five times. [48sts]

Rows 17–18: Work as for Tss.

Row 19: Work as for Row 2. [46sts]

Repeat Rows 17–19 twice. [42sts]

Row 26–28: Work as for Tss.

Row 29: Work as for Row 2.

Repeat Rows 26–29 three times. [34sts]

Work 12 rows as for Tss or to length required without sleeve band and cuff.

Do not fasten off, and place the last loop remaining at the completion of the last row on to the 6.00mm crochet hook.

Sleeve band

The sleeve band is formed along both sides of the sleeve and along the armhole edge of the sleeve head and is worked with the same colour sequence as used for the side bands and the first 3 rows of the fronts-and-neck band (that is, first by using M and then C1 and C2).

With RS facing and the 6.00mm crochet hook, work double crochet up the adjacent long side of the sleeve by placing 1dc in each row end. Continue by working across the sleeve head (which will be positioned at the armhole edge when the garment is assembled) by working 1dc into each stitch and increasing at both corners by working 1dc or 2dc as appropriate. Continue by working double crochet down the other side of the sleeve, ensuring that the same number of stitches is worked on both sides of the sleeve. Fasten off M.

Join C1 with 1slst to the start of the row just worked, make 1ch, and work 1dc in each stitch to the end of the row. Fasten off C1.

Join C2 with 1slst to the start of the row just worked, make 1ch, and work 1dc in each stitch to the end of the row. Fasten off C2.

Cuff

The cuff is worked across both sleeve-band ends and the last row of the sleeve.

With RS facing and the 5.00mm crochet hook, attach M with 1slst to the corner of the first sleeve band.

Row 1: Make 1ch (counts as the first stitch), work 2htr across the sleeve-band row end, 1htr in each stitch of the sleeve by inserting the hook under each vertical strand in turn to pull up a loop for working each dc (to avoid holes) to the start of the second sleeve-band, 3htr across the sleeve-band row end, 2ch at the end of the row, and turn. [40sts]

Row 2: *Work 1RtrF in the next stitch, and 1RtrB in the following stitch; repeat from * to the end of the row, make 2ch, and turn.

Repeat Row 2 six times, omitting the turning chain at the end of the last row. Check that the raised trebles form continuous columns of stitches.

Fasten off.

Sleeve-to-body joins

Align the centre top of one sleeve to the centre of one armhole of the body. Using markers at the start, end and centre of the armhole and sleeve top, to ensure that the number of stitches on each side of the central armhole marker matches that on each side of the central sleeve-top marker. With markers or a length of yarn, anchor the sleeve head to the armhole prior to working the join.

With RS facing and the 6.00mm crochet hook, join C3 with 1slst to the endmost stitch of one side of the sleeve and corresponding stitch of the body, work 1dc into each stitch across the row by inserting the hook through both the sleeve stitch and the armhole stitch at each stitch position; do not turn the work at the end of the row. Check whether all of the stitches of both the armhole and sleeve top are anchored and that there are the same number of stitches for the armhole and sleeve top included in the join.

Place the last loop on to the 5.00mm crochet hook, and work crab stitch in each dc of the previous row to the end of the row. Fasten off.

Repeat this process for the second sleeve and other armhole.

Having joined both sleeves to the garment body, the coat is still a flat piece.

Side-and-sleeve seams

With the back positioned behind the fronts, fold the left sleeve in half from the sleeve head to the cuff, ensuring that the edges of the sleeve and corners of the cuff are properly aligned. The shoulder seam should not sit precisely at the top of the shoulder but slightly towards the back, for a better fit. Ensure that the edges and bottom corners of the Left Front and Back are properly aligned.

With RS facing and the 6.00mm crochet hook, attach C3 with 1slst to the bottom corner of the side of the Left Front, and work the left side seam by working 1dc through each pair of aligned stitches of the Left Front and Back in turn until reaching the start of the sleeve at the end of the underarm.

Continue joining the side seam on to the sleeve by working 1dc through each pair of aligned stitches or row ends of the left and right sides of the folded sleeve in turn, to completely join the sleeve sides from the underarm to the end of the cuff. If any bulk appears at the point where the sleeve and left side meet, it may be necessary to work a decrease prior to completing the join in order to remove the bulk, but ideally avoid this.

Still with RS facing, place the last loop on to the 5.00mm crochet hook, make 1ch, and work crab stitch to the end of the row (that is, along the entire length of the join). Fasten off.

Repeat this process to work the seam for the right sleeve and right side of the garment as follows.

Work the right side-and-sleeve seam as for the left sleeve-and-side seam, attaching C3 to the corner of the cuff, and working from the cuff to the bottom corner of the side of the Right Front.

Detail of the back neck band of the Colourful Textured Car Coat.

David showing the back of the Colourful Textured Car Coat.

CHAPTER 6

CONTINUING TUNISIAN CROCHET CREATIVELY

The previous chapters have provided many basic and advanced techniques in Tunisian crochet. Now, it is time to put all of these skills into practical use by combining them with other crafts. Tunisian crochet is ideal for colour blending, which allows pictorial work to be achieved, perhaps as a wall hanging, an art-to-wear garment or simply a cushion cover, with all of the colour-blending effect achieved from the start of the project. There is no limit to the creative possibilities of Tunisian crochet.

A base of Tunisian simple stitch can be a perfect foundation upon which to add a variety of other techniques. Methodical and logically minded people who prefer working to a plan will find that for projects worked with Tunisian simple stitch they can get creative with designs requiring the use of graph paper, charts and other calculations. With its regular square look on one side, Tunisian simple stitch offers many opportunities for planned designs, a base for cross-stitch embroidery being just one.

Not everyone enjoys working to plans and having to calculate prior to beginning a project, in which case an intuitive way of being creative will appeal. Surface crochet is one way to add a design to form a picture or motif. An overlayer of lace – be it crocheted or, alternatively, bought fabric lace – can work well over experimental pieces of heavily textured Tunisian in strong colours, to soften the final appearance. Tunisian offers the possibility of using multiple strands of differently coloured, thinner threads together to form one strand and working with it as for a single purchased yarn, which further increases Tunisian crochet's colour-blending possibilities. Blending colours in such a way is ideal for creating facsimiles of pictures.

Before explaining how to combine different crafts with Tunisian crochet, there are a couple of ways to use the stitch techniques already learned that could be beneficial. These are the use of different stitch heights within a piece and the use of an overlay. The overlay idea has multiple possibilities for use, one of which is to soften areas of colour, acting as a camouflage. An open net fabric can allow heavily embossed Tunisian fabrics containing irregular bobbles such as clusters, puff stitches, and so on, to poke through the lace as part of an overall design.

The secret is to have fun. Let your imagination run riot, and throw any preconceived ideas out of the window. If you have gone through the pages of this book in methodical order, you will have an enormous amount of technique ability and experience already, if you have tried all of the different ideas presented. You now have the opportunity to explore uncharted waters and find answers for projects so far not attempted!

OPPOSITE PAGE: This crop top worked with textured, space-dyed yarn demonstrates some of the techniques presented in this chapter and elsewhere in the book. The fabric could just as well be used as the basis for a picture or in combination with surface crochet.

Stitch Heights

The most obvious use of varying stitch height would be to use a taller Tunisian crochet stitch to create a diagonal slope on the edge of a piece of Tunisian crochet that requires shaping, for instance, to create the intended shape during decreasing or increasing at an armhole or neck edge. If a taller Tunisian crochet stitch is not used instead of the main stitch of the fabric, the stitch may be too short, causing the edge to pucker. Occasionally, in a creative piece of Tunisian crochet artwork, if an unexpected hole appears, the use of different stitch heights can mitigate or prevent this from happening when these different stitches are placed either in the same row or on the next row.

Ripple design

Varying the height of Tunisian crochet stitches to create repetitive patterns is fun to do, but it brings with it challenges that do not occur when varying stitch heights in ordinary crochet. Use of one such stitch pattern would be as a ripple design, when varying the stitch heights replaces other methods of making curves in Tunisian crochet. It is recommended that you try working the following trial piece to understand the intended anomaly occurring when introducing a variety of stitch heights within a fabric of Tunisian crochet.

Although one row of a contrast colour worked only with Tss should, in theory, produce a straight stripe, when worked between rows of another colour that include varying stitch heights, the contrast row has the illusion of creating ripples. The main colour, on the other hand, worked in the varying heights of Tunisian crochet stitches, forms a line of textured ovals or flattened wheels.

Trial piece of ripple design

With M, make a slip knot and place it on to a crochet hook of an appropriate size for the yarn, and make a length of chain stitches of a number that can be divided by 4 plus 1. Place the last chain on to a Tunisian crochet hook of an appropriate size for the yarn.

Row 1, Stage 1: Counting the loop on the hook as equivalent to 1Tss and by picking up 1 loop and placing on to the hook from under the top strand only of each chain in turn, *work 1Ttr, 1Tdtr, 1Ttr, and 1Tss; repeat from * to the end of the row.

Row 1, Stage 2: Remove all of the loops as for Tss, changing to using C to work off the last 2 loops on the hook.

Row 2: Work as for Tss, changing to using M to work off the last 2 loops of the row.

Row 3, Stage 1: Make 2ch (to lift the hook; equivalent to 1Tdtr) and, by working under the next vertical strand or into the next stitch, as necessary, in turn, *work 1Ttr, 1Tss, 1Ttr, and 1Tdtr; repeat from * to the end of the row.

Row 3, Stage 2: Remove all of the loops as for Tss, changing to using C to work off the last 2 loops on the hook.

Repeat Rows 2–3 until the fabric is of the desired length.

The ripple design, featuring different stitch heights, breaks up the usual stripe effect of two rows worked with different colours.

Free-Form Tunisian Crochet

Free-form crochet, whether traditional crochet or Tunisian crochet, is recognized as a way of creating attractive small pieces of textured crochet containing a variety of textured stitches that can eventually be placed together to form a complete article. These finished items can range from being brooches through to full-length coats.

It is rare to see this kind of crochet worked wholly with Tunisian, because Tunisian crochet stitches have to be completed in two stages. As it is necessary to have all of the loops placed on the hook prior to their removal, some of the directional changes typical of free-form crochet may be limited. However, it is an area that can be developed if it appeals to you, as it gives an opportunity to experiment and then still use any unsatisfactory experiments as part of a larger project. Follow Steps 1–6 given for free-form Tunisian crochet first, before putting together the resulting pieces.

Often at the Step 6 stage, there may be gaps in the fabric. Any trial pieces that fall short of what was initially required can be scrunched up to fill these gaps. This is particularly useful if the trial piece has been worked with a 4-ply yarn or finer, or, if a larger Tunisian crochet hook has been used when attempting a trial piece with DK-weight yarn. Utilizing any 'mistakes' (or as I call them 'happy accidents') can save time if there are spaces in a larger design, alleviating the need to crochet more Tunisian crochet pieces as fillers.

Steps to making free-form Tunisian crochet

Many of the trial pieces presented throughout this book contain regularly spaced texture and could be used as a fabric base for exploring this technique, but remember that true free-form crochet has no such uniformity. Removing the regularity of repeating stitch patterns is the start of making a piece of free-form crochet in Tunisian.

Step 1: Make a piece of Tunisian crochet containing texture, embossed stitches and stitch patterns, added randomly.

Step 2: Having mastered how to be free with the introduction of texture, move on to playing with small patches of colour. Do this by working only a few stitches over a few rows with one colour. Then, attach another colour by linking it to the side of the small amount of Tunisian crochet just worked, continuing at a 90-degree angle to that of the crochet worked so far or going in the same stitching direction, and link to the sides of the existing rows as the fabric grows.

Step 3: Continue to work as for Steps 1–2, but make the fabric adopt an irregular shape.

Step 4: Produce a number of these free-form Tunisian crochet pieces, making sure they are kept small.

Step 5: On a large surface, spread out all of the pieces of free-form Tunisian crochet made. Stand back to observe them, and see whether they are forming a pattern that represents some part of a component of your life. Aspects of nature or the elements often spring to mind.

Step 6: Arrange these pieces in a pleasing way, bearing in mind any design theme that came to mind from Step 5, and pin them to a disused pillowcase, or to a sheet if you have made a large number of free-form pieces.

Step 7: Connect the pieces together by sewing or with crochet, to form a complete whole.

Although the end result might be a picture, free-form crochet is a technique in itself and should not be confused with making a picture.

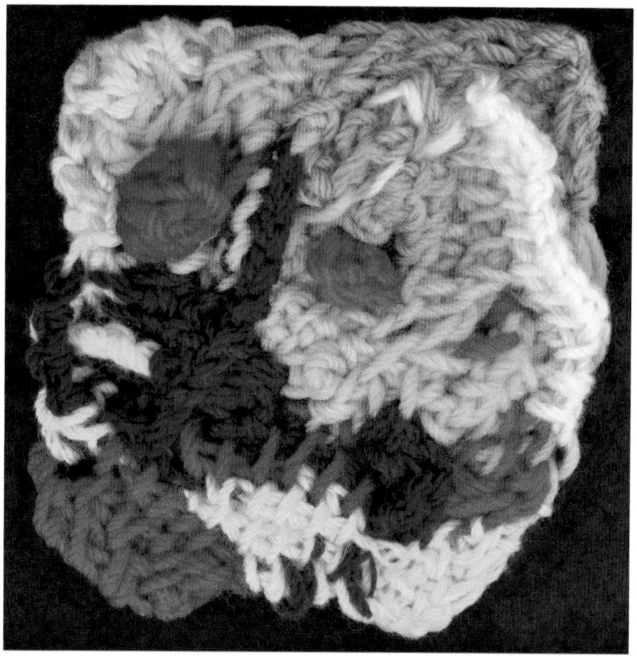

An example of free-form Tunisian crochet, made by use of whatever colour, stitch or technique desired whilst producing the fabric. An overlay can soften the colours.

An example of free-form traditional crochet and Tunisian crochet within a large ring. Remember that any technique can be combined to fill a ring with free-form-style crochet.

Making a Picture

Preparation before any crocheting takes place

Whether you plan on producing an abstract picture or a facsimile of a photograph or a printed picture in a magazine, it is the preparation and planning that will make it a success. The first thing required is a shallow, flat box into which you can place your yarns. Often the lid of a box will suffice, but it is essential that you can see *all* of the yarns placed into it, including any tiny balls. Any leftover scraps of yarn that may be required can be placed in a see-through bag or container, rather than being left loose where they can get tangled. A wire tray can be used as an alternative, but line it with some form of white paper, to prevent the smaller pieces of yarn from falling through.

It can take many days or even weeks to find exactly the right yarns, in the right colour and texture needed, for a small but vital portion of the picture. It is essential to achieve this part of the procedure first, even though a particular yarn can often be elusive. Unless the missing yarn is a critical portion of the picture that needs to be included during the early stage of the crochet, the production of the picture can begin whilst you are still searching. However, be sure that you know you can get what you need before you begin, or all of your work up to the point of needing this yarn could be wasted.

When all the yarns are visibly put together, it should be obvious that they will require different hook sizes to be used in order to crochet them as desired. Therefore, in another clear container, place the hooks that you think will be in demand, plus any small additional items such as stitch markers, a tape measure and scissors. If the design needs to include buttons and beads, these also have to be added to the container, in readiness. There is nothing more off-putting than, having got partway through a project, being unable to find that one item you know is around 'somewhere'. That item can be what prevents the project from ever getting finished.

Although everything is visible, it is highly recommended that you make a note of why you have chosen each yarn, along with a suggestion as to where it would be used in the picture. Similarly, any buttons or beads included in the second container should have a reference to where they are thought to be needed. The hook choices may be straightforward; however, as the picture is being planned, ideas of using a smaller or larger hook for a particular yarn or area within the picture might occur, and these need to be added to your notes.

General information for constructing a picture

The example being presented is a pillow, which means that the fabric does not have to hang – it simply has to be dense enough to have the padding inserted without the colour of the padding showing through. Where there are intended open sections of crochet, the padding needs to be covered with a fabric that enhances the picture design and does not detract from it.

A hanging picture may need to be placed on to a secure backing such as iron-on tailor's or dressmaker's fabric. If the picture is to be hung in a damp place, the connection of the backing to the picture may need some reinforcing with one or two sewn catch stitches. It is also possible to have the finished piece framed.

Art-to-wear garments and unsupported hangings demand that the following guidelines be followed, if the project is to avoid being distorted by gravity over time. Tunisian crochet is less likely to distort as quickly as classic crochet, but nevertheless over a period of time distortion can still occur.

- A sky needs to look light and ethereal, but the physical weight of the yarn used needs to be heavy.
- Unless a three-dimensional object is to be included, the sky should be smooth and flat.
- Combine a fluffy mohair, angora, or brushed acrylic, which are light in weight, with a heavier smooth yarn. This gives the appearance of lightness and might even be selected for some cloud imagery.
- Smaller quantities of a colour give the illusion of being somewhere in the distance.
- Work more than one yarn together at a time to give additional support, and this approach is also perfect for blending and merging colours. Employing Tunisian tweed stitch, along with using more than one colour at a time, is what makes Tunisian perfect for presenting all kinds of illusions and likenesses to a memory or a photograph.
- A single colour of a dark yarn will appear heavier than its physical weight, but will sustain a lightweight yarn added as surface crochet.
- The use of heavily textured yarn as the base of a picture reduces the amount of surface crochet that later needs to be added. Also, heavily textured yarns are often light in physical weight, which is essential if the base of the garment or hanging is not to drag down the upper area and distort the shape of the picture.

Crocheting the picture

When a picture is being worked with Tunisian crochet, there is less freedom for producing a facsimile than if it were to be created using classic-crochet techniques. The rectangular pillow selected as an example allows the range of possibilities and techniques that Tunisian offers, giving an opportunity to explore and increase your practical skills. Inevitably, the steps given in the following procedure for making the pillow cover are only one way of achieving the end result; any art form relies on the intuition of the creator; therefore, these steps as given for the pillow are purely guidelines. If you are a total beginner with this area of crochet, then guidelines can be good for aiding a first attempt.

Taking the picture on the pillow as an illustration of how to achieve any desired imagery, note that for practical purposes the pillow itself needed to be wider than the working section being explained, to allow it to be able to contain the inner pad, but the pillow itself is not taller than the crocheted fabric. The dominating factor for its size was its eventual resting place, which is on a bed, to add colour to a bedroom.

This picture is inspired by nature. The scene is a tidal coastline of rocks and pebbles that blends sea and sky in the distance. The vegetation survives the few times in the year that the high tides wash over it.

Procedure

Step 1: Have a clear idea of what you are attempting to produce. It can be inspiration from a photo, a postcard or something that is in your mind's eye. If the latter, put as much as you can of the picture that your mind can see on to paper. Do this before the image disappears, because the memory is a fickle thing.

Step 2: Know where the completed item will be displayed.

Step 3: Have the collection of intended yarns, hooks and materials ready for use.

Step 4: Make a template of the exact size of the finished picture with either paper or fabric. There does not need to be any markings on it, but it essential that you have this size template to drop your work on to as it progresses. For an art-to-wear garment, this template can be for just a section of the finished piece.

Step 5: The picture can be worked in any direction, from left to right, right to left, top to bottom or bottom to top. Because the picture is being made with Tunisian crochet, it is advisable not to complicate the direction of work. Let the variety of yarns and colours make the difference to the complexity and movement of the design.

Step 6: If a border of any depth is to later be added to the picture as a frame, fold (or pin) your size template to reflect the depth of the eventual border.

Step 7: The featured pillow was worked from bottom to top. With a hook large enough to be able to accommodate the thicker textured yarn. Use a large crochet hook to make a length of chain stitches the whole width of the pillow.

Step 8: With a heavily textured yarn, the whole length of chain was used for working a row of Tss. This was the only time that the whole of Stage 1 of a row was worked with one yarn.

Step 9: Removing the loops of this first row required four or five different textured yarns to be added, to represent the foam of the sea water, soil and pebbles, ending with a yarn that would be included for a pool of water. After working every few stitches, the original textured yarn would be used, so that it could reach the place where the pool of water would be made.

Step 10: Using three thin yarns held together as one yarn, to represent the colour of a pool of water, the remaining loops were removed. Work continued with this mixture of threads, to pick up loops over the ones removed with this colour, plus two more loops beyond the edge of the water area, and the mixture of yarns no longer in use were left in place along the row, in readiness for working Stage 2.

Step 11: Returning to the original yarn, loops were picked up in irregular numbers, using all of the other attached yarns to pick up loops throughout the rest of the row. This approach prevents any regular colour blocks from forming and at the same time stabilizes the stitches of all of the different yarns in use.

The finished picture pillow.

Step 12: Because all the other yarns were then securely attached to the fabric, it was possible to remove all of the loops of yarn on the hook with the original yarn, until the water area was reached again. The water yarns were kept attached to the work but unworked. Ideally, place the remainder of any still-attached yarns in a clear ziplock bag or small container, so that they stay together and do not slide around or get caught into the rest of the design.

Step 13: A major advantage of working Tunisian crochet with a single-ended hook is that the work is not turned, thus eliminating the occurrence of large amounts of yarn getting tangled and knotted. Having put the remainder of the water yarns somewhere safe, it was possible to focus on making the next area of the picture requiring similar techniques and yarns. In this instance, partial rows were worked, mixing whatever coloured and textured yarns previously selected as necessary. Working something similar to the pillow, this would be done over the next 5 or 6 rows requiring completion.

Step 14: After completing the sixth row, it was necessary to work in partial rows to achieve the emergence of the rough triangle shape that is present at the left of the picture.

Step 15: Flowers, shells and other crocheted embossed elements could be worked at the same time as the main part of the fabric design, using the technique given for bobbles worked over 2 or 3 rows, covered in Chapter 5 (in particular, *see* the section 'Monochromatic textured patterns').

Step 16: Before introducing the yarn for the flat area of red sandstone beyond the rocks, the yarns for the pool of water were returned to. The area was completed by allowing just one or two stitches to be worked with each yarn, incorporating each colour and yarn, to avoid the appearance of straight edges. Nature is rarely made up of straight architectural lines but, as in all things, even nature can break this rule, as in the Giant's Causeway in Northern Ireland.

Step 17: The red-sandstone area was worked with no harsh red patches. For all of the stitches made with the red yarn, either the red yarn was worked together with another yarn or the stitches were blended with neighbouring ones worked with totally different yarns. Some deep blue was added, to give the impression of deeper pools of water.

Step 18: The rocky area gives the impression of both a sturdy plant growing from it and, with the addition of a lighter strand of yarn to some of the stitches, that fronds emerging from the sea are growing there. The sturdy plant was made with surface crochet (as covered in the next section), and its position, plus those of all other areas of surface crochet, was marked in advance with a stitch marker once sufficient fabric had been worked to form the area that the surface crochet was to sit upon. The fernlike fronds were made with long Tunisian stitches or lengths of chain stitches. In this instance, the yarn was one containing tufts of fibres trapped in the plying process and giving the appearance of budding or small leaves.

Step 19: The work was continued by incorporating the stitches of the dry sand and darker land mass prior to its merging into the sea area. It is most important that neither the sea area nor the sky have a single-colour appearance. Two space-dyed yarns, each with a short colour change, worked together as one, were integrated into the fabric to produce the effect required. Often the combination of a thin, smooth yarn and a softly spun, puffier yarn works well. If one of the yarns has been dyed in a closely matching and appropriate colour range and is combined with a short-length space-dyed yarn, the two yarns used together can produce an excellent illusion of a sky.

Step 20: Once the intended size of the piece had been reached, it was time to add any extra materials. For this pillow, the trunk of the tree was worked with surface crochet. A very-long-haired mohair was added for balance throughout the composition. It is arguable that this could be seen as a sea urchin, say, or a cloud, so what is at the top of this branch will depend on the particular observer.

Step 21: Finally, the picture was edged all round with double crochet worked with an earthy colour. A light border would give the impression of the piece still being unfinished, whilst the darker colours are making a statement of its completion. As this fabric was for a pillow, the second round of stitches was applied once the back of the pillow had been attached.

Surface Crochet

A similar result to that of free-form crochet can be obtained by working surface crochet. To be pedantic, this could be placed in the section 'Combining crafts', as it fuses classic crochet with Tunisian crochet. Surface crochet is a term used when crocheting into a base that need not be one that has been crocheted. Any kind of material into which a hook can be inserted can be used for the working of surface crochet.

Tunisian crochet, particularly Tunisian simple stitch, provides an excellent base for surface crochet. The surface crochet that was incorporated into the picture pillow of the previous section was achieved by having the yarn underneath the picture fabric and the hook being inserted through the fabric from the top. A selection of closely worked chains consisting of different yarns were worked closely together lying side by side to gave the desired result. However, surface crochet is normally used to enable many forms of embossed embellishment to be formed.

Having made a background of Tunisian simple stitch, all manner of stitch patterns can be added to produce the three-dimensional effect needed. Although where to put the stitch patterns is up to the designer, it is possible to illustrate how to introduce surface-crochet worked on to a Tunisian crochet background. Obviously, both the project and the embellishment must belong to the creator of the article being made.

Surface crochet is achieved by using a standard crochet hook. The size needs to be small enough to be inserted into the work but at the same time large enough to accommodate the yarn being used in the hook head. It is advisable to try the yarn, hook and stitches to be used on an inconspicuous area of the background, prior to inserting the hook into the central focus of the fabric. The aim is to produce a neat finished design of crochet excellence. If the first attempts are not satisfactory, this is normally because there are plucked threads and distorted stitches on the most important part of the Tunisian background.

Depending upon your design, it may not be possible to work more that a small amount of surface crochet at a time. Because of the yarn being on top of the work, it is necessary to finish off the yarn for each small section before starting to work in another place. Otherwise, the surface of the picture becomes cluttered in an undesirable way with the planned design gets lost and mistakes are likely to happen.

Occasionally, say, when working a bunch of flowers, it may be possible to carry the yarn in use in the direction of the stem of another flower. Make sure that the yarn lies across

The hook has been inserted into the Tunisian fabric to collect the yarn, to start a new area of surface crochet.

Pull both strands of the surface-crochet yarn through the loop just made to firmly secure the yarn in place.

Having worked two chains to lift the hook above the surface of the fabric sufficiently to work surface crochet, work one treble in the same place.

Add three more trebles, to be ready to shape the stitches into a small popcorn, or leave the stitches ungathered, to be laid flat against the fabric's surface.

Having first inserted the hook into the starting chain, collect the unattached loop at the end of the group of stitches.

Pull the loop through the top of the starting chain to join the stitches into a small open-ended ball.

the surface of the fabric in the direction the stem needs to go, for it to look natural. It then becomes possible to anchor a thin strand of the yarn by working over it with another yarn or colour. Alternatively, finish the yarn in use, pulling the end through to the back of the fabric, to be secured later, and start afresh with a new yarn where needed.

As mentioned in the information of the 'Making a picture' section, it is advisable to place a marker where each area of surface crochet is to be worked. A good idea is to attach a tiny piece of the selected yarn for working the surface crochet to the marker, in order to jog the memory when reaching that area at a later date.

Once the surface crochet worked with a particular yarn has been finished, pull both the short starting end and the newly cut finished end through to the back of the work. Start each section of surface crochet by inserting the hook under two strands of the Tunisian fabric, to give it a secure base. More importantly, using these two strands rather than one to secure the yarn helps prevent the Tunisian background from becoming distorted.

Because of the frequent starting and finishing of yarn to produce the desired surface-crochet effects, it is recommended that the first chain is worked with the short end of the yarn as well as the yarn coming from the ball, as demonstrated in the accompanying images.

Even though it is essential for the surface-crochet design to lie flat on the background fabric when completed, without distorting it, it is normally better to fold the Tunisian fabric near the place where the surface crochet is going to be added. Treat the fold as though it is the top edge of a line of crochet, inserting the hook into the fabric in the same way that the hook would be inserted into each stitch of a row of double crochet.

Surface-crochet popcorns can be formed for representing a wide number of items. For instance, as the hook is inserted under the same stitches of the background every time, when many stitches are joined together, they form cups. These can be made with a different number of stitches, from three or four, to represent the buds of a flower, or, with many more stitches, to simulate moon craters, open flowers, and so on. The stitches do not all have to be made to the same height; varying stitch heights give the edge of the popcorn a natural look. When the popcorns are produced to create cup-like containers, they are suitable to hold beads, small gems and polished stones.

The same principle can be adopted without the top of the stitches being brought together and closed, as for a completed popcorn. This allows the mini-motif of surface-crochet stitches to be made to lie flat against the background fabric, covering a larger area and achieving a different effect. This idea is suitable for depicting seascapes, especially those representing the observer peering through water and looking at a variety of shells and pebbles. Also, if the stitches are not closed into traditional popcorns, they can be useful in representing the petals of a flower, along with a crochet or purchased bead placed in the centre to represent the pollen at the flower centre.

In the example on page 134, included to demonstrate the method of working surface crochet, a small popcorn is made to form a bud-like knob.

Having attached the yarn to the background where the popcorn is to be made, work 2ch to give height to the following stitches, and work 4tr in the same place on the fabric. Without joining these stitches into a popcorn, the collection of stitches can be encouraged to lie flat on the background, to form a wedge shape or fan.

To form these stitches into a cup shape, remove the hook from the last loop made, being careful to ensure that the stitches do not come undone. Insert the hook into the top of the 2ch made at the start of the group of stitches and also through the loop that is now loose at the end of the group of stitches. Pull this loose loop through the top of the foundation chain, to join the stitches of the group together, so that they form a small open-ended ball.

This little three-dimensional knob can stand alone, to give detail and height to a particular part of the picture. It can form the centre of a large flower, when petal shapes are worked around it. These petal shapes can be made to lie flat, so that the centre stands proud. Alternatively the petals themselves can be anchored only on the edge near the popcorn knob. Another use for this little decoration would be as a fastener on a garment: one little knob can be worked near the edge of a garment on each side, with a figure-of-eight-shaped chain added to link them into a fastener.

Even though the same yarn used to close the little popcorn might still be needed nearby for working more surface-crochet, the yarn will have to be cut first and the ends involved with the popcorn be completely secured before the yarn can continue to be used. The yarn cannot be carried over the surface to the next place where stitches need to be made, otherwise the intended design and effect produced will be altered. Neither can a large loop be carried across the back of the Tunisian crochet fabric being used as a base, because that could get trapped by other carrying threads and later prevent the base from lying flat.

The tiny popcorn currently stands alone, ready to be incorporated into a surface-crochet section of the design.

An example of how three-dimensional knobs of surface-crochet stitches can be effectively used with a loop of chain stitches to form a fastener.

Notice how the working yarn is being directly worked into the surface crochet that has already been formed.

To break up a patch of surface crochet that was too dominant, the same yarn as used for the nearby little popcorn was selected, to give harmony to this area of the design.

A crab-stitch edging is being added to an area of already worked surface crochet, for an interesting addition of detail.

Reattach the yarn to the Tunisian crochet background by picking up two, or more, strands of the background fabric, as shown.

Anchor the same yarn to the point where it is needed for working further surface crochet. In this instance, the yarn is being added to give shadow and depth to some surface crochet that has already been worked. The hoop of chain stitches was made in readiness to enable another yarn to be worked into it at a later stage. Just as making a picture with Tunisian crochet requires planning, the same amount of planning is required when embellishing with surface crochet if the intended result is to be achieved without undue stress.

One of the joys of working surface crochet is that it can be added later. What is already worked directly into the background can be crocheted over, to add more depth, colour or detail. Occasionally, the colour may stand out too harshly, but then, with another colour and thinner yarn, it can be softened. Similarly, if a continuous line of crocheted stitches seems to be too long, it can be broken up by using another colour and yarn to change it. Be aware of adding too many yarns, or too much colour, because this can distract the eye and take away from the effect being aimed for.

Sometimes, it may be sensible to continue to work with the same yarn, allowing it to bring different areas of the design together. Having already used a yarn for the little popcorn to add depth and shadow to the design, it has been used again to break up a length of surface crochet that had begun to obscure the reason for it being there in the first place. In this instance, the changes are focusing on the surface crochet closest to the original popcorn. Knowing in advance that just a little bit further along the background this particular yarn is going to be required, it may be possible to carry it along on the surface as part of the design. Here, crab stitch was ideal for working along the edge of a large, open motif, allowing the yarn to be in place ready for the next addition needing to be worked directly into the Tunisian crochet background.

Having reached the place where a group of leaves are intended to be worked directly into the Tunisian crochet background, the hook is first inserted through the Tunisian stitches to pick up at least two strands of the background, to attach the yarn securely. Once the yarn is firmly anchored into the Tunisian crochet background, two chains and three unfinished trebles are made in the same place; these are then pulled together as a treble cluster, to form the shape of a leaf. The hook is again inserted into the Tunisian crochet background to attach the completed leaf, before being moved on to the next design area.

If more leaves are to be added in the same place, it is possible to link the yarn from the tip of the leaf just made, behind the bulk of this leaf, to be attached again into the background fabric, thus allowing another leaf to be worked from the same starting place.

For surface crochet, the yarn is worked on top of the background fabric, and the hook is also used above the surface of this fabric. However, it is also possible to work a fine line of thin chains attached to the surface of the background fabric, to form an outline. This technique requires the yarn to be held under the background fabric and the crochet hook being worked from above. To achieve this effect, insert the hook from above the background fabric at the point where the start of the chain needs to be made. Collect the yarn from underneath the background fabric (having first cut and relocated the working yarn, as necessary), and pull through a loop of yarn to lie on top of the fabric. With the hook still holding this loop, reinsert the hook into the fabric from above, a short distance away from where the hook was first inserted, and again pull through a loop of yarn to the front of the work and also through the loop still on the hook. Continue in this manner to work additional chains, until the desired chain length is reached. Depending on the design, the chains can be short and wide and therefore close together or be stretched and long, to make a narrower chain. As always, to achieve a good result it is necessary to choose the technique that is right for the design. If the length of each chain is too long, the line of the chain can look untidy, whereas, if the length of each chain is too short, the line of the chain could become too thick and dense.

Surface crochet can be off-putting for some people, but perhaps trying to add a little to a small item or gift could be one way to gain confidence in the process before moving on to larger projects and applications.

Once secure, the yarn is used to make a three-treble cluster in the same place on the background fabric.

First making sure that the leaf is lying flat, as desired, attach it to the background fabric.

A Tunisian crochet pouch decorated with a little bit of surface crochet makes it unique. '

Combining Crafts

Hard-material crafts

Items made of hard materials such as leather, wood, ceramics and metal can all incorporate Tunisian crochet, as explored in the following sections with suggestions of possible applications. All that is required is a series of holes into which to insert the classic crochet hook, to enable a row of double crochet to be made. The double-crochet stitches act as a foundation chain from which to work Tunisian crochet. The articles that can include Tunisian crochet in this way are endless.

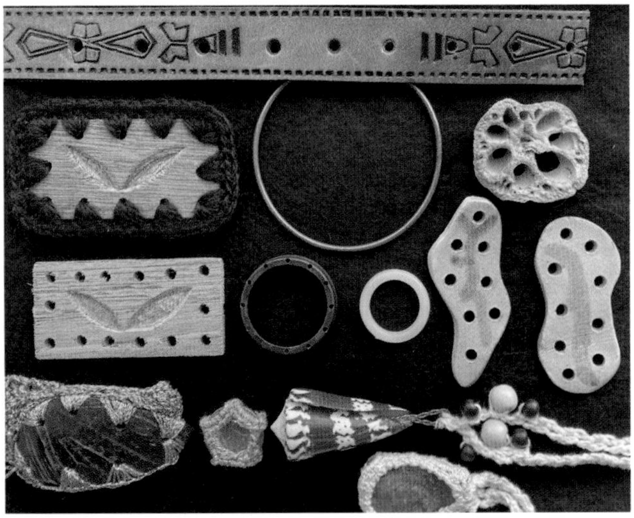

A selection of hard materials that can be used in combination with Tunisian crochet. Top to bottom: (left) tooled leather with holes, wooden pieces with holes and with and without edgings, coconut shell with drilled holes and an already added edging; (middle) three types of metal and plastic rings, crochet-covered coin, shell and beads in combination with thread, pebble; (right) seed casing with natural holes, ceramic tiles fired with holes in place. The holes present in hard materials can be used for first adding traditional-crochet stitches from which Tunisian crochet can be worked.

Leather

There are many possibilities for combining Tunisian crochet with leather.

- A strip of stiff leather, whether left plain or decoratively tooled, can have one side punched to be used as a waistband. Once a row of double crochet has been added to the holed side of the leather, Tunisian crochet can be worked to form either a top or as a skirt, depending on which side of the waistband features the punched holes.
- Soft leather can be used for the palms of gloves, with the backs worked in Tunisian crochet.
- Strips of flat leather, often to be found in do-it-yourself shops, can be used as an alternative to cord. They can be plaited to make the handle of a Tunisian crochet tote bag, or a classic crochet hook can be inserted between the plaited strands to make the necessary row of double crochet from which to work a Tunisian crochet design.
- Reels of narrow, rounded leather can be purchased in many different colours and worked as a 4-ply knitting yarn. This material works well for the production of a Tunisian fabric, but beware: it is less accommodating than yarn made with a fibre.
- Any kind of leather can be utilized to make a unique frame for a Tunisian crochet picture.

I am sure that you can think of many more ways to combine leather and Tunisian crochet!

Wood

Wood is another hard material that can be combined with Tunisian crochet. As for leather, it also has the possibility to be pliable.

- Tunisian crochet pictures can be framed with pieces of wood.
- Wooden chairs with drop-in seats are perfect to cover with Tunisian crochet. Use a smaller crochet hook and a yarn that is heavily twisted and hard-wearing such as a crepe yarn. If you have a set of chairs, there is the option of using the same colours of yarn for all four chair seats but using a different stitch pattern for each one.
- Thin sheets of wood can have a motif cut out to be used as a stencil or overlay for a background of Tunisian crochet.
- The bark of some trees can be peeled into thin strips, like the strands that peel off a stick of rhubarb. Tunisian can be worked with a large hook and with a hard-wearing yarn. Once the loops are on the hook, a strip can be threaded through, getting trapped as the loops are removed.
- When strips of thin wood are soaked and softened, they can be used as a yarn in the same way that bamboo and cane made from natural materials are used for soft furnishing, such as cane seating. This time, however, the thin strips could be used for crochet.

Raffia and other natural materials fit into this selection of hard-material crafts.

Ceramics

Believe it or not, ceramics and Tunisian crochet work well together. If you are a potter or have a friend who is, you have a wonderful opportunity to design small pieces of ceramics such as tiles, which need to be glazed and fired, having first added holes to allow a crochet hook to be inserted later.

- Small rectangles of thicker pottery can be linked together to form a belt or waistband, similar to that described in the leather section.
- Plain square ceramic tiles can have Tunisian crochet added as a border or to cover the upper or lower side. Once the Tunisian crochet is added, the tile can be used as a coaster. The side with the Tunisian crochet can be at the back of the tile, to stop a highly polished table from getting scratched, or on the top, to prevent a cup from slipping.
- A larger tile can be made as a table centre, to go with coordinating coasters.
- Ceramic and glass beads are ideal to be added to the base of a Tunisian crochet hanging, to keep the fabric taut.
- Handmade and fired ceramic shapes can be incorporated into a Tunisian crochet picture.

Metal

Uses for metal combined with Tunisian crochet are possibly easier to envisage.

- Buckles can be purchased and added to a piece of Tunisian crochet, as a fastener, for example, a Tunisian belt.
- Tunisian can be worked inside a metal ring. These can be purchased from a very small size, where only thread and a fine Tunisian crochet hook would work, or one as large as fifty centimetres in diameter or larger. The smaller rings are useful for embellishment or even for use as buttons.
- A picture worked inside a large ring has no restrictions other than the background of its resting place. Whether it is to hang in a window, or against a coloured wall, the position of the finished picture needs to be taken into account at the onset. Work what is to go inside the ring first, ensuring that the picture is really tight within the ring. Any moisture in the air will make the fabric heavier and could therefore distort the picture over time. Cover the ring with double-crochet stitches worked with a complementary yarn, or bind it with ribbon, prior to securing the Tunisian crochet picture to the ring.
- Metal frames for handbags and purses can be purchased, to which Tunisian crochet fabric can be attached.

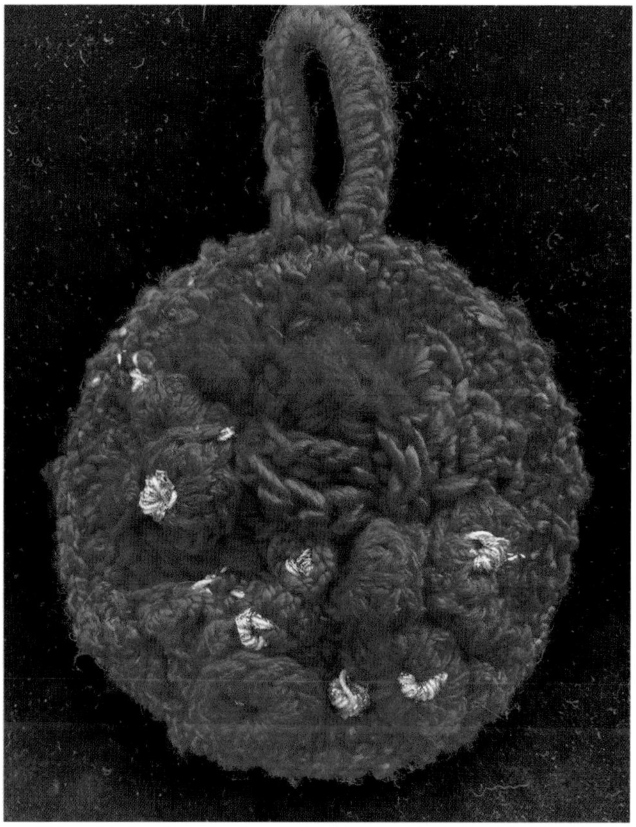

An example of free-form traditional crochet and Tunisian crochet within a small ring. Remember that any technique can be combined to fill a ring with free-form-style crochet.

A selection of soft materials that can be used in combination with Tunisian crochet. Top (left to right): mohair fabric, canvas, checked-pattern fabric (insert the hook under the lines of white threads), felt, lace; bottom (left to right) muslin; open-weave fabric.

- Clasps for jewellery can also be obtained, and, with fine Tunisian crochet hooks and jewellery wire, a Tunisian crochet decoration can be made. For those with nimble fingers, pieces of costume jewellery featuring lurex or jewellery wire worked with Tunisian crochet and finished with metal clasps allow exploration of yet another branch of Tunisian.

Soft-material crafts

Crafts worked with soft materials include crochet, knitting, cross-stitch embroidery, dressmaking/tailoring, patchwork, felting, lace-making, tatting, macramé, and many more. It is impossible to cover every one of these in detail, even though Tunisian can be combined with them all. The most popular soft crafts are listed below, along with ideas and suggestions on how to fuse the two crafts.

Crochet

Crochet worked with a short, traditional hook has, of necessity, been covered previously. However, it makes sense to list some ideas where a section of Tunisian crochet is attractively combined with the classic form of crochet.

- A yoke of Tunisian can hold together an open, even lacy, crochet addition for the bodice of a dress. This is an attractive idea for a special-occasion baby dress, to prevent food and saliva falling through the design. A crochet yoke worked in Tunisian is also easier to wipe clean.
- Rectangular panels of Tunisian crochet can be shaped with classic crochet insertions. Crochet is not restricted by having more loops on the hook than the one that is being worked in the process, thus making it easier to adjust and shape.
- Broomstick crochet is worked on a large knitting needle to produce rows of large holes. Interspersing rows of broomstick crochet with narrow bands of Tunisian crochet is a simple matter, because both techniques require having all of the loops on the hook (or needle) during one step of the process of making one complete row. The result is quite stunning and can be used for garments and accessories, as well as for a range of soft furnishings, such as curtains, bed coverings, pillows, throws and knee rugs.
- The loops on each side of a length of hairpin crochet can connect to Tunisian crochet in a similar way as that of broomstick crochet that has Tunisian added. This can be achieved by sliding a Tunisian crochet hook through the loops on one side of the hairpin strip, then connecting the yarn at the end of the strip and removing the loops that are now on the Tunisian crochet hook as for working Tss.
- Over a heavily embossed Tunisian crochet background, an overlay of open crochet worked with a classic crochet hook is easier to manipulate than attempting to produce such an overlay with Tunisian lace. An overlay fabric of open crochet is ideal to use when:
  - camouflaging colours that are clashing within a Tunisian base fabric,
  - allowing interesting bobble stitches of various types to poke through the lacy overlay as a design feature,
  - to give an illusion of three dimensions, for example, for a picture.

Knitting

Classic or traditional crochet is successfully added to knitting for embellishment and to replace the buttonhole band and button band of a knitted garment. However, this does not work so well for Tunisian crochet, as the fabric has a tendency to not lie flat. Therefore it is only occasionally that it would be advantageous to combine Tunisian crochet with knitting. However, for those who have not mastered the art of knitting but like a particular knitting pattern, it is possible to achieve a facsimile of a knitting pattern by following these steps.

1. Use an equivalent yarn as that recommended in the pattern, i.e. of the same yarn weight and fibre type.
2. Select a Tunisian crochet hook that is double that of the knitting-needle size recommended in the pattern.
3. Photocopy the pattern, if you can, so that you can mark on the copy and keep the original pattern fresh, to be referred to as necessary at a later date.
4. Select the relevant size to be worked. If the grading of the sizes is in sequence (for example, 12, 14, 16, 18, and so on), choose one size larger than you would usually select. However, if the sizes are given as small, medium, large, and so on, work the size that you would normally select.

5. Where possible, work the two fronts and the back as one piece, to avoid seaming the pieces.
6. Halve the number of stitches given for the cast on row and follow the pattern following the points below.
7. The number of rows should also be halved, so be very careful when working out any pattern repeats.
8. Check whether the armhole will be deep enough and, if necessary, add one or two repeats of relevant parts of the instructions, to achieve the necessary depth.
9. Before joining any seams, check whether the neck requires any adjusting.
10. Finish the item as described in the knitting pattern, for example, by using a classic crochet hook for working the cuffs and borders.

Dressmaking and tailoring

Although it is possible to replace any one piece of the paper patterns used in dressmaking and tailoring, the pattern pieces usually contain detailed shaping. Detailed shaping for Tunisian crochet is challenging, and it is therefore often better to add Tunisian crochet as an embellishment rather than combine it as part of a garment made with dressmaking or tailoring techniques until you feel confident and skilled with shaping.

Cross-stitch embroidery

The beauty of Tunisian simple stitch is the uniformity of the little squares that are present on the smooth surface of the fabric. These little squares can be used as one uses canvas. Although cross-stitch embroidery can be worked on almost any material, Tunisian simple stitch is a perfect background on which to add colour using sewn cross-stitches.

The Tunisian simple stitch can be worked in a single colour, as for the following Baby Blanket, or in different colours, as shown with the featured cushion. For the cushion, a paisley motif was added to break up some of the blocks of colour present, to balance the colours used throughout the cushion and prevent a patchwork appearance from emerging. By using the colours from the other sections of the cushion for the paisley cross-stitch being worked on the white squares, there is cohesion and harmony, linking together the colours across the different areas of the cushion. The neutral grey columns separating the larger patches of colour provide the stillness necessary when working with strong colours.

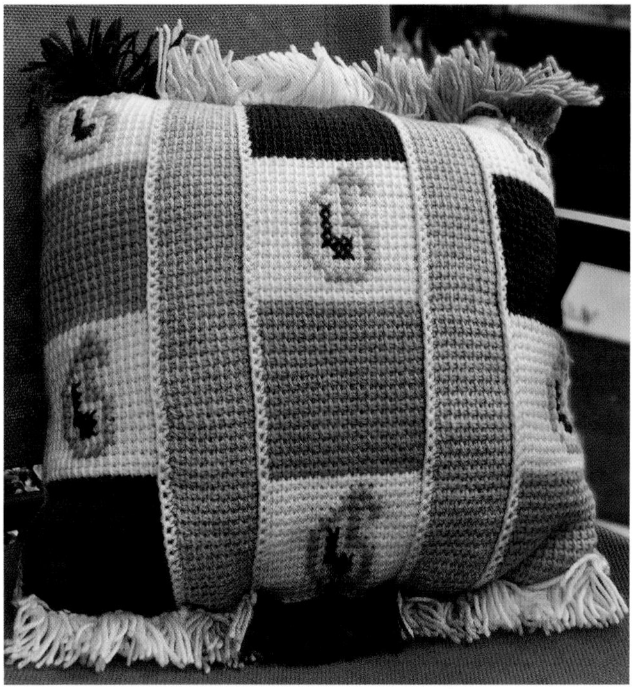

This cushion features paisley motifs that are worked with cross-stitch embroidery on a background of Tunisian simple stitch.

The colour of the Baby Blanket comes only from the embroidered cross-stitches and the addition of a multicoloured eyelash yarn for the inner band that is worked with surface crochet. The seven differently coloured balloons, corresponding to each of the colour bands in a rainbow, and a cheerful clown form the overall sewn cross-stitch design. Any colour added to the background would have detracted from the desired effect.

Cross-stitch embroidery on a background of Tunisian simple stitch can be worked in two ways. Both the paisley motif and the baby-blanket design are worked in the traditionally accepted manner, to allow unbroken blocks of colour to form. However, cross-stitch embroidery on a background of Tunisian simple stitch can be produced to introduce shadows. The techniques for working both methods are given, as the shadow technique works well on pictures featuring any imagery of nature as seen through a mist.

Classic cross-stitch

Select a large-eyed blunt sewing needle, such as one of those used for knitting and tapestry embroidery. Have the yarn to be used ready, along with a sharp and pointed pair of scissors.

Inserting the needle at the right-hand side of the squares allows the cross-stitch yarn to cover the vertical strand of the Tunisian simple stitch.

At this stage of working the cross-stitch, the same points of the squares are ready to be used again to complete the row of cross-stitches.

In the process of completing the row of cross-stitches.

Step 1: Insert the needle, threaded with the chosen yarn, from the back of the work through the bottom right-hand corner of the first Tss square to be covered with a cross-stitch.
Step 2: Draw the yarn to the front of the work, leaving enough of a yarn end at the back of the work to be secured later.
Step 3: From the front of the work, insert the needle from the top right-hand corner of the adjacent square on the left under the two horizontal strands that form the equals sign of this stitch, formed during Stage 2 of working Tss, and bring the needle out at the bottom right-hand corner of the same square, as shown. This takes the yarn over the vertical strand that is characteristic of Tunisian simple stitch.
Step 4: Repeat this process, working across the row from right to left, until the last square of the row to be worked and covered by a cross-stitch has been reached. It is important to work all of the squares with this one half of the cross-stitch first, before working the second half, in order to maintain an even and unified finish for the stitches.
Step 5: The second halves of the cross-stitches can now be worked. Return to the start of the row of cross-stitches by inserting the sewing needle from the top right-hand corner of the current square under the two horizontal strands of the equals sign and bringing the needle out at the bottom right-hand corner of the same square, which is essentially utilizing the same points of making the stitch as before. This will complete the first cross and again cover the same vertical strand of the Tss as covered by the first half of the cross.
Step 6: Repeat this process, working across the row from left to right and utilizing the same points of making the stitches as before, until the intended block of colour is completed.
Step 7: When the yarn is no longer required, having completed the block of colour, take the needle through to the back of the work and secure the resulting yarn end and also the yarn end left at the start of the row.

Shadow cross-stitch

Now and again, a block of colour can be too dense. This can be made less so by using the method of shadow cross-stitch, a process that works well on a background of Tunisian simple stitch, because the vertical lines of Tss can be left exposed. The cross-stitches then sink into the fabric, to give the impression that those stitches are further away.

Shadow cross-stitch is most effect for pictures needing to give the impression of there being a heat haze or mist. Often, this effect is enhanced if the background is worked with a mohair, brushed acrylic or even a single-colour eyelash yarn.

Steps 1–2: To produce shadow cross-stitch on a background of Tunisian simple stitch, work Steps 1–2 as for classic cross-stitch, so that the yarn emerges through the first Tss square to be covered by a shadow cross-stitch at the bottom right-hand corner.

Step 3: Insert the needle from the top left-hand corner of the same square, under the adjacent left-hand vertical strand and bringing it out at the bottom right-hand corner of the next square. This takes the yarn under the adjacent vertical strand, allowing it to remain visible.

Step 4: Repeat this process, working across the row from right to left, until the last square of the row to be worked and covered by a shadow cross-stitch has been reached.

Step 5: Complete the shadow cross-stitches by inserting the sewing needle from the top right-hand corner of the current square under the adjacent right-hand vertical strand and bringing it out at the bottom left-hand corner of the next square, to place the second half of the shadow cross-stitch over the first half of the shadow cross-stitch of this square. This forms a sunken cross-stitch, still leaving the vertical strands visible.

Step 6: Repeat this process, working across the row from left to right and utilizing the top right-hand corner of the current square and the bottom left-hand corner of the next square, as for Step 5, until the area of colour needed to be applied by this method has been completed.

Step 7: Work as for Step 7 for classic cross-stitch.

Inserting the needle in this way allows the vertical strand of the Tunisian simple stitch to stay exposed.

In the process of completing the row of shadow cross-stitches.

BABY BLANKET

The Baby Blanket, with its eyelash-yarn surface-crochet border that is offset from the blanket edging.

Materials

3 × 100g balls West Yorkshire Spinners ColourLab DK (225m/100g) in M
Small amounts of a DK-weight yarn in each of the seven colours of the rainbow, for the balloons, and small amounts of yarn, including a little black, for the clown, to work the cross-stitch embroidery
Small amount of a bubble yarn, or any long-haired, textured yarn as a substitute, to work the embroidery for the clown's hair
Approximately 25g colourful eyelash yarn, to work the surface-crochet border
5.00mm crochet hook
6.00mm crochet hook
7.00mm Tunisian crochet hook
Tapestry sewing needle
Optional: An iron-on cotton or lining fabric, to back the Tunisian crochet base of the blanket

Tension

Measured over Tss: approximately 14 stitches and 13 rows to 10cm
Note that the stated tension is close to reality but may not be 100-per-cent precise, because of the softness of the yarn, the particular size of the Tunisian crochet hook used and the large area that the blanket covers.

Size

50cm/19½in × 70cm/27½in, excluding the crocheted edging

Pattern instructions

Base of Tunisian simple stitch

With M, make a slip knot, place it on to the 6.00mm crochet hook, and work 79ch. Place the last chain on to the 7.00mm Tunisian crochet hook.

Rows 1–95: Work as for Tss.

Row 96: Work 1dc under each vertical strand to the end of the row, and do not break off the yarn.

Keeping RS facing, continue to work double crochet around all four sides of the blanket, including the top of the blanket that already has a double-crochet row worked along it, by working 1dc into each stitch or row end in turn. Join the last loop on the hook to the top of the first dc of the round with 1slst, make 1ch, and turn the work.

With WS facing, work 1dc in each stitch of the previous round, but work 2dc at each corner. Join the last loop on the hook to the top of the first dc of the round with 1slst, make 1ch, and turn the work.

With RS facing, work 1dc in each stitch of the previous round, but work 1dc and 1tr at each corner (to give a sharper point). Join the last loop on the hook to the top of the first dc of the round with 1slst.

Keeping RS facing, work 1 crab stitch in each stitch of the previous round in turn, without increasing at the corners, to the end of the round. Fasten off.

Sew in all yarn ends.

Eyelash-yarn border

The eyelash-yarn border is offset from the edge of the crocheted edging of the blanket, so the double-crochet edging rounds and the outermost row or column of the Tss base need to be ignored; the eyelash-yarn border is to be worked around all four sides of the next row or column of the Tss base away from the edge of the blanket. You may find it useful to temporarily mark the corner stitches of the path that the eyelash yarn will follow with stitch markers or short lengths of yarn when being worked into the underlying Tss rows and columns.

With the 5.00mm crochet hook (the smaller hook size is necessary to achieve the correct tension), attach the eyelash yarn under any of the vertical strands marked out for the path when identified working the colourful eyelash-yarn border. To form this surface-crochet border around all four sides of the Tss base, work 1dc under each vertical strand around the identified path of stitches. Fasten off.

Sew in all yarn ends.

Balloons and clown embroidery embellishments

Follow the provided chart to place and work the cross-stitch embroidery embellishments of the balloons and clown.

Use black to embroider a belt between the orange of the clown's trousers and turquoise top.

Add the hair either by working surface crochet or sewing.

The indigo or the black yarn can be used to embroider the strings of the balloons.

To form the eyes, a small amount of black yarn can be knotted and the ends pulled through to the back, so that the knot forms an eye on the front of the work.

Chart of the balloons and clown embroidery embellishments for the Baby Blanket.

The proportions of the face are not conducive to including the big smiling mouth synonymous with a clown; however, a small double backstitch worked over two squares works well to represent the mouth.

Optional finishing

If desired, a fabric backing can be attached to cover the Tunisian background for the blanket, but leave the crochet edging unlined.

A close-up of the face-and-hair details of the clown.

By working the stitching as directed, the strings of the balloons are held by the clown.

A perfect gift – a facecloth with a corner detail of Tunisian lace, to hold a bar of soap.

Bathroom gift

Tunisian lace can be more of a challenge for some people, so, once it has been mastered, it is satisfying to utilize the trial piece used for learning, rather than putting it aside with no vision for its future use.

The trial piece of Tunisian crochet lace is large enough to cover a bar of soap. Consider adding a border of double crochet and crab stitch (or a crocheted shell edge) around the entire piece, then fold over one of the narrow edges to provide a design detail and reinforce this edge. Stitch the bordered piece of Tunisian lace on to a corner of a terry-towelling facecloth by working sewn stitching along the two long edges and the bottom narrow edge, leaving the folded-over edge unattached, to form a pocket into which the soap can be inserted.

The lace fabric allows the perfume of the soap to linger in the atmosphere. The idea can be used for fabrics constructed from many other Tunisian stitch patterns, including those that are a little denser but still allow the perfume and lather of the soap to escape.

Adding Crochet to Another Article

Many of the techniques described throughout this book include instructions for producing a trial piece, to allow that technique to become familiar to you. Some of these techniques have been accompanied by suggestions of to how to incorporate either the technique or even the practice piece itself into a functional item.

Appliqué

Extend this idea of using the stitch-pattern trial pieces by using them to brighten up garments, sewing them in place for use as pockets or simply as decoration. Any of the colourful pieces worked when mastering a technique or when experimenting need not be wasted, as they can be appliquéd on to articles to give them a new lease of life.

Tunisian crochet lace is perfect for use on a lampshade.

The inside of the lined lampshade with its Tunisian lace outer cover.

Lampshade cover

Having mastered Tunisian lace, beautiful lampshades can be made. Lampshade frames are available at larger craft shops and online suppliers. Plain-white coated rings for the base and a matching lampshade ring to slip over the bulb socket are readily available, and the rings can be bought singly or as a pair. The lampshade pictured has a plain ring at the top, to allow it to sit over the bulb socket. The lampshade could be reversed if required to be used as a light shade in a ceiling fixture. Alternatively, attach a piece of Tunisian crochet lace as an overlay to brighten up the lampshade of an existing lamp.

Although lampshade frames can be purchased with supports between the plain ring and the one that will sit over the socket, they are, unfortunately, not so readily available. However, there is no need to be deterred, as a short length of fine, stiff, flameproof parchment can be purchased to support the two rings. The parchment is ideal to hold the two rings in place, but it is necessary to take the colour of the parchment into consideration when making the Tunisian lace cover. Another alternative would be to use an old lampshade that can be stripped, cleaned and, if necessary, painted white, before adding the new fabric to the lampshade frame.

To make a lampshade cover, first work a trial tension piece, remembering that measuring an accurate tension for a lace pattern is not always possible. This tension check is necessary to enable the design to be worked out carefully, particularly if the lampshade frame has metal supports.

Any lampshade struts need to be hidden. Rows of double crochet between the Tunisian lampshade panels successfully achieve this.

Allow the supports to be covered with a denser stitch than that used for the Tunisian lace panels between the supports, which is what allows the light to shine through. The fact that Tunisian crochet lace has some inherent give in the fabric is an advantage when working out the design, because it can usually be stretched or eased, as required, during the final assembly.

The featured lampshade has supports, and the design was worked with four rows of double crochet to separate the Tunisian lace panels. The inside of the drum was covered with a heat-resistant muslin first, bringing the fabric edges to the front. The crochet sheath was made slightly smaller than the measurements of the lampshade surface, to allow the fabric to be stretched firmly into position as it was attached.

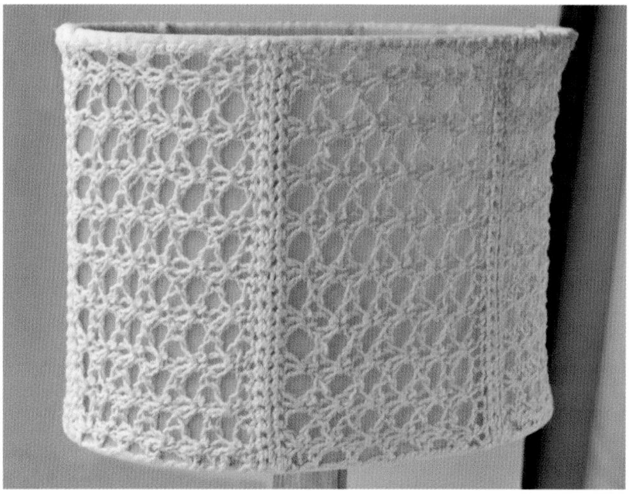

A close-up of the fabric of the Tunisian lace lampshade cover.

BIBLIOGRAPHY AND FURTHER READING

For those interested in searching for further information about Tunisian crochet, the books listed below are a starting point.

Busy Needles magazine series (Marshall Cavendish, 1981) de Dillmont, T., *Encyclopedia of Needlework* (Running Press, 1884)

This title contains the first known reference to 'Tunisian crochet' instead of 'tricot'.

Golden Hands Encyclopedia of Crafts magazine series (Marshall Cavendish, 1975)

Klickmann, F. (ed.), *The Home Art Book of Fancy Stitchery* (The Girl's Own Paper, 1912)

Rivers Turnball, *Selected Works Of Mdlle. Riego On 19th c. Crochet, Knitting, & Lace Work* (Lacis Publications, 1904)

The Harmony Guide to Knitting Stitches (Lyric Books, 1987)

Turner, P., *Crochet for the Absolute Beginner* (Search Press, 2014). ISBN: 978-1782210900

This title contains all of the instructions needed for working classic crochet stitches.

Turner, P., *Crocheted Lace: Techniques, Patterns and Projects* (B T Batsford, 2003). (Reprinted by Dover Publications, 2015). ISBN: 978-1564775764

This title contains information about working with fine threads.

Turner, P., *Tasteful Tunisian* (Crochet Design, 1992). ISBN: 978-1874080855

Turner, P., *Tunisian Crochet* (Search Press, 1987). ISBN: 978-0855325985

Turner, P., *Crochet, Shire Album 126* (Shire Publications, 1984). ISBN: 978-0852636978

In my book *Crochet, Shire Album 126*, a validated history of crochet up to the time of publication is included and covers in detail the first time that the photograph of Queen Victoria was given permission to be published.

Wilkins, D., *The Railway Knitting Workbook* (Friesen Press, 2015)

Pauline Turner's Crochet Design website: https://www.crochet.co.uk/

Pauline Turner's Crochet Design Facebook page: https://www.facebook.com/paulineturnercrochetdesign

ACKNOWLEDGEMENTS

My heartfelt and totally inadequate thanks go to:

Photographer: Fredrik Holm, for the photography, and, impressively, he also made, as a first attempt at Tunisian crochet, a sweater for himself.

Models: Alex Dobson and Elsa Holm, who gave up a weekend from their university studies to model several of the book's patterns.

Olivia, Thomas, William Ritsan, Joyce Cane and David Rush who (living close to Pauline Turner) came to the rescue as models during the pandemic.

Supplier: West Yorkshire Spinners, for supplying much of the yarn for the projects and stitch examples.

Åsa Sandberg and Helen Jordan, for their constant support and for putting up with the disruptions that I caused.

Beverley, who looked after my nails.

Also, my family, who rarely heard from me during the time of preparing this book.

The International Diploma in Crochet students, who gave permission for reference to be made to their study of Tunisian crochet:

Barbara Tennant, an early graduate of the International Diploma in Crochet, for allowing me to use a point from her final research paper on the history of Tunisian crochet.

Angela Creber and Maris Groter, for allowing patterns that they designed to be the inspiration for and be adapted as included projects (the Colourful Textured Car Coat and the All-Square Sleeveless Jacket, respectively).

Without the encouragement and support of many other people, this book could not have been written.

I am also thankful for: The gracious permission of Her Majesty the Queen for the reproduction of the photograph of Queen Victoria from the Royal Archives.

INDEX

RELATED TITLES FROM CROWOOD

978 1 78500 549 7

978 1 78500963 1

978 1 78500 802 3

978 1 78500 455 1

978 1 78500 507 7

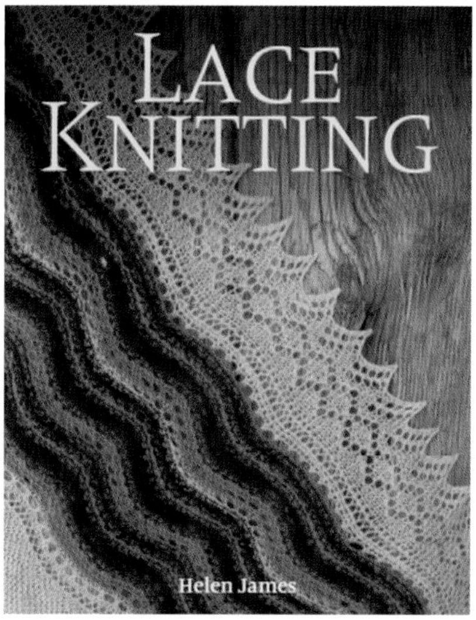

978 1 78500 571 8